Children, Families, and Public Policy in the 90s

This book may be ordered from:

THOMPSON Educational Publishing, Inc.

Publishing for the Social Sciences and the Humanities
11 Briarcroft Road, TORONTO, ONTARIO M6S 1H3
Telephone (416) 766-2763 / Fax: (416) 766-0398

Children, Families, and Public Policy in The 90s

Edited by

Laura C. Johnson and Dick Barnhorst
*The Child, Youth, and Family Policy Research
Centre, Toronto, Ontario*

With a *Foreword* by
Senator Lorna Marsden

Thompson Educational Publishing, Inc.
Toronto

Copyright © Thompson Educational Publishing, Inc. 1991

Additional copies of this publication may be obtained from:
  Thompson Educational Publishing, Inc.,
  11 Briarcroft Road, Toronto,
  Ontario, Canada M6S 1H3
  Telephone (416)766-2763 Fax: (416) 766-0398

Please write for a full catalogue of publications.

Canadian Cataloguing in Publication Data

Children, families and public policy in the 90s

Includes bibliographical references.
ISBN 1-55077-015-2

1. Family policy - Ontario. 2. Children - Government policy - Ontario. 3. Ontario - Social policy. I. Johnson, Laura Climenko, 1943 II. Barnhorst, Richard, 1947

HV700.C3C48 1990   362.82'561'09713   C90094918-X

Cover illustration: *Christopher* by Horst Guilhauman; oil on canvas, 1984. ©Horst Guilhauman. Courtesy of Horst Guilhauman.

ISBN 1-55077-015-2 Paper

Printed in Canada.
1 2 3 4 5   94 93 92 91 90

TABLE OF CONTENTS

LIST OF CONTRIBUTORS

EDITORS

Dick Barnhorst is a lawyer and Executive Director of the Child, Youth and Family Policy Research Centre, Toronto, Ontario. Formerly, he held a senior policy position with the Ontario Ministry of Community and Social Services where he played a key role in the development of Ontario's Child and Family Services Act. He has written and taught in the areas of children's law and family law.

Laura C. Johnson is a sociologist and Research Director of the Child, Youth and Family Policy Research Centre, Toronto, Ontario. Her areas of research include social policy issues related to parental employment, child care and youth employment.

CONTRIBUTORS

Nicholas Bala is Professor at the Faculty of Law at Queen's University, Kingston, Ontario. He has written extensively on family and children's law, specializing in issues related to juvenile justice and child abuse.

Michael H. Boyle is Associate Professor in the Department of Psychiatry at McMaster University, Hamilton, Ontario. His past work has involved research in the areas of clinical epidemiology and community health. His current area of interest is the epidemiology of childhood psychiatric disorders.

Peter Jaffe is Director of the London Family Court, and Adjunct Professor in the Department of Psychology and Psychiatry at the University of Western Ontario, London, Ontario. His recent pursuits involve primary prevention of family violence.

Irene Kyle is a child care consultant with a special interest in child care and family support programs, family policy, strategic planning and program development. She was formerly a Senior Policy Analyst with the Ontario Ministry of Community and Social Services.

Donna S. Lero is Professor in the Department of Family Studies at the University of Guelph, Guelph, Ontario. She is currently Project Director for the National Child Care Survey. Her teaching and research relates to work on the family and child care.

Lorna Marsden is Professor of Sociology at the University of Toronto, Toronto, Ontario. She is a Senator in the Parliament of Canada. She is a founding member of the Child, Youth and Family Policy Research Centre and currently sits on its Board of Directors.

Allan M. Maslove is Professor at the School of Public Administration at Carleton University, Ottawa, Ontario. He is the author of numerous articles and several books in the area of tax policy and budgeting.

Kevin McQuillan is Associate Professor in the Department of Sociology at the University of Western Ontario, London, Ontario. He is also a Research Associate of the Population Studies Centre at the University of Western Ontario. His major area of interest is the demographic aspects of family change.

Penny Moss is Executive Director of the Ontario Public School Boards' Association. She was chair of the Toronto Board of Education and vice-chair of the Metropolitan Toronto School Board. She is an experienced public speaker and workshop leader in the area of education policy issues.

Donald Rutledge is former Associate Director of the Toronto Board of Education. He has been involved in developing the Toronto Board's policies in many areas, including multiculturalism, religious observances, affirmative action, the evaluation of student achievement known as Benchmarks. He is currently a Professor at Ontario Institute for Studies in Education, Toronto, Ontario.

Pamela J. Sloan is a graduate of McGill and Cambridge Universities. She has worked in the private sector and with the provincial and federal governments. She established Hill Sloan Associates Inc., Toronto, Ontario, an economic and management consulting firm in 1985.

Wayne Warry is Assistant Professor in the Department of Anthropology at McMaster University, Hamilton, Ontario. He has taught Native Studies at Trent University, Peterborough, Ontario. He is an applied anthropologist and a Native affairs consultant specializing in the fields of Native health and mental health and in justice-related issues.

David A. Wolfe is Associate Professor of Psychology and Psychiatry and co-director of clinical training at the University of Western Ontario, London, Ontario. He is the Director of Research at the Institute for the Prevention of Child Abuse. His research interests involve intervention and the study of child maltreatment.

Foreword

CHILD, YOUTH, AND FAMILY NEXUS

There is a great body of knowledge among social scientists and social researchers in Canada. For the most part, it is not available to those members of the community in advocacy groups and in public policy positions who could benefit from such knowledge. Much more is known from psychology, early childhood education, sociology and economics about the importance of good child care than turns up in child care policy at any level of government. One objective of the Child, Youth and Family Policy Research Centre is to build the linkages among those people carrying out important research, the public policy makers who need that knowledge to propose their programs, and the advocacy groups for children, youth and families who equally need that knowledge to use in their attempts to influence the public agenda.

Canada is not a country rich in free-standing policy institutes of the kind so familiar to us from the U.S.A. such as the Ford Foundation, the Russell Sage Foundation, the Population Council, the Brookings Institution and many others. We must try to build such institutions to raise the quality of information, ideas and assessments available for social and economic policy and planning.

At present no rewards accrue to academic researchers for public policy research and so the standards and habits of academic research vary greatly from those required in the policy research setting. Among the problems here are the time scale involved in the production of research, the standards by which research is judged, and the need to provide some clear cut and unambiguous answers instead of a series of qualifiers for every finding. This is an ambitious task that the Child, Youth and Family Policy Research Centre has set itself.

Let me offer an example of the problem. Most of the questions asked on the policy side of children, youth and family now concern the end points, questions about health, poverty, education and income support programs. But equally important—and the kind of contribution that this Centre can make—is the question of how the various levels of government interact in a fiscal way to produce the resources that make many of those programs possible. Every federal budget changes something in social services spending and personal income taxes and therefore affects personal disposable income and a variety of government programs. Each federal budget leads provincial governments to change their own fiscal plans and expenditures to accommodate the changes made federally. Of course, the transfer is not simply one way and municipalities react equally to the changes made at the federal and provincial levels. For example, when the federal dollars for family allowance or other family benefit programs are changed the tax system of some provinces means that those dollars disappear in pre-tax deductions. In other provinces it is post-tax deductions. The amount taken off by provinces varies. In a recent Senate study, entitled *Analysis of Child and Family Benefits in Canada: A Working Document*, it was shown that the people of Alberta received more of the federal dollars expended in this way than the other provinces or at least did at the time of the study. Because this fiscal balance changes and alters on a very frequent basis, it is important not only for Treasury Board officials, social services ministries and policy makers in the provinces, but also advocacy groups, to be made aware of what is going on. By what is going on I mean not only the exact amounts that are shifting, which soon become obvious, but the process by which it goes on and the way in which that process can be influenced.

This type of project strikes me as being central to the kind of service that the Child, Youth and Family Policy Research Centre can provide. This can be straightforward analysis. It can maintain the same standards and objectives that are maintained in other kinds of research. But it can provide what no current organization is providing—a public discussion of the linkages between budgets at all levels, fiscal transfers, and therefore the dollars that reach the hands of children, youth and families, those who work with them and those who work on their behalf.

If the kind of research proposed above were successful, after every federal, provincial and municipal budget some well-informed citizen would know almost right away what the effect would be and would be able to talk about it while people were still interested. The present book represents our first attempt to bring together all those interested in developing the culture of information and research essential to improving the lives of children, youth and families.

The Child, Youth and Family Policy Research Centre is filling a need that is currently not filled by anyone in this country. It has an ambitious agenda: to develop the kind of culture of research which Canada has only to a limited extent and which, where it does exist, exists in the interest of corporations, powerful sectors such as agriculture, or very senior policy makers. What we are aiming for is a different kind of analysis for different groups of people. This book is a contribution to that objective.

Lorna Marsden
Founding Board Member
*The Child, Youth and Family Policy
Research Centre*

PREFACE

The individual chapters in this volume review the findings of available research on particular policy issues pertaining to children, youth and families in Canada. The authors establish the social context in which policy issues emerge and then identify what they believe to be the most critical policy issues.

In the first chapter Allan Maslove analyzes the Ontario government's social policy expenditures, with particular reference to programs relating to children, youth and families. After providing a general introduction to the economic and political contexts of the budgeting process, Maslove reviews economic and budgetary patterns in the province over the past decade. Maslove observes that in the 1970s targeted social spending tended to be given an economic rationale by government; by the middle of the 1980s there was a shift toward addressing social issues such as child care in their own right. This change is attributed, in part, to the change in government and the increasing influence of women's groups and social policy advocates. Over the past decade, social services has been the third largest claim on the Ontario budget, following health and education spending. This general category, which includes expenditures on children, youth and families, has remained relatively stable over the decade, although there has been relative growth in provincial Ministry of Community and Social Services spending on programming for children and families. Maslove concludes with a discussion of some of the possible budgeting effects of several major social and political developments.

The dramatic increase in maternal labour force participation constitutes one of the major social changes of recent decades. Donna Lero and Irene Kyle document this demographic trend in Ontario. One result of this pattern is that increasing numbers of employed parents are experiencing difficulty reconciling their work and family roles. Lero and Kyle examine the notion of family policy in the Canadian context, focusing on two substantive policy areas: work-family linkages and child care. In each area they review existing research and elucidate the key policy issues. They conclude that while there is some evidence of new and creative approaches, "the challenge of providing equitable access to necessary services and benefits that support families remains."

Michael Boyle addresses several fundamental issues in the field of children's mental health and observes that "little scientific basis exists for what is done."

Basic questions persist about the value of the classifications of childhood psychopathology. There is only limited information about the scope and magnitude of child mental disorders in the general population. There appears to be "a dramatic mismatch" between the use of children's mental health services and community need. The literature on the impact of mental health interventions for children does not demonstrate that such interventions are effective. There are also deeply rooted structural deficiencies in the provision of services, including problems of funding, coordination and responsiveness. Boyle concludes with suggestions in four areas: measurement priorities, research priorities, policy priorities and new initiatives.

Nicholas Bala provides the context for his discussion of justice issues by reviewing key social and legal changes relating to children and families in Canada. Bala notes that recent years have been characterized by "revolutionary change" in the laws governing families and children. Children and parental separation is the first of three justice areas examined by Bala. Policy issues which arise in this area include custody and access issues, mechanisms for resolution of parental disputes and child support. The second area reviewed by Bala is child welfare, including issues of child protection, prevention of child abuse and prosecution of abusers, and adoption. Young offenders is the third area considered, including discussion of the implementation of this legislation in Ontario. In each of these three areas Bala reviews existing research findings and identifies areas where additional research or data collection is needed.

Penny Moss and Donald Rutledge's review of policy issues in education begins with a rationale for change. Public satisfaction with Ontario's educational system has declined over the past decade. There is increasing public concern about educational outcomes in an increasingly technological and economically competitive society. Moss and Rutledge review critical policy issues currently under debate, including: streaming, equity, drop-outs, teacher education and evaluation of student achievement. Their chapter concludes with an integrated proposal for educational reform through a restructuring of schooling.

Kevin McQuillan reviews trends in family income in Ontario over the fifteen year period from 1970-1985. He compares the income patterns of poor families with families as a whole and examines the social characteristics of poor families. Families of young workers and mother-led families are shown to be at particular risk of poverty. McQuillan examines various alternative explanations for changing income patterns, noting the central role which labour market factors play in the evolution of family income patterns. He concludes that" ... the general thrust of social policy should be directed toward helping those on assistance and, young family heads in particular, to participate in the labour force."

Pamela Sloan observes that the school-to-work transition emerged as a distinct area of public policy in the late 1970s and early 1980s when "exceptionally high rates of youth unemployment ... challenged the assumption that education alone would assure young people access to the labour markets." Current concern with technological change in Ontario has again elevated the policy significance of this issue. Sloan provides a demographic profile of Ontario's youth and describes patterns of youth employment over the past decade. Comparisons are made between the employment patterns of youth and adults in the Ontario labour market. Sloan reviews past and current policy responses, citing program evaluation data where available. She develops an ambitious agenda for public policy that is based on multi-sectoral initiatives.

Wayne Warry examines policy issues concerning Native children and families in the context of Native goals of self-determination and self-government. He begins with an overview of the nature of Native communities in Ontario, the status of Native child health and welfare and the concept of self-government. He then focuses on the child welfare system and child health care. Native children continue to be over-represented in the child welfare system but the percentage of Native children in care has been decreasing, in part due to the development of Native child and family service agencies. Native organizations view Ontario's Child and Family Services Act as progressive, leading legislation but the government has not fully developed the Act's potential to advance Native aspirations. Warry argues that improving Native child health care requires a holistic approach which includes traditional Indian health practices and a link between individual and community health. He concludes with a call for "participatory research" which gives Native communities control over the research process and enables Native people to obtain research skills.

David Wolfe and Peter Jaffe consider the psycho-social needs of children in the care of the state. The authors describe the various service systems, and present some information on risk factors which appear to influence the chances of a child's entry into the care of the state. Wolfe and Jaffe identify five major policy areas in this field including: (1) decision-making and services relating to children's admission to care; (2) the provision of adequate services to children, parents and foster parents of children in care; (3) the need for service coordination for multi-problem children and youth; (4) the needs of young people leaving care and the gap in service for youth aged 16 to 18 years; and (5) needed research and program evaluation. This review concludes that there is a basic question ... "whether the state has been concerned enough about effectiveness and interventions that ensure the rights of children and parents."

The Child, Youth and Family Policy Research Centre is founded on the premise that public policies for children and families should be grounded solidly in research. The Centre's inaugural project documents existing knowledge and research gaps in key policy areas affecting children and families. It is hoped that readers of *Children, Families and Public Policy in the 90s*—researchers, students of public policy, policy makers, advocates, and others—will find this volume useful in their own efforts to improve the well-being of children and families in Canada.

Laura C. Johnson and Dick Barnhorst
The Child, Youth, and Family Policy
Research Centre, Toronto, Ontario

1

HOW QUEEN'S PARK SPENDS
The Economic and Political Context

Allan M. Maslove

Why does the Ontario government spend as much as it does on issues relating to children, youth and families? Why does it not spend more? Why does the Ontario tax system not provide more benefits to families? Why does it provide as much as it does? In order to address questions such as these, it is first necessary to understand the budget of the Ontario government, how it is determined, and what economic, financial and political factors bear on its development.

This chapter will discuss the economic and political context of Queen's Park budgets over roughly the last decade, and the budgetary patterns that have emerged in this environment. It will also briefly discuss the place of social programming generally and child, youth and family policy specifically within the overall budgetary pattern. This discussion is required to prepare one to address questions such as those posed at the outset. The chapter concludes with a brief discussion of the possible budgetary effects of several major social and political developments.

Three caveats are in order before we proceed. First, the aim is not to explain budget allocations and revenue structures "down to the penny;" indeed such precision is impossible. Rather, the aim is to describe more generally the factors that "explain" the Ontario budget picture and to understand the strengths and weaknesses of various policy concerns as claims on that budget. Secondly, while it does deal with budgetary pressures and constraints, the paper does not discuss the budget process per se. Analyses of process are available elsewhere.[1] Third, it is important to appreciate that budget numbers are not always a good indicator of the effect of a particular program, and that not all government actions have significant budgetary dimensions. For example, the Ontario rent control program has had a major effect on the market for rental accommodation in the province, which in turn has affected the well-being of families, yet the budgetary implications of this program are very small relative to the total. Similarly, the solutions to important problems such as child abuse lie mainly outside the domain of government budgets.

---

[1] M.J. Prince, "The Bland Stops Here: Ontario Budgeting in the Davis Era, 1971–85," in Allan M. Maslove (ed.), *Budgeting in the Provinces: Leadership and the Premiers* (IPAC, 1989).

Table 1-1: Selected Economic Statistics

Year	GDP/PDP Growth Rates (%)[1]		Unemployment Rates[2]		Inflation Rates (CPI Increase)[3]				Average Weekly Earnings[4]
	Canada	Ontario	Canada	Ontario	Canada	Ottawa	Toronto	Thun. Bay	Ont. as % of Can.
1988	9.7	10.9	7.8	5.0	4.1	4.2	5.1	4.2	104.0
1987	9.3	11.2	8.8	6.1	4.4	4.0	5.6	3.2	103.4
1986	6.4	10.5	9.5	7.0	4.1	4.0	4.7	3.4	101.7
1985	7.5	8.4	10.5	8.0	4.0	4.1	3.9	4.4	100.8
1984	10.0	12.3	11.2	9.0	4.4	5.0	4.8	4.9	100.2
1983	7.9	10.7	11.8	10.3	5.8	6.7	6.0	6.1	99.0
1982	5.1	4.2	11.0	9.7	10.8	9.9	11.3	10.4	99.6
1981	14.8	14.6	7.5	6.6	12.5	11.9	12.5	11.7	97.7
1980	12.1	10.2	7.5	6.8	10.2	9.6	10.2	9.8	97.9
1979	14.5	12.9	7.4	6.5	9.2	8.9	9.2	8.8	98.7
1978	11.5	9.2	8.3	7.2	8.8	8.4	8.5	8.1	99.5
1977	9.4	8.3	8.1	7.0	7.9	8.1	7.8	7.8	99.9

Sources:
[1] Provincial Economics Accounts, Statistics Canada.
[2] Historical Labour Force Statistics, Statistics Canada.
[3] Consumer Prices and Price Indexes, Statistics Canada.
[4] Labour Force Statistics, Statistics Canada (Industrial Composite Average Weekly Earnings as of December).

The Economic and Political Context of Ontario Budgeting

Ontario boasts the largest and most diversified economy of any province in Canada. Because of this diversity average incomes in Ontario are higher than the national average and the Ontario economy is less susceptible to shocks in any one area than are most of the other provincial economies. This economic strength and diversity has important implications for budgeting in Ontario. In provinces in which one economic sector is dominant, budgeting and policy directed to that sector often become closely intertwined. In comparison, Ontario's diversity gives its government more room to manoeuvre in its budgetary policy.

A brief comparison of the Ontario and national economies over the last ten years is presented in Table 1–1. The rates of change of gross domestic product (GDP) and provincial domestic product (PDP) indicate that the 1982–83 recession (which was broadly based and widespread) was somewhat more severe in Ontario than in Canada as a whole, but that the recovery in Ontario has been much stronger and more rapid than the national average. While lingering depressed agricultural and resource markets have hindered the recoveries of several provinces, Ontario's strength in other areas has led its recovery.

The table also shows that unemployment rates in Ontario are consistently below the national average,[2] again reflecting the diversity of the Ontario economy. Average wage rates, which were below the national average during the recession of the early 1980s, have risen more rapidly in Ontario since then. This trend is consistent with the stronger recovery of the provincial economy since about 1983.

Finally, Table 1–1 compares inflation rates in Canada as a whole with those in three Ontario cities (no provincial inflation rates are available). No consistent differences between Ontario cities as a group and the national average are evident; indeed, the differences across cities are at least as prominent. In large part, local differences are the result of the local land and housing markets, which in turn reflect the levels of activity in the local economies.

Table 1–2 compares income levels and distributions in Ontario and Canada. Average family income levels in Ontario are historically higher than those in Canada as a whole (1983, reflecting the recession, is the exception). The proportion of Ontario families living below the poverty line is also consistently lower than the national average. These income data reflect the general economic data in the previous table. In particular, the higher Ontario family incomes reflect the lower unemployment rates in the province, and the highly urbanized population with a correspondingly high percentage of households with two earners. The distribution of incomes data also show that consistently more families in Ontario are in higher income groups than is the case for Canada as a whole. For example,

---

[2] The differences between Ontario and the rest of Canada are in fact somewhat greater than the data in Tables 1–1 and 1–2 suggest because the national data include Ontario. Unfortunately, there is no straightforward way to present corresponding data for "Canada excluding Ontario."

Table 1–2: Selected Income Statistics

A. Average Family Incomes

	Average Family Income		% of Families at or Below Poverty Level[3]	
	Canada[1]	Ontario[2]	Canada	Ontario
1986	40,356	45,078	12.3	8.7
1983	34,748	34,457	14.0	11.9
1981	30,440	32,170	12.0	9.9
1980	27,579	28,854	12.2	10.2

[1] National council of Welfare, Poverty Profile 1988, Minister of Supply and Services Canada, 1988.
[2] Ontario Statistics 1986, Ministry of Treasury and Economics Ontario, 1987.
[3] Poverty Profile 1988.

B. Income Distributions
(% of families by income range)

	1980		1983		1986		1988	
Income	Can.	Ont.	Can.	Ont.	Can.	Ont.	Can.	Ont.
Under $5,000	2.8	2.7	1.6	1.3	1.0	0.9	0.8	0.8
$5,000–10,000	10.0	7.6	5.4	4.6	3.8	2.7	2.5	1.5
$10,000–15,000	10.7	9.6	10.4	8.4	7.8	5.4	5.2	3.5
$15,000–20,000	12.7	10.9	9.7	9.2	8.9	7.5	8.0	5.8
$20,000–30,000	27.0	28.7	21.1	20.4	17.4	14.7	15.1	12.6
$30,000–45,000	25.2	28.0	26.8	27.9	26.3	26.9	24.1	22.6
$45,000 and over	11.7	12.6	-	-	-	-	-	-
$45,000–60,000	-	-	14.9	15.8	17.9	20.6	19.7	21.1
$60,000 and over	-	-	10.1	12.4	-	-	-	-
$60,000–75,000	-	-	-	-	9.0	10.9	11.4	13.3
$75,000 and over	-	-	-	-	7.8	10.5	13.0	18.8

Source: Statistics Canada, Income Distributions by Size in Canada.

Table 1–2 shows that in 1988, Ontario had fewer families in all income groups below $45,000, and more in all income groups above that level.

The character of the Ontario economy affects both the revenue and expenditure sides of Queen's Park budgets. First, because it ranks as a wealthy province, Ontario receives less in federal government grants than do other provinces, both in per capita terms and as a proportion of total revenues. For example, Ontario receives no equalization payments and little in terms of Ottawa's regional development spending. Thus, compared to other provinces, Ontario generates a very high percentage of its revenues from its own taxes and other revenue sources.

Ontario's high "own-revenues" not surprisingly give rise to a situation in which the revenue side of the budget receives much more attention than is the case in other provinces. This is reinforced by the fact that a Keynesian-style short-term provincial stabilization policy is likely to be more efficacious in the Ontario economy than elsewhere because of its size relative to Canada as a whole. Keynesian policy in other provinces is severely restrained by the extreme "openness"[3] of their regional economies, which means that most of the effects of provincial stabilization policies will "leak out" to other provinces and internationally. Ontario, while it is still an extremely open economy, offers somewhat more scope for the provincial government to practice stabilization policy effectively because more of the effects occur within the province.

Thus, in most provinces (and certainly the smaller ones) budgeting is very much an expenditure-side exercise, consisting of tailoring government spending to the predicted revenue flows that can be expected from Ottawa and the provincial tax system. Ontario budgeting, in contrast, involves both sides of the ledger to a greater extent. Tax policy decisions are taken with an eye to their effect on the provincial economy, and expenditure aggregates are determined in light of the tax policy adopted and the deficit that the government is prepared to countenance. In this regard, Ontario is closer to the federal government than it is to several of the smaller provinces.[4] In a later section, some of the specifics of Ontario revenue budgeting will be discussed in more detail.

A continuing theme throughout the period (actually beginning in the budget speech of 1975)[5] has been public-sector restraint. Successive treasurers have taken the position that restraining government spending, containing the deficit, and limiting the size of the public service are prerequisites for a strong private sector. The evidence shows that government spending in per capita terms is less in Ontario than in any other province.[6] Public employment relative to population size has been reduced.[7] Thus, while restraint has been a contentious practice in many provinces in recent years, Ontario governments in their typical non-confrontational style, have been effectively restraining spending and public-sector employment for many years.

In part, this long-standing restraint program reflects a basic conservative approach to government. The traditional approach to budgeting in Ontario, like the approach to governing in general, has been small-c conservative. Ontario treasurers have repeatedly sounded the themes of small government, good management

---

[3]　The term "openness" refers to an economy subject to large inflows and outflows of goods and resources (including capital and possibly labour). In effect, openness means that markets for the relevant goods and services extend beyond the borders of the (provincial) jurisdiction.

[4]　M.J. Prince, *op. cit.*

[5]　The April 1975 Budget Speech of the Treasurer D'Arcy McKeough introduced a program of spending restraint and the government's intention to reduce the number of Ontario public servants.

[6]　Allan M. Maslove, "Introduction: Budgeting in the Provinces," in Maslove, *op. cit.*

[7]　In 1977 there were 10.3 employees in Ontario government ministries per 1,000 population. In 1986 there were 8.9. The actual number of employees declined by more than 4,000. (Calculated from data in *Ontario Statistics*.)

in the public sector, and the importance of maintaining and enhancing the competitiveness of the Ontario economy. In the mid–1970s this philosophy was expressed in terms of combating inflation and easing adjustment to the dramatic increases in energy costs. In the late 1970s and since, and especially during the period of the recession in the early 1980s, the specifics have been industrial adjustment and productivity increases through technology and labour force training.

The conservative approach to government is also reflected in the perceived need to contain the province's budgetary deficit. With the onset of the economic difficulties of the last half of the 1970s and the 1980s, Ontario was faced with the prospect of significantly increasing budgetary deficits. Successive treasurers in the Conservative governments of those years were alarmed by this prospect. Continuous deficits violated their own views about fiscal responsibility.

Of more immediate political concern, a growing deficit would threaten the province's credit rating. Ontario has traditionally been accorded the highest credit rating by the agencies that publish these lists.[8] There is both a substantive and political dimension to these ratings. With respect to the first, the stronger the credit rating the lower the rate at which the province can borrow money in international markets. More importantly, at least in the case of Ontario, is the political dimension. A high credit rating is viewed as a "stamp of approval" by the financial community, endorsing the government's management of the province's finances. Governments and treasurers certainly use good credit ratings as evidence supporting their policies, and in fair turnabout, the opposition parties quickly point to any down-grading of the credit rating as evidence of the government's financial mismanagement; this was certainly the case when Ontario temporarily lost is highest-level credit rating in 1985. The credit rating is thus an important political constraint on the government's budgetary policy. It affects not only the size of the deficit it is willing to incur, but also the types of expenditures it selects, because the rating firms tend to look less favourably on social spending than they do on spending intended to promote economic development.

The final element in setting the budgetary context is that of federal-provincial fiscal and economic relations. Three aspects are relevant to our discussion. First, the province of Ontario, and other provinces, are often put in the position of responding to macro-economic policies adopted by the federal government. The regional economic effects of federal measures will, in turn, affect the revenue flows and expenditures of the provincial governments. They must respond to maintain their own fiscal plans. In addition, because the Canadian economy is regionally differentiated, not all provinces look for the same policy initiatives from Ottawa. Most of them, therefore, are always partially disappointed by fed-

---

[8] The Moody's and Standard and Poors Investor's Services are the two leading credit rating agencies. Historically, both agencies accorded their highest ratings to the Government of Ontario. In the fall of 1985 Standard and Poors dropped Ontario's rating one notch. In the summer of 1986 the rating was restored.

eral actions. As noted earlier, Ontario is large enough to respond to these disappointments (to a limited extent) by adopting countervailing fiscal measures of its own.

Second, provincial budgets are directly affected by the transfers (cash and tax points) they receive from Ottawa. Ontario, because it receives relatively little of its budgetary revenues in this form, is less vulnerable than other provinces to federal shifts in these areas. Nevertheless, Ontario receives large transfers through the Established Programs Financing (EPF) arrangements (approximately $2.6 billion in 1989–90)[9] and a variety of other programs (approximately $2.7 billion in 1989–90). The inter-governmental politics surrounding EPF are a case study of the larger federal-provincial budgetary relationships. For this reason, EPF merits brief discussion.

Under EPF, the federal government makes cash and income tax point transfers to each provincial government. The total entitlement of each province is calculated according to its per capita spending on health care and post-secondary education in a base year, increased at a rate related to GNP and provincial population growth. The position argued by the federal government is that these funds are intended to support provincial spending in these two service areas and that the provinces are obligated to match federal funds in each area. The provincial view is that EPF funds are, in fact, like any other general revenues of the government and can be spent according to provincial priorities. The EPF legislation supports this provincial position.[10]

However, the provinces, including Ontario, like to have it both ways. Whenever Ottawa cuts or threatens to reduce the expected flows of EPF funds, the provincial response is that their health care and post-secondary education systems are threatened. On one level, this response can be viewed simply as a provincial bargaining response, intended to prompt Ottawa to reverse the EPF cuts and maintain provincial revenue flows. On another level, however, one can also see it as a response to the provinces' attempt to squeeze health and post-secondary education spending while shifting the blame to the federal government.

The third area of federal-provincial budgetary relationships relates to the collection of joint programs between the two orders of government. It is these programs that are most often referred to in terms such as "federal-provincial

---

[9] This amount represents the cash transfer from Ottawa to Queen's Park. The EPF arrangements also include a tax point transfer from the federal to the provincial government that is worth approximately the same amount in revenues. These revenues are not recorded separately; they are part of the province's personal and corporate income tax receipts.

[10] For an excellent discussion of EPF with respect to post-secondary education see, A.W. Johnson, "Giving Greater Point and Purpose to the Federal Financing of Post-Secondary Education and Research in Canada" Secretary of State, 1985. For a discussion on this aspect of EPF more generally see, Allan M. Maslove and Bohodar Rubashewsky, "Cooperation and Confrontation: The Challenges of Fiscal Federalism," in M. Prince (ed.), *How Ottawa Spends: 1986–87* (Toronto: Methuen, 1986).

fiscal coordination." They include expenditure programs such as the Canada Assistance Plan (CAP)[11] under which both orders of government agree on the financial arrangements for social welfare support. There are also revenue programs such as the tax collection agreements under which the federal government collects tax revenues on behalf of the provinces (the personal income tax in the case of Ontario). From time to time the federal and provincial governments collaborate on special measures of limited duration; perhaps the best recent examples are in the imposition of wage and price controls.

These examples of coordination are often cited as evidence of the harmonious system of fiscal federalism that has evolved in Canada, and to a considerable degree that is, in fact, the case. From our perspective, it is also important to recognize that the cooperative arrangements also constrain budgetary decision-making. The CAP agreement, for example, defines many of the conditions under which social welfare programs are delivered, and the province is not at liberty to change these aspects of program design (many of which have budgetary implications) unilaterally. Tax collection agreements require the provincial government to define its tax base identically to the federal base. In the case of the personal income tax, the province has some freedom to offer tax credits and to determine its own rates,[12] but Ontario's definition of the base (taxable income) must be the same as the federal government's definition.

Given this economic and political environment, it is useful to discuss briefly the approach to social policy spending taken in Ontario budgets. While one does not find a direct discussion of the government's philosophical approach to social policy in budget speeches, it is possible to obtain a sense of the priority accorded to these issues. In the middle and late 1970s, social spending tended to be grouped into two categories. The universal services such as health care were treated as basic public services, requiring continued public support to maintain adequate service levels. This stance reflects the clear signals that the public values these services highly.[13]

---

[11] Of the $2.7 billion in non-EPF transfers referred to above, the CAP transfer accounts for about $1.8 billion.

[12] Provincial personal income tax rates are not levied against the tax base directly but as a percentage of the "Basic Federal Tax" which is calculated from the tax base (taxable income).

[13] For public opinion poll evidence that services such as health care enjoy strong public support see, Richard Johnston, *Public Opinion and Public Policy in Canada: Questions of Confidence* (Toronto: University of Toronto Press in association with the Royal Commission on the Economic Union and Development Prospects for Canada, 1986). During the 1988 election campaign, the strong public reaction to fears that the Canada-U.S. Free Trade Agreement would threaten a number of Canada's social programs provides further evidence of strong support.

Other more targeted programs tended to be treated as instruments of economic policy rather than as priorities in their own right. The best example of this latter approach is youth employment policy. With great regularity budget speeches in this period contained announcements of new, renewed, and adjusted programs for the employment and training of young people between the ages of 15 and 24.[14] The rhetoric used in presenting these programs typically viewed them as measures intended to deal with the economic problems facing the economy at the time. Similarly, announcements of social housing initiatives were presented in terms of their favourable effect on the housing market and employment in the construction industry.

By the middle of the 1980s, an apparent shift in approach could be detected. Concerns such as social housing and day care were more likely to be addressed in their own right rather than as means to some other economic objective. In part this shift coincided with the activities of various cabinet members seeking to succeed Premier Davis; in part it coincided with the later election of the Liberal government, with its different perspectives and priorities. But the shift also was likely related to the stronger voices of women's groups and social policy advocates in the 1980s.

The Ontario Spending Record

Having examined the political and economic background to the Ontario budgetary process, in this section and the next we turn to the budgetary evidence. Table 1–3 presents the record of Ontario government spending by function from 1978–79 to 1989–90. Over the entire period the largest claim on the budget has been health care spending, accounting for over 30% of the total at the end of the period. Moreover, for virtually all of the period the portion of total spending allocated to health care has been increasing. Several factors are relevant to the size and growth of Ontario health spending. First, it is clearly a service of utmost importance and concern to Ontarians, and as a result, the "health lobby" is very strong. Second, because medical services are labour intensive, and because there is limited scope for productivity increases, the costs of medical services tend to increase over time with average wage rates in the economy; offsetting productivity gains cannot be relied upon systematically as they can in (for example) manufacturing activities.[15] Third, on a technical level, it is difficult to conduct informative program evaluations or management audits in most health service areas because of difficulties in measuring outputs and therefore effectiveness and efficiency. As a result, the budget decision-makers have less information against

---

[14] For example, youth employment and training initiatives were included in the budget speeches of 1978, 1982, 1984, and 1985. Each offered new or revamped programs. the regularity with which these initiatives appeared is testimony to the political importance accorded to the problem of youth employment. It may also be testimony to the lack of success of a succession of programs.

[15] W.J. Baumol, "Macroeconomics of Unbalanced Growth: The Anatomy of Urban Crisis," *American Economic Review*, v. 57, pp. 415–425, 1967.

Table 1-3: Ontario Government Spending by Function

Year	78–79	79–80	80–81	81–82	82–83	83–84	84–85	85–86	86–87	87–88 (p)	88–89 (p)	89–90 (p)
General Services[1]	690.6	827.4	750.6	906.7	972.9	1021.8	1061.9	1374.0	1428.3	1504.9	1935.2	2311.6
% of total budget	4.5	4.9	4.1	4.3	4.0	3.9	3.7	4.1	4.1	4.0	4.6	5.1
% increase over previous year	(8.8)	19.8	(9.3)	20.8	7.3	5.0	3.9	29.4	4.0	5.4	28.6	19.5
Protection of Persons and Property	496.4	556.8	622.5	710.6	856.1	905.6	945.0	1052.6	1198.3	1346.9	1489.4	1828.3
% of total budget	3.3	3.3	3.4	3.4	3.5	3.4	3.3	3.2	3.4	3.5	3.5	4.0
% increase over previous year	2.4	12.2	11.8	14.2	20.5	5.8	4.4	11.4	13.8	12.4	10.6	22.8
Transportation and Communication	1053.2	1131.1	1223.3	1399.1	1532.4	1566.7	1599.4	1711.6	1798.4	1775.9	1986.9	2288.4
% of total budget	6.8	6.7	6.6	6.6	6.3	5.9	5.6	5.1	5.2	4.7	4.7	5.1
% increase over previous year	2.7	7.4	8.2	14.4	9.5	2.2	2.1	7.0	5.1	(1.3)	11.9	15.2
Health	4069.0	4343.0	4989.5	5948.4	6930.3	7779.3	8575.1	9605.7	10788.0	11862.7	13102.4	14287.7
% of total budget	26.5	25.8	27.1	28.1	28.5	29.3	29.9	28.9	31.0	31.2	31.2	31.6
% increase over previous year	9.2	6.7	14.9	19.2	16.5	12.3	10.2	12.0	12.3	10.0	10.5	9.0
Social Services	2167.6	2332.3	2900.5	3055.9	3554.4	3997.6	4391.8	4768.2	5350.1	6110.0	6474.4	7749.3
% of total budget	14.1	13.9	15.7	14.4	14.6	15.1	15.3	14.3	15.4	16.1	15.4	17.1
% increase over previous year	7.4	7.6	24.4	5.4	16.3	12.5	9.9	8.6	12.2	14.2	6.0	19.7

Education	3446.4	3672.9	3849.0	4390.6	4825.8	5235.4	5440.2	7436.1	6608.4	6794.0	7624.5	7841.9
% of total	22.4	21.9	20.9	20.7	19.9	19.7	19.0	22.4	19.0	17.9	18.1	17.3
% increase over previous year	6.6	6.6	4.8	14.1	9.9	8.5	3.9	36.7	(11.1)	2.8	12.2	2.9
Resource Conservation & Indust. Devel.	394.8	586.5	595.3	673.5	875.6	767.6	792.5	952.7	1109.0	1235.7	1277.1	1347.6
% of total budget	2.6	3.5	3.2	3.2	36.7	2.9	2.8	2.9	3.2	3.3	3.0	3.0
% increase over previous year	0.1	48.5	1.5	13.1	30.0	(12.3)	3.2	20.2	16.4	11.4	3.4	5.5
Regional Planning and Development	328.3	176.6	205.3	193.5	310.4	291.6	231.1	128.1	183.7	210.0	272.2	285.2
% of total budget	212	1.1	1.1	0.9	1.3	11.1	0.8	0.4	0.5	0.6	0.6	0.6
% increase over pevious year	128.9	(46.2)	16.3	(5.7)	60.4	(6.1)	(20.7)	(44.6)	43.4	14.3	29.6	4.8
Debt Charges	1554.9	1804.1	2092.4	2350.9	2871.6	3343.1	3955.9	4285.5	4445.5	5043.7	5092.6	5258.3
% of total budget	10.1	10.7	11.4	11.1	11.8	12.6	13.8	12.9	12.8	13.3	12.1	11.6
% increase over previous year	18.4	16.0	16.0	12.4	22.1	16.4	18.3	8.3	3.7	13.5	1.0	3.3
General Purpose Transfers to Local Govts	481.4	647.1	416.5	659.8	654.8	721.5	751.8	784.4	827.8	857.0	1318.0	494.9
% of total budget	3.2	3.9	2.3	3.1	2.7	2.7	2.6	2.4	2.4	2.3	3.1	1.1
% increase over previous year	30.0	34.4	(35.6)	58.4	(0.8)	10.2	4.2	4.3	5.5)	3.5	53.8	(62.5)

Year	78–79	79–80	80–81	81–82	82–83	83–84	84–85	85–86	86–87	87–88 (p)	88–89 (p)	89–90 (p)
All Other Expenditures	694.7	728.5	775.4	886.4	907.6	907.2	949.7	1161.4	1056.8	1245.4	1441.7	1567.4
% of total budget	4.5	4.3	4.2	4.2	3.7	3.4	3.3	3.5	3.0	3.3	3.4	3.5
% increase over previous year	5.7	4.9	6.4	14.3	2.4	(0.0)	4.7	22.3	(9.0)	17.8	15.8	8.7
Total Gross Expenditure[2]	15377.3	16806.3	18420.3	21175.4	24291.9	26537.4	28694.4	33260.3	34794.3	37986.2	42014.4	45260.6
% increase over previous year	8.8	9.3	9.6	15.0	14.7	9.2	8.1	15.9	4.6	9.2	10.6	7.7

[1] Dollar values are in millions.
[2] Includes environment, recreation and culture expenditures.

Source: Statistics Canada, Provincial Government Finance, Revenue, and Expenditure, various years.

which to judge the requests of the health care providers than is the case in many other functions funded by the public sector.

Finally, the much predicted aging of the population has begun to occur in Ontario and elsewhere in Canada. Since people tend to utilize more health care services as they grow older, the per capita demands on the health care system are increasing. Moreover, we know that this trend is just beginning and will continue for many years.[16] The budgetary pressures from health care are therefore likely to increase further rather than ease or even level off.

Education spending constitutes the second largest claim on the Ontario budget. While education spending has accounted for more than one-fifth of total spending, its relative size has declined quite steadily over the period shown in Table 1–3. This relative decline is attributable most directly to the levelling (and in some areas actual decline) of the school age population. If there is anything remarkable in this pattern it is that the level of education spending has been as robust as it has, given the enrolment patterns. This stability is testament to the rigidities inherent in the annual rolling budget compromises.[17] Between 1976 and 1987 education spending (primary and secondary) in current dollars increased by 71.8%, and the CPI increased by about 72%. Thus, in real terms, total education spending was roughly constant and real spending per student increased.

The third large program area in the provincial budget is social services. The largest ministry included within this functional category is Community and Social Services. Because many child, youth and family programs are located within this ministry, we will examine its spending in more detail below. At this point it is sufficient to note that social spending (which also includes Housing, Citizenship and Culture, and other ministries with smaller budgets) as a portion of the budget total has remained increased over the years shown in the table but in an irregular pattern.

Debt service costs are the final "big" claim on the budget, and the portion of the budget dedicated to these payments has increased noticeably over the period. In the last half of the 1970s and early 1980s, the increase could largely be explained by high interest rates; in the years immediately following, the increased budget deficit resulting from the recession was the primary factor. In the most recent years shown in the table, this claim on the budget has stabilized.

Overall, spending increases have been relatively modest, given that the rates shown in Table 1–3 include both real increases and inflation. Expenditures increased more rapidly in 1981–82 and 1982–83, reflecting in part the effect of the

---

[16] In 1977 in Ontario there were 764.5 thousand people aged 65 or over (9.2% of the total population). In 1986, there were 1,005.6 thousand over the age of 65 (11.0%). The projection for 2001 is 1,318.5 thousand (1.4 million) people (13.0%). Calculations based on data from *Ontario Statistics*, 1986.

[17] In 1977 there were 2.2 million children in Ontario between the ages of 5 and 19. In 1986 there were 1.9 million, a decline of 13.7%. From 1977–78 to 1984–85 elementary and secondary school enrolment in Ontario declined by 9.4%.

Table 1–4: Provincial Government Transfers and Grants

Year	78–79	79–80	80–81	81–82	82–83	83–84	84–85	85–86[2]	86–87	87–88	88–89
Municipalities and Agencies[1]	1627.0	1747.0	1918.4	2178.6	2535.8	2774.2	2912.0	2338.0	2874.0	3863.0*	4163.0*
% ot total budget	11.5	11.4	11.4	11.1	11.3	11.3	11.0	8.1	9.3	11.1	10.7
% Increase/decrease	6.7	7.4	9.8	13.6	16.4	9.4	5.0	(19.7)	22.9	34.4	7.8
Hospitals	2146.0	2317.8	2639.2	3194.6	3643.0	4042.3	4440.2	4875.4	5345.5	6026.7	6500.5
$ of total budget	15.2	15.1	15.7	16.3	16.2	16.5	16.8	16.9	17.2	17.2	16.8
% increase/decrease	4.4	8.0	13.9	21.0	14.0	11.0	9.8	9.8	9.6	12.7	7.9
Elementary & Secondary Educ.	1954.5	2057.7	2280.9	2549.1	2812.3	3014.3	3218.6	3251.0	3726.0	3818.4	4453.8
% of total budget	13.8	13.4	13.6	13.0	12.5	12.3	12.2	11.3	12.0	10.9	11.5
% increase/decrease	4.3	5.3	10.8	11.8	10.3	7.2	6.8	1.0	14.6	2.5	16.6
Post Secondary Education	1266.3	1333.3	1425.2	1572.1	1794.0	1932.4	2028.5	2049.3	2241.4	2385.9	2662.7
% of total budget	8.9	8.7	8.5	8.0	8.0	7.9	7.7	7.1	7.2	6.8	6.8
% increase/decrease	8.4	5.3	6.9	10.3	14.1	7.7	5.0	1.0	9.4	6.4	11.6
Subtotal	6993.8	7455.8	8263.7	9494.4	10785.1	11763.2	12599.3	12513.7	14186.9	16094.0	17780.0
% of total budget	49.4	48.6	49.1	48.3	47.9	47.9	47.7	43.4	45.7	46.1	45.9

OHIP[3]	1023.3	1122.1	1334.3	1543.0	1846.5	2149.3	2416.4	2723.7	3177.4	3628.2	3936.5
Suppl. Health Care Coverage	246.6	289.6	342.8	427.6	522.6	603.0	652.2	772.0	913.0		
% of total budget	9.0	9.2	10.0	10.0	10.5	11.2	11.6	12.1	13.2	10.4	10.2
% increase/decrease	14.3	11.2	18.8	17.5	20.2	16.2	11.5	13.9	17.0	14.2	8.5
Transfers to Individuals	1797.6	2152.5	2115.7	2798.1	3264.2	3523.7	3785.2	5849.4	5119.6	N/A	N/A
% of total budget	12.7	14.0	12.6	14.2	14.5	14.4	14.3	19.0	16.5		
% increase/decrease	8.8	19.7	(1.71)	32.3	16.7	7.9	7.4	45.0	(6.7)		
Total Transfers	10061.3	11020.0	12056.5	14263.1	16418.4	18039.2	19453.1	21498.8	23396.9	25365.7	28519.2
% of total budget	71.1	71.8	71.6	72.6	72.9	73.5	73.6	74.4	75.4	72.6	73.6
% increase/decrease	7.2	9.5	9.4	18.3	15.1	9.9	7.8	10.5	8.8	8.4	12.4
Total Budget	14156.9	15345.9	16835.8	19650.8	22509.2	24553.2	26436.9	28890.0	31031.0	34941.9	38734.9

Sources:

* Estimated.
[1] Ontario Statistics 1986, Ministry of Treasury and Economics Ontario, 1987.
[2] Data 85/86 and subsequent years obtained from Pubic Accounts, Ontario.
[3] OHIP and supplementary data were collected from Public Accounts, Ontario.

recession of those years. A more rapid increase also occurred in 1985–86, the first year of the minority Liberal government.

Table 1–4 presents data on provincial grants and transfers. These are of three general types. First are the grants paid to other governments and public organizations, including municipalities, school boards, universities and hospitals. These grants account for almost one-half of the total provincial budget. Second are the grants to fund the Ontario Health Insurance Plan (OHIP) and other health care activities. The main claim on these funds are the payments to medical practitioners. Third are the transfers to individuals, mainly in the form of social welfare support. Together these grants and transfers constitute almost three-quarters of the total budgetary expenditures of the provincial government.

The latter two categories of payments are often characterized as examples of statutory expenditures over which the government has no discretion. This is clearly an overstatement, but they do represent commitments over which the government has limited control in the short run. Once rates of reimbursement or benefit levels are determined, the spending totals are essentially demand driven rather than government determined. The government can, in normal circumstances, certainly forecast the expenditures with a high degree of accuracy; nevertheless, little control over them can be exercised until the next opportunity arises to revise payment levels.

The grants to municipalities and other public institutions are of particular interest. In the first instance, the recipients of these funds are the elected and appointed officials of the respective agencies. These groups act as special interest representatives vis à vis the provincial government, lobbying for more funds in competition with each other and the other functions for which the province is responsible. They are extremely well informed about the particular service areas because they represent the agencies that directly deliver the services to individuals and families.

The elected officials in the recipient organizations (e.g. municipal councils and school boards), because they are elected, possess a special legitimacy which strengthens their positions as "lobbyists." The appointed officials share with their counterparts in the respective provincial ministries, common professional interests and views. Finally, the recipient organizations interact closely with the relevant provincial agencies in ways that would be completely inappropriate for private-sector interest groups. These factors together make these groups particularly effective claimants on the provincial budget, restricting effective provincial discretion accordingly.

Any estimate of an actual "family and youth budget" must resolve two major problems. First, the definition of this budget is not at all obvious. Family and youth oriented spending could certainly be defined to include major portions of health and education spending, social services such as housing, and even some industrial development expenditures such as youth employment initiatives. Second, once a working definition is determined, constructing budgetary classifications that depart from the standard functional and ministry categories would

Table 1–5: Ministry of Community and Social Services Spending ($ million)

	1980–81	1983–84	1986–87	1987–88	1988–89
Policy Development and Administration	35.0	52.3	67.0	78.6	100.4
% of Ministry budget	2.3	2.2	2.0	2.1	2.3
Income Maintenance	731.9	1210.2	1642.4	1911.8	2167.2
% of Ministry budget	47.9	50.4	50.0	50.6	50.3
Adult's Social Services	187.2	293.4	449.5	567.3	619.2
% of Ministry budget	12.1	12.2	13.7	15.0	14.4
Children's Social Services	310.9	433.5	608.5	659.8	802.8
% of Ministry budget	20.3	18.0	18.5	17.5	18.6
Developmental Services	263.2	412.4	517.4	557.2	622.1
%of Ministry budget	17.2	17.2	15.8	14.8	14.4
Ministry Budget as % of Total Budget	9.1	9.8	10.6	10.8	11.1

Source: Ontario Public Accounts

Table 1–6: Ontario Government Revenue by Source

Year	78–79	79–80	80–81	81–82	82–83	83–84	84–85	85–86	86–87	87–88 (p)	88–89 (p)	89–90 (p)
Personal Income Taxes[1]	3514.7	3652.5	4038.0	5182.5	6132.9	6274.2	6545.2	7523.7	8892.9	10139.1	12047.0	13080.0
% of total revenues	25.3	23.1	23.5	26.5	28.7	26.6	24.7	25.8	27.1	27.8	29.0	29.0
% increase over previous year	22.3	3.9	10.6	28.3	18.3	2.3	4.3	14.9	18.2	14.0	18.8	8.6
Corporation Income Taxes	957.7	1256.0	1410.9	1396.7	992.6	1228.1	1595.9	1937.9	2476.2	2851.0	3390.0	3896.0
% of total revenues	6.9	7.9	8.2	7.1	4.6	5.2	6.0	6.6	7.5	7.8	8.2	8.6
% increase over previous year	21.2	31.1	12.3	(1.0)	(28.9)	23.7	29.9	21.4	27.8	15.1	18.9	14.9
General Sales Tax	1735.2	2436.6	2590.8	2882.9	3455.0	3917.3	4470.1	5073.5	5654.5	6305.0	7776.0	8679.0
% of total revenues	12.5	15.4	15.1	14.7	16.2	16.6	16.9	17.4	17.2	17.3	18.7	19.2
% increase over previous year	(10.8)	40.4	6.3	11.3	19.8	13.4	14.1	13.5	11.5	11.5	23.3	11.6
Motive Fuel Taxes	630.8	734.6	745.8	925.3	1028.8	1140.9	1182.6	1215.2	1250.2	133.0	1535.2	1739.0
% of total revenues	4.5	4.6	4.3	4.7	4.8	4.8	4.5	4.2	3.8	3.6	3.7	3.9
% increase over previous year	3.8	16.5	1.5	24.1	11.2	10.9	3.7	2.8	2.9	6.4	15.4	13.3
Health Insurance Contributions	977.2	1008.7	1032.2	1147.2	1327.7	1438.1	1542.9	1581.0	1627.7	1723.0	1744.0	1850.0
% of total revenues	7.0	6.4	6.0	5.9	6.2	6.1	5.8	5.4	5.0	4.7	4.2	4.1
% increase over previous year	17.7	3.2	2.3	11.1	15.7	8.3	7.3	2.5	3.0	5.9	1.2	6.1

Workers' Compensation

Contributions	570.3	613.4	569.3	657.9	763.7	860.1	1135.8	1398.4	1712.5	2092.0	2201.0	2300.0
% of total revenues	4.1	3.9	3.3	3.4	3.6	3.7	4.3	4.8	5.2	5.7	5.3	5.1
% increase over previous year	(3.3)	7.6	(7.2)	15.6	16.1	12.6	32.1	123.1	22.5	22.2	5.2	4.5
Transfers From Other Governments	2405.9	2755.9	3090.2	3296.3	3252.4	4086.4	4536.4	4616.4	4800.9	5192.3	5351.1	5759.0
% of total revenues	17.3	17.3	18.0	16.8	15.2	17.4	17.1	15.8	14.6	14.2	12.9	12.8
% increase over previous year	8.8	14.5	12.1	6.7	(1.3)	25.6	11.0	1.8	4.0	8.2	3.1	7.6
Other Revenues[2]	3104.7	3344.0	3725.1	4095.6	4423.6	4606.6	5493.8	5843.6	6925.2	6681.9	7514.0	7863.1
% of total revenues	22.3	21.2	21.7	20.9	20.7	19.6	20.7	20.0	19.6	18.3	18.1	17.4
% increase over previous year	18.5	7.7	11.4	9.9	8.0	4.1	19.3	6.4	10.0	4.0	12.5	4.6
Total Gross General Revenues	13896.5	15801.7	17202.3	19584.4	21376.7	23551.7	26502.7	29189.7	32840.1	36514.3	41558.3	45166.1
% increase over previous year	11.0	13.7	8.8	13.8	9.2	10.2	12.5	10.1	12.5	11.2	13.8	8.7
Total Revenues Minus Expenditures	(1480.8)	(1004.6)	(1218.0)	(1591.0)	(2915.2)	(2985.7)	(2191.7)	(4070.6)	(1954.2)	(1471.9)	(456.1)	(94.5)
% of total revenues	10.7	6.4	7.1	8.1	13.6	12.7	8.3	13.9	5.6	4.0	1.1	0.2
% increase over previous year	1.1	(32.2)	21.2	30.6	83.2	2.4	(26.6)	85.7	(52.0)	(24.7)	(69.0)	(79.3)

[1] Dollar values are in millions.
[2] Other revenues include natural resource revenues, privileges, licences and permits, liquor board profits, alcohol and tobacco taxes, returns on investments, and other own-source revenue.
Source: Statistics Canada, Provincial Government Finance, Revenue, and Expenditure, various years.

require access to data that are much more disaggregated than those available in published sources.

However, it may still be instructive to examine briefly the spending of the ministry most directly involved in child, youth and family policy (at least narrowly defined). Table 1–5 presents some detail on the spending of the provincial Ministry of Community and Social Services. About one-half the Ministry's budget is allocated to income maintenance, which includes General Welfare Assistance (GWA) and Family Benefits (FB). The provincial costs for the first program, which is administered by the municipalities, accounts for about 80% of total benefits; the remainder comes from municipal budgets. GWA is intended for individuals and families deemed to be in need on a short-term or emergency basis. Recipients must be available to accept employment. Family Benefits are funded fully by the province. These payments are for family units in long-term need (e.g. disabled persons).[18]

The adults' social services category in Table 1–5 includes funding for homes and support services for the aged, and vocational and rehabilitation programs for the disabled. Children's social services include funding for child welfare services (Children's Aid Societies, correctional and other services), nurseries and child care facilities. Developmental services include residential care and support services for developmentally handicapped adults and children. Collectively, spending on these programs has increased faster than overall government spending between 1980–81 and 1988–89, thus increasing their share of the total budget.

The Ontario Revenue System

The overview of Ontario government revenues in Table 1–6 highlights several trends that are of interest in the current discussion. First, transfers from other governments, almost entirely Ottawa, which were already low compared to other provinces declined as a proportion of total revenues over the period shown. In part, this reflects the slower rate of increase of federal transfers in recent years as Ottawa attempts to deal with its own budgetary deficit; in part, it reflects the rather healthy growth rate in the provinces' two major sources of own revenues, personal income taxes and the general sales tax.

Personal income taxes as a share of total revenues tended to increase over the period shown, except for the recessionary period of the early 1980s. Similarly,

---

[18] These services and proposals for reform are discussed in detail in the recent report of the Social Assistance Review Committee. See, *Transitions*, Ontario Ministry of Community and Social Services, 1988.

sales tax revenues have increased over the period, partly as a reflection of higher consumer spending as incomes and population have grown, and partly because of the increases in tax rates and the broadening of the tax base that occurred during the period.[19] In relative terms, reliance on health insurance premiums decreased over the period. In the earlier years shown in Table 1–6, governments periodically increased the OHIP contribution rates in order to maintain the relative revenue flows from this tax, but more recently, the Liberal government explicitly adopted a policy of reducing reliance on these revenues.[20]

While any more definite conclusion would depend upon a formal tax incidence analysis, it would appear that no clear changes in the distributive effect of the Ontario tax system can be discerned. Increasing personal income taxes (in relative terms) would tend to increase the progressivity of the overall tax system.[21] The reduced role of health insurance premiums would tend to move the system in the same direction, though less clearly so because low-income individuals and families are exempted from the premiums. On the other hand, the relative increase in sales tax revenues would make the system less progressive. Thus, the combined effects of these shifts would likely be marginal. Certainly, other than the policy noted above with respect to OHIP premiums, there does not appear to be any explicit strategy by the government to alter its revenue structure.

We noted earlier that the federal-provincial tax collection agreements required participating provinces to adopt the federally determined income tax base. This still leaves the province with options to employ tax credits and reductions to tailor the tax structure to a limited extent. Ontario provides a tax reduction that eliminates the provincial portion of the income tax for low-income individuals. It also offers tax credits to low-income families to offset property taxes or rents, and sales taxes.[22]

Finally in this section, we briefly comment on the deficit measure in Table 1–6 (total gross revenues minus total gross expenditures). The values fluctuate

---

[19] The extent to which Ontario Treasurers utilize the retail sales tax as an instrument of policy is probably not generally recognized. during the period covered in this analysis (1976–87), every Budget Speech contained adjustments to the sales tax base. Adjustments to the tax rate were less frequent. For the last nine months of 1975 the rate was lowered from 7% to 5% to provide some stimulus to the economy, and in May 1988 the rate was increased to 8%.

[20] Budget Speech, May 1986, p. 13. In January 1990, OHIP contributions were completely eliminated and a new payroll tax was implemented.

[21] Progressivity is used here in the technical sense to mean that the effective rate of tax (taxes paid as a percentage of incomes) increases with incomes.

[22] More recent budgets appear to focus more attention on the possibilities of using tax measures as instruments of social policy.

widely because they reflect sensitivities to economic conditions on both sides of the budget. In periods of recession, revenues from some sources (e.g. corporate income taxes) decline, and some expenditures (e.g. social welfare) increase. Thus we see a large increase in the deficit in the early 1980s. It then stabilized for a period of years,[23] and then began a rapid decline in the later years shown in the table.[24]

Conclusions and Prospects

Overall, Ontario spending patterns are clearly stable, and changes in budgetary allocations (in relative terms) are small and gradual. Nonetheless, some changes do occur and cumulatively over time they can be substantial.

A government budget should be interpreted as an equilibrium or compromise among competing needs and interests. As such, the best predictor of next year's budget is this year's, because the system cannot possibly reopen all the issues that form the consensus on an annual basis. Thus, despite the advent of the "rational budgeters" and policy analysts, the budgetary process remains, at its heart, a political competition, and social spending competes for budgetary dollars against all other provincial responsibilities.

In this ongoing political budget compromise, the status quo assumes a strong and prominent position. Existing programs deliver benefits to people who quickly come to view these benefits as entitlements. In contrast, new or challenger programs have potential beneficiaries, many of whom may not be identifiable or aware of their potential benefits before the fact. This asymmetry in the political budget competition helps to explain the patterns of budgetary stability.

A continuing theme during the years included in this analysis, and one which is likely to continue into the future, is restraint. In Ontario's case, restraint has meant gradually returning to a balanced budget without resorting to politically difficult tax increases or painful expenditure cuts. This typically non-confrontational Ontario government style probably serves to strengthen the inherent rigidities in the budget; more dramatic budget surgery could potentially create more room for new programs than the adopted strategy of holding tight reigns on existing programs.

Yet new programs do emerge. Funding priorities do change. New issues emerge on the political agenda and governments respond to them through their budgets.[25] For example, in the social policy area, child care is obviously an emerging issue. The Ontario government has not yet signalled how deeply it is

---

[23] The "actual" deficit for 1985–86 is about $1.2 billion less than is shown in Table 1–6. In that fiscal year the provincial government "wrote off" approximately that amount of unfunded loans and advances that had been previously extended to school boards. As well, the actual amount of education spending in Table 1–3 is overstated by that amount for 1985–86.

[24] The budget for 1990-1 anticipated a small surplus.

[25] Of course, governments also respond in other ways. Regulation and study, for example, may be substitutes for budgetary action, or at least, delaying tactics.

willing to become involved in this area, in part because thus far the federal government has yet to proceed with its program. Ultimately, the provincial response will be shaped by the strength of the pressure exerted by the child care advocates and the financial role that Ottawa will play. The federal role, in turn, may be dependent on the pattern of federal-provincial relations in the post-Meech Lake period. This is discussed briefly below.

Future social policy will also be shaped by the aging of the population. Ontario, like the rest of Canada, is near the beginning of a major shift in its demographic structure. As noted earlier, over the next fifteen to twenty years, the number of people aged 65 or over will rise substantially, as will the old age dependency ratio.[26] One could predict with some confidence that this shift will lead to increased demands on government to increase spending on programs of special concern to the elderly, such as health care and appropriate housing, and possibly also protection services. This, in turn, would imply less emphasis, if only in a relative sense, on services targeted to children, youths and families. Populations in the young age groups are projected to decline or remain constant over the same period.[27] However, the population declines coupled with budget rigidities may lead to the curious result that, for a time at least, spending on functions of interest to children and families will increase in per capita terms.

Finally, two major developments have the potential to affect significantly the Ontario budget in general, and social programs spending in particular. They are the Canada-U.S. Free Trade Agreement and federal-provincial relations. The Free Trade Agreement and its provisions will, to some extent, restrict the economic development and adjustment policies adopted by the federal and provincial governments. One can only speculate how binding these restrictions will be.

At the same time Canadian governments will need to continue to respond to demands arising from structural adjustments in the economy, some of which will arise as a result of the Agreement and some of which would have occurred in any event. Governments will be expected to respond to these economic adjustments and to ease the associated personal and community costs. Politically, no government will be able to turn its back on such demands. If the Free Trade Agreement turns out not to be restrictive with respect to economic policies and policy instruments except in marginal ways, then existing budgetary patterns may not be disturbed significantly. But, if the Agreement turns out to be more restrictive,

---

[26] The "old age dependency rations" is generally defined as the ratio of the population aged 65 and over to some definition of the working age population.

[27] In 1986 there were 3.4 million persons in Ontario under the age of 25. They constituted 37.2% of the province's total population. In the year 2001, the population in this age group is projected to be 3.2 million, or 31.2% of the total. Within this group, the population between the ages of 5 and 14 will increase, while those younger and older will decrease. Calculations are based on data from *Ontario Statistics, 1986*.

then it is more likely that other avenues of assistance will be developed. At least some of these will involve aid to individuals in their own right as distinct from aid to workers in a particular industry. Social programs could thus be directly affected by Free Trade, but the results may be quite different from that which many critics of the Agreement have argued. In particular social programs may expand as substitutes for economic policies.[28]

At least some of these programs, those that involve the delivery of services as distinct from cash transfer programs to individuals, fall almost entirely under provincial jurisdiction. Examples include education and training, labour market supports such as child care services, and investment in the renewal of municipal infrastructures. The role of provinces as social service providers may thus expand to replace economic policy instruments lost at both the federal and provincial levels. The effect on the distribution of provincial expenditures is clear. On the revenue side, one might expect larger transfers from the federal government.

However, on this point, federal-provincial fiscal relations may be moving in the opposite direction. In the wake of the Meech Lake Accord collapse, the provinces seem to be intent on asserting and enhancing their powers at the expense of Ottawa. Rather than support this thrust through shared programs and other similar arrangements, the federal government may opt to focus on programs over which it has exclusive jurisdiction. In the social area these are, for the most part, programs of direct financial payments to individuals and families (e.g., Old Age Security pensions, Family Allowance benefits, tax credits, UI).

In this scenario, provincial governments would thus have to rely more on their own resources to provide expanded or new social services in their areas of jurisdiction. Another possibility could be the development of bilateral agreements between Ottawa and individual provinces. These would essentially be contracts between the two governments specifying the cost sharing and delivery arrangements for specific programs. They could be viewed as successors to the General Development Agreements formerly concluded between Ottawa and individual provinces, which specified arrangements, including funding for regional development. If federal-provincial social policy was to develop in this fashion, the variance across provinces in standards and per capita funding would increase.

Discussing future developments in the delivery of social programs is obviously highly speculative. However, it is clear that Free Trade and the state of federal-provincial relations individually and especially together, represent major changes in the context in which social policy is formulated. Their potential effects on social policy budgets may be equally great.

---

[28] Elsewhere the author and a colleague have developed the argument that governments' ability to develop and fund social programs themselves is unlikely to be restricted by the Free Trade Agreement. N.H. Lithwick and A.M. Maslove, "The Sum of the Parts: Free Trade and Meech Lake," K.A. Graham (ed.), *How Ottawa Spends, 1989–90*, (1989, Carleton University Press).

WORK, FAMILIES AND CHILD CARE IN ONTARIO

Donna S. Lero and Irene Kyle

There can be little doubt that the social and economic changes families have been experiencing in Canada and in the industrialized world since the 1950s have had profound effects. Changes in women's labour force participation and the increased rate of separation and divorce, as well as changes in social attitudes and economic conditions, have combined to produce a new modal family form—one in which parents require additional support, including child care as a basic feature of everyday life. Increasing numbers of individuals, employers, and government departments are, at least, considering what actions may be taken to ameliorate the problems that result when social and economic realities and changing expectations outstrip existing policies, benefits, and services.

It is a difficult time for many working parents and for their children. It is also difficult for those who do not approve of, nor understand, the new realities and pressures families are facing or the new value of gender equality. Hence, the continuing debates about the extent to which parents (i.e., women) should be expected to make sacrifices if they "choose" to have and rear children, and the extent to which society (i.e., government through taxpayers) has a collective responsibility for ensuring that all children are properly cared for and educated. The fact that such debates are occurring at a time when concerns about deficit reduction and the need to be competitive in the international marketplace predominate, further complicates and constrains large-scale policy development in this value-laden area. The results are manifested in a lack of agreement and considerable ambivalence about what actions should be taken and by whom, what costs should be incurred, and what are the appropriate roles and responsibilities of parents, government, and the private sector. Consequently, the development and funding of a comprehensive child care system has been blocked or slowed to a considerable extent, and access to desirable benefits and services (such as parental leave, part-time work with pro-rated benefits, subsidized child care, and child care information and referral services) is not equitably distributed to parents across the province or those employed in different sectors of the economy.

This chapter will examine ways in which family-related social policy in Ontario can best be used to support the role of parents. First, we will provide a demographic portrait of Ontario's families. Second, we will discuss some fundamental issues underlying the construction and implementation of family-related social policies in Ontario and in Canada. The remainder of the chapter is devoted to two main areas in which policies, benefits and services can and do support the parenting role. They are the harmonization of work and family roles, and the provision of child care services and family resource programs. Our intentions are to provide information about current needs and concerns, to describe existing programs and policies, to identify critical issues and controversies where they exist, and finally to suggest specific questions or concerns that should be included in a policy-relevant research agenda.

I. ONTARIO'S FAMILIES

General Demographics

More than 1,000,000 of Ontario's census families have children under 18 years of age, according to the last (1986) census; 871,227 had at least one child 12 years of age or younger as of December, 1985.[1] Of those families, approximately 48.7% have only one child, 40.2% have 2 children, and 11.1% have 3 or more children.[2] Ontario contains by far the largest proportion of Canada's families with children 12 years of age or younger, accounting for 34.14% of all such families in Canada.[3] About 85% of families with children under 18 in Ontario are considered two-parent families, while one in seven is headed by a single parent: 12.6% are headed by a female single parent; another 2.2% are headed by a single male.[4]

Data from the 1981 census indicate that 34.4% of Ontario's children under 14 years of age live in rural areas or small cities with populations of less than 30,000; 8.4% live in moderate size cities of 30,000–99,999; and 57.2% live in larger cities. Almost 41% of Ontario children under 14 years old live in the larger Toronto area.[5] One factor that contributes to Ontario's richness is its heterogeneity. Approximately 17.2% of Ontario's population report having a language other

---

[1] Statistics Canada (1986). "Families: Part One" in The Nation. Ottawa: Population and Dwelling Characteristics, Census 1986, Statistics Canada (extracted from Table 4).

[2] Statistics Canada (December, 1985). Special tabulation for the National Child Care Study.

[3] Ibid.

[4] Statistics Canada (1986) *supra* note 2.

[5] Abramovitch, Rona (November,1987). *An Overview of Rural Child Care Needs and Preferences*. Ontario: Ministry of Community and Social Services (extracted from table 1, p.39).

than English or French as their mother tongue. This compares with 13.1% of all Canadians.[6] Approximately 2% of Ontario's population is estimated to be of Native descent, including those residing on and off reserves.[7] Ethnic diversity contributes to the complexity of designing appropriate family policies and services.

Changing Family Needs and Social Circumstances

Ontario's families have been experiencing a number of changes that contribute to the need for new measures to assist them in raising their children. Although today's families tend to have fewer children than their parents, at the same time, they have lost many of their traditional sources of support. In recent years Ontario families have become quite mobile, with parents often moving to seek training or job opportunities. Escalating housing prices in large urban areas in many cases has necessitated two full-time incomes and has contributed to an increasing trend for young families to move to smaller cities or suburban areas from which one or both parents may commute to work.

The poor remain a major concern in Ontario even with the improvements in unemployment and economic growth that have occurred over the last four years. Despite the province's relative wealth and a reduction in the poverty rate among families from 11.9% in 1983 to 8.7% in 1986, 13.4% of children in Ontario are poor, according to Statistics Canada low-income cut-off points. While Ontario's child poverty rate is the lowest in Canada, the total number of poor children who live in Ontario (268,700) amounts to 26.4% of all of Canada's poor children.[8] Province-specific analyses of child poverty produced by the Social Planning Council of Metropolitan Toronto (1986) indicated that, contrary to popular belief, in 1984 more than two thirds of Ontario's poor children lived in families in which the head was employed either full-time or part-time. Thus, children of the "working poor"—families in which a single parent's or both parents' wages are insufficient to meet the necessities of life—comprised the largest group of poor children in Ontario.

The burden is greatest for lone parent families, especially single mothers. The choice for these mothers is work or social assistance, and given the income differential between men and women workers and women's concentration in lower paying jobs, work is no guarantee of solvency. According to labour force

---

[6] Statistics Canada (February, 1985). *Canada, the Provinces, and the Territories: A Statistical Profile*. Ottawa: Small Area Data Program, Statistics Canada (extracted from Table 1.4, p.12).

[7] Personal Communication (March, 1989). Ottawa: Department of Indian Affairs and Northern Development.

[8] National Council of Welfare (April, 1988). *Poverty Profile 1988: A Report by the National Council of Welfare*. Ottawa: National Council of Welfare (extracted from Table K, p.28).

statistics, 63.8% of single mothers with children under 16 are either employed or looking for work, and 85% of those with jobs are employed full time.[9] Yet, the poverty rate among single mothers with children in Ontario, at last estimate, was an abysmal 55.3%.

Parts of Ontario, most notably Toronto, have received a large number of refugee and immigrant families. Currently, 38% of Toronto's population is foreign-born. Statistics show that 50% of new immigrants are in their child-bearing years (25–44 years of age). In many instances, both parents must work in order to establish themselves and provide even minimal security for their families. The need for these parents to work, combined with their separation from relatives and their newness in the community makes finding reliable, affordable child care arrangements essential. In addition, many immigrant parents require day care services to enable them (and/or their children) to participate in language classes or in training programs to ease their adjustment to life in Canada.

Dramatic changes in women's labour force participation in Ontario, as in Canada as a whole, have resulted in families consciously juggling their scarce resources (money, time, and energy) to ensure the economic, physical, and psychological well-being of family members. In the 1950s, 11% of married women worked outside the home. By 1980, the percentage had risen to about 50%. In 1988, 67.3% of women with children under 16 were employed in the paid labour force.[10] The labour force participation rate of mothers whose youngest child was less than three years old was 58.4% in 1988. The corresponding rates of employment for women whose youngest child is 3–5 years old, and 6–15 years old are 64.3% and 74.3%, respectively.[11]

These changes are not confined to urban areas, but affect families in all areas of the province. For example, the study, *Women in Rural Life* (Ministry of Agriculture and Food, 1984) noted that in 1981, 54.7% of rural women in Ontario worked either full- or part-time. For farm women, the figure was even higher, at 61.8%. Concerns about child care in rural communities are acute. In addition to child care that is needed on a regular basis, there are major concerns about child care during peak seasons, and about the safety of children in "workplaces" that are increasingly highly mechanized.

Changes in women's labour force participation are also reflected in the structure and functioning of two parent families. According to national figures drawn from the 1981 census, the "traditional" breadwinner family consisting of a single

---

[9] Statistics Canada (May, 1989). *Labour Force Annual Averages, 1981–1988*. Ottawa: Household Surveys Division, Statistics Canada. (Extracted from Table 8, p. 135; and Table 61A, pp. 96–97.)

[10] Ibid.

[11] Ibid.

male wage earner and an at-home spouse is now *atypical*, accounting for only 16% of all Canadian families. (This proportion is only slightly larger than the proportion of single parent families.)[12] The rate of change has been truly remark-able. Only twenty years earlier, 1961 census figures indicated that 65% of Cana-dian families conformed to the traditional, male breadwinner model.

Women have been entering the labour force for a variety of reasons. The most obvious one is to provide essential income—especially in single parent families and in those in which the husband is unemployed, disabled, or unable to provide sufficient income. Among dual earner families, wives' incomes are estimated to account for approximately one-third of total family income and, in a not insignif-icant number of cases, is essential to keep the family from falling below existing poverty lines.[13] Besides economic reasons, most women also say their involve-ment in the labour force provides them with a personal sense of satisfaction and achievement. Women in their child-bearing years are among the best-educated members of Canadian society, and increasingly, women view themselves as hav-ing a strong commitment *both* to the world of work and to their families.

In summary, the new reality is that most mothers with young children now are engaged in paid employment—usually in a full-time job, and that almost 60% of two-parent families in Canada with children younger than 5 years of age are dual earner families. In addition to changes in roles and expectations occurring within the home, parents now must depend on others for support in order to fulfil their two major functions, which Gwen Morgan describes as "the economic responsi-bility to work, to support family members, and to maintain family autonomy; and the responsibility to care for the physical and psychological needs of children in a stable and nurturing environment" (1986: 157). Government policies and pro-visions, social assistance programs, the structure and availability of child care services, and benefits and services in the workplace can help or hinder; but to date, they have not kept pace with the changes that have taken place in Canadian society.

II. FAMILY POLICIES/FAMILY PERSPECTIVES

As others have noted, it is difficult to identify a subset of public policies or social policies that are explicitly formulated solely to support the well-being of families (Kamerman and Kahn, 1978). It is recognized, however, that policies in many diverse areas (health, education, employment, income distribution, immi-gration, housing, pay equity, etc.) do affect children and families in significant ways. Moreover, most social policies are implicitly family policies because they are based on certain assumptions about the pattern of relationships presumed to

---

[12] Townson, Monica (January, 1987). *Women's Labour Force Participation, Fertility Rates, and the Implications for Economic Development and Government Policy.* Ottawa: Institute for Research on Public Policy, Table 3, p.30.

[13] Status of Women, Canada (1986). *Report of the Task Force on Child Care.* Ottawa: Canada Government Publishing Centre.

exist between the sexes, and the division of labour males and females have, or "should have," both in and outside the family.

Many Canadian policies (especially those pertaining to child and family welfare) have a long history that typically includes an early period of reliance on the family itself, and then kin, the church, and various community groups and charitable organizations to meet the needs of society's unfortunate members. When the resources of families and communities are inadequate to provide support or are depleted (as they were during the Great Depression or during wartime; or as they have become, due to the reduction in volunteers and unpaid service workers that has occurred as a by-product of women's increased labour force participation), pressure builds for government to respond by authorizing fiscal expenditures and implementing programs. Pressures may also mount for other institutional changes, e.g., in the workplace and/or in educational settings.

Historically, then, many child and family related policies are likely to be problem-driven or reactive, rather than proactive. These policies are conceived and modified over time in response to changing political, economic and social pressures. As often as not, policies developed to address complex social issues by different government departments at different times, and those developed and implemented by more than one level of government, are likely to be uncoordinated, leading to further disparities and the need for additional policy changes.

There are several reasons that explain why Canada has no national family policy. One is that having a national policy presupposes having a shared goal or set of goals that can be used as a framework for policy development. The diversity of family types and values among Canadians who, themselves, come from many traditions and cultures and reside in regions and provinces with different priorities and perspectives militates against this. A second factor is the historical division of federal and provincial responsibility under the *British North America Act*, and now the Constitution, which has resulted in the involvement of different levels of government in the development, implementation, and funding of services. Third, Canadians have traditionally held the view that families should assume full responsibility for child-rearing, and that government should not become involved unless serious problems are evident. Finally, reliable data about families and children have not been available for policy planning purposes and for evaluating existing programs and policies. Quebec's recent introduction of a set of policies and programs that are family-focused serves as an interesting contrast to Canada as a whole and to Ontario in this regard.

In the absence of a specific, explicitly formulated family policy, Kamerman (1980) has identified clusters or packages of benefits and services (i.e. income transfers, child care services, and employment leave policies) that, in combination, go beyond any single policy strategy to address the major needs of families. Moreover, she and others (Bronfenbrenner and Weiss, 1983; Spakes, 1983) have suggested that despite the initial goals of any particular policy (or set of policies), its (their) effects can be evaluated empirically by:

a) identifying the scope and status of families and children to whom it is (they are) addressed,

b) documenting how the policy(s) influence(s) families and other social institutions responsible for providing services or benefits to families, and

c) determining what specific, measurable effects (both intended and unintended) result or are likely to result for families and for the development of children.

An analysis and review of *all* policies that do, or might support the parenting role is clearly unrealistic. For the purposes of this chapter, however, we can at least identify the major difficulties and needs of families that should be addressed, and indicate to what extent existing policies are effective in doing so. One fundamental assumption is that the function of caring for children (and other dependent family members) must be valued and supported *explicitly*. Based on that premise, family-related policies should ensure that parents (and women, particulary), are not penalized for bearing and rearing children, and that children's health and well-being are not jeopardized by their parents' involvement in activities that ensure their family's survival and contribute to our collective economic and social welfare. Specifically, this means that policies should address:

- The need for financial assistance to help ease the costs of raising children;
- The need to provide high quality, developmentally appropriate care for children while parents are working or engaged in education or retraining;
- The need to make possible a more equitable sharing between men and women of home and family tasks and responsibilities;
- The need to facilitate a better balance between work and home so that adults may fulfil their roles as parents without either gender suffering penalties in the labour market; and
- The need to recognize, maintain and strengthen the range of formal and informal social support mechanisms that can assist family members to care for each other, and for other members of their community.[14]

Assistance with the Cost of Raising Children

Historically, the federal and provincial governments have recognized the need to provide some financial assistance to families, as is evident in the gradual accumulation of a number of tax measures and financial benefits, beginning as early as 1917. General measures include the Married Exemption; Equivalent to Married Exemption; the Child Tax Exemption (Exemption for Dependent Children); Family Benefits (Mother's Allowance); Family Allowance; and the Refundable Child Tax Credit. Measures to support working parents include day care subsidies under the Canada Assistance Plan; the Child Care Expense Deduc-

---

[14] List adapted from S.B. Kamerman (1983: 61).

tion, and UIC Maternity Leave Benefits. Many of these provisions were introduced in recognition of the fact that the cost of raising children is a particularly
onerous one for young families (especially single earner families), who tend to
be in one of the most economically vulnerable stages in the family life cycle.
Other, more recent measures such as employment equity and pay equity legislation are intended to reduce the wage gap between men and women and provide
more income to working women.

As Eichler (1988) has shown, however, lack of consistency in how specific
tax measures are applied (i.e. who may claim/must claim tax exemptions or
credits and the structure of the benefits themselves) militate against any consistent effect. The playing out of progressive and regressive elements actually results in less overall benefit being given to lower income families, and a dip
occurring so that families in the highest income group derive greater benefit than
those earning less. Family Benefits and other levels of social assistance have
been criticized as insufficient, resulting in incomes that are far below the poverty
cut-offs.

Assistance with the cost of child care is also inadequate. According to information presented by the National Council on Welfare (1988), a study commissioned by the Special Committee on Child Care concluded that only 12% of the
preschool children of working parents eligible for a full child care subsidy in
1987 in Ontario were actually receiving it (1988: 11). It is not known what
proportion of families do not or can not claim the federal child care expense
deduction, either because their caregiver is a relative, or because the caregiver
does not provide receipts. Until 1988, the maximum amount allowable was
$2,000 per child, which is significantly less than the estimated out-of-pocket cost
of licensed care. (Changes introduced in the 1988 tax year increased the maximum deduction to $4,000 for children under the age of 6.) While this increase is
welcome, many parents and day care advocates had hoped that the deduction
would be changed to a credit, since deductions are regressive, benefitting higher
income families more than those who can barely afford child care costs. Finally,
the UIC Maternity Leave Benefit level (17 weeks of maternity benefits at 60% of
insurable earnings with a two-week waiting period), is far from generous and is
not available to adopting parents.

Provisions for Adequate Supplies of High Quality Child Care for Working Parents

The Ontario Standing Committee on Social Development and the Select
Committee on Health have gathered extensive information about the urgent need
both for more day care spaces, and for a variety of child care services and
support programs across Ontario. Many parents in Ontario are precluded from
using care in a licensed child care setting or approved private home day arrangement because spaces are either not available or not affordable. Quality concerns,
even in licensed programs, are evident. While specific, reliable data on child care
in Ontario is not yet available, it is clear that child care is a major problem for

many working parents, and that dramatic improvements in the quantity, quality and range of services is essential.

The Need to Encourage a More Equitable Sharing Between Men and Women of Home and Family Tasks and Responsibilities

Gender equality both at home and in the workplace depends on many factors, including changed societal attitudes and expectations. While attitude change can not be legislated, obstacles or impediments to paternal involvement in child rearing can be reduced. Corporate attitudes need to be re-examined, in particular, and benefits and flexibility should be extended as routinely to men as to women. Leave policies, for example, could allow fathers to take time off at the time of birth or adoption, and provide both parents with a number of flexible leave days or part days to enable them to be with a sick child, cope with changes in child care arrangements, attend school meetings, etc. Presently, there is considerable inequity in the availability of paternal and parental leave, other than maternity leave. Maternity leave is the only type of statutory leave presently covered in the *Employment Standards Act* of Ontario.

The Need to Facilitate a Better Balance Between Work and Family Life

Much of Section III of this chapter deals with this issue. At present, whatever balance exists seems to occur in spite of the lack of policies, benefits, and services that would assist in this regard. Both men and women need to have real choices in order to have greater control over the structure of their lives. Innovative work schedules, part-time work with pro-rated benefits, job sharing, and sensitivity to the fact that people are more than just workers are some of the options that are being raised. These suggestions include provisions to ensure that employees who opt for reduced time commitments or parental leave do not suffer by losing their positions, seniority, or other benefits, or get derailed into dead end "mommy tract" roles that can perpetuate economic and social discrimination against women.

Recognizing and Strengthening Social Support Mechanisms

Our increasingly complex world sometimes seems to act as a cyclotron that fragments people further from each other at a time when they need increasing support. Social support can be obtained from co-workers and from the workplace in ways that are not detrimental to productivity. The recent introduction of Employee Assistance Programs is one example of a corporate initiative that was designed to provide confidential assistance to employees to help them with personal and family problems. Community or workplace-based resource and referral services can provide parents with help when selecting child care arrangements and offer support and advice about parenting. Similar services and family-related seminars can help families meet the needs of elderly or disabled family members. And yet funds for some of the most critical services to families—such as marital and family therapy, debt and credit counselling, women's shelters, visiting homemakers, and treatment services for children—are often extremely tenuous. While much of this chapter deals with supports and flexible benefits that are emerging in large corporations, a comprehensive approach to supporting parents must start with ensuring that community-based safety net, supportive, and preventive resources are functional and are available to all families.

III. RECONCILING WORK AND FAMILY LIFE

Forces for Change

Bowen (1988) has reminded us that there was a period in the first part of this century when companies showed considerable concern about the welfare of their employees' families. Company "welfarism" or paternalism began to decrease in the early 1930s, and, with rare exception, has been replaced with the view that work and family life are separate spheres. Until very recently, most companies conveyed the message that a worker was to check her/his family persona at the door, and that personal matters were to be dealt with on the employee's own time and in a way that did not hamper work activities. A tacit rule in most large corporations (as well as government departments and other work environments) has been that those who expect to climb the corporate ladder should be prepared to put in long hours, relocate or travel as needed, and ensure that family problems don't interfere with work. This doctrine of separation between home and work is, however, increasingly outmoded. Currently, a number of private employers and policy makers have become interested in developing workplace policies and support programs which would enable people to harmonize their work and family responsibilities. Yet, recognition that there is a problem and/or acceptance of the view that employers should provide additional flexibility and benefits to parents is still quite uneven.

There are three driving forces stimulating interest and activity among more innovative employers. They are: a commitment to gender equality; demographic changes in the labour force, and employers' concerns about productivity, employee morale, and recruiting and maintaining skilled workers in a period of projected labour shortages.

The commitment to gender equality is evident in the principles and statements that have been adopted by Canada's First Ministers in a series of meetings oriented towards ensuring economic equality for women. In November of 1987, the First Ministers directed their Status of Women Ministers to "develop strategies that would address the changing relationship between work and family life." Future policies and programs would be based on the premise that "family and other social responsibilities should be shared by both men and women, and that both workers with dependents and workers without dependents should have equality of opportunity and equality of treatment." Each jurisdiction agreed to develop a strategy according to its own priorities that would address the "changes required in areas such as attitude, programs, services and legislation to promote the harmonious fulfilment of employment and family responsibilities." These statements indicate that measures which better enable workers (of both sexes) to fulfil family responsibilities are viewed as essential if the goal of achieving economic equality for women is to be met. As a result of the meeting, The Ministers Responsible for the Status of Women were to initiate discussions with all relevant ministries, and to table comprehensive strategies at a First Ministers' Conference to be held in 1988.

In Ontario, the Ontario Women's Directorate, an advocacy agency working within the provincial government, assumed the role of coordinating this initiative, and has chaired an interministerial committee made up of representatives of 12 ministries and other departments. To date, they have embarked upon a number of initiatives, including the production of a bibliography on work and family responsibilities; the development of a handbook to increase employer awareness of the issues; assistance with a conference on Work and Family Responsibilities convened in December, 1988; co-sponsorship of a research project with the Conference Board of Canada designed to investigate employment practices that currently impede or enhance the harmonization of work and family responsibilities; review of Ontario's *Employment Standards Act* (1988), and encouragement of other Ontario government initiatives in its role as a model employer. Unfortunately, the 1988 meeting of First Ministers at which prioritized strategies were to be tabled was postponed due to the federal election. Since then, other pressing matters (the Meech Lake Accord, anticipated effects of the Free Trade Agreement) have displaced these efforts on the agenda.

The increasing prevalence of mothers in the labour force has literally forced employers to be more aware of the extent to which work and family lives are interrelated. However, it is not just women who are affected by family responsibilities. Although mothers still are more likely to take time off from work to care for a sick child or to be affected by changes in child care arrangements, an increasing proportion of fathers are affected as well. It has been suggested that women's participation in the labour force, particularly in full-time jobs, has removed the shield that once served to maintain fathers' distance from these problems. Moreover, the dual earner family lifestyle and general social changes have encouraged men to re-evaluate the importance of their involvement in child-rearing, as opposed to the primacy of their work role.

Parents who are having difficulty balancing work and family responsibilities experience role strain or work-family interference. This means that they are likely to have difficulty coordinating the practical demands of work and family life, and to experience negative psychological spillover in the form of fatigue, guilt, irritability, and depression. Health consequences may result, as well as reduced marital satisfaction and decreased parental competence. Children are also affected. They may be rushed from home to caregivers and back again, and receive less individual attention and sensitive care when they need it most. While specific causes and effects of work-family interference vary depending on the unique mix of stressors and supports that are operating for particular individuals, the consequences are serious, and seem to affect a significant proportion of employees. Various studies have suggested that the prevalence rate of work-family interference may be as high as 25–45% of employed parents (Burden & Googins, 1985; Emlen & Koren, 1984; Hughes & Galinsky, 1988). Employers' awareness of these problems is based on effects experienced in the workplace. These consequences include absenteeism, lateness, employees' preoccupation with family problems while at work, decreased commitment to a career, lower employee morale, and decreased job satisfaction. Ultimately, employers are concerned not only with lost productivity resulting from all the above, but with the stability of their work force, especially among highly skilled workers and those in upper management positions.

If employers are not motivated to support and accommodate workers with family responsibilities now, they soon will be, according to recent projections made by the Hudson Institute in New York (1988). On the basis of demographic trends (the baby bust and an aging population), and assumptions of continued economic growth, particularly in the service sector, projections of work force characteristics in the 21st century have been made. It is now predicted that two-thirds of the new entrants into the work force between 1988 and the year 2000 will be women, who will be assuming a greater proportion of higher paying professional and technical jobs. Demands for day care and parental and family responsibility leave are projected to increase, as will interest in part-time, flexible, and stay-at-home jobs. Self-interest, if no other motive, then, should encourage employers to provide workplace options and benefits in order to recruit and maintain a skilled work force in a competitive market and to ensure their own productivity.

What Does Research Tell Us About Work/Family Linkages?

The research that has been conducted to date is starting to paint a relatively clear picture of the prevalence of work/family interference, the factors that contribute to it, and its effects, especially in the workplace. One caveat is that almost all the research has been conducted in large (American) corporations, and study samples seem to over-represent white collar, managerial and professional occupations. Little is known, for example, about work/family conflict in small businesses and among the self-employed.

Canadian research is particularly sparse. Several surveys do provide information about the prevalence of workplace supports in Canada (Rothman Beach Associates, 1984; SPR Associates, Inc., 1986). Abramovitch and Johnson (1989) have recently conducted a work and family life survey in Metropolitan Toronto that explores the relationship between parental work variables (hours worked, work schedules, etc.) and parent-child interaction patterns; Frankel's investigation of work-family fit has been noted.

Two studies of national scope are currently in progress that will make significant contributions to our understanding of the relationships between work and family life in Canada. An extensive project being conducted by the Conference Board of Canada (1988) includes two surveys—one of employers, the other of employees. The employee survey focuses on the extent of workers' responsibilities for dependent family members, how they currently manage to meet those responsibilities while fulfilling their workplace obligations, and the difficulties they have in doing so. Employees will also be asked about those policies, practices, and benefits that would be most helpful to them in alleviating the conflicts they experience. A parallel survey will probe employers' expectations and perceptions, perceived human resource problems (absenteeism, low morale, employee stress, current policies, practices and benefits), and employer opinions about the effectiveness of these workplace supports.

As well, the National Child Care Survey (Lero, Pence, Goelman & Brockman, 1988) that is currently in progress will examine the relationships between work, family, and child care in a nationally representative sample of families with at least one child 12 years of age or younger. Detailed information will be collected about each parent's work involvement, including the actual schedule of their work hours and the availability of specific workplace benefits. Multivariate analyses will be conducted to determine the effects of work, family, and child care arrangements on mothers' experienced "work/family/child care tension." In addition, the study will investigate the extent to which difficulties experienced with child care arrangements over the last year have contributed to mothers' and fathers' absenteeism, worry while at work, commitment to their careers, etc.

Prevalence and Indicators of Work/Family Interference

Recent research studies are quite consistent in suggesting that a significant proportion of employees who are parents routinely experience work/family conflict, or work/family interference, as defined previously. Some specific findings from the literature are as follows:

- 26% of a U.S. national sample of working parents said that work has strained their marriage and family life, resulting in a lack of time with family/children (Harris & Associates, 1981).
- Among parents with children under 6, 68% of mothers and 51% of fathers said they experienced some or a great deal of interference between work and family life (Galinsky, Hughes & Shinn, 1986).
- 37% of mothers in a Toronto study with full-time jobs said they felt conflict quite often or very often between being a mother and having a job. To maintain their working hours, mothers cut back on their leisure and sleep time (Michelson, 1985).
- While at work, over one third of parent employees worry about their children always or most of the time (Burden & Googins, 1985).
- Among employees with children 18 and under, 77% of the women and 73% of the men had dealt with family issues during working hours, and 48% of the women and 25% of the men had experienced a loss of productivity at work because of child care issues (Fernandez, 1986).

- Instances of missed days at work, tardiness, leaving work early and dealing with family issues during work hours were strongly related to employees' difficulties in coping with child care and handling dual family-work roles (Fernandez, 1986).
- Among a sample of 109 Toronto workers, 69% of whom rated their own work/family fit as good or very good, 67% said they felt drained when coming home from work; 52% worry often about their children and their care while at work; 43% say they are dissatisfied with the amount of time available for them to spend with their children. Most of these workers said that when faced with work/family conflicts, they usually sacrificed family roles (and then felt badly about it) (Frankel, 1988).

Factors that Contribute to Work/Family Interference

The variety of factors that contribute to work/family interference can be classified as stemming primarily from workplace factors, family factors, and child care factors. A few studies (Crouter, 1984; Galinsky, 1986) support a suggestion of asymmetrical effects. Specifically, it seems that workplace factors are most likely to affect men's feelings of work/family conflict, resulting in disturbances in family functioning. In contrast, it is hypothesized that women are more strongly affected by family and child care variables, resulting in negative effects on their work (i.e. increased absenteeism, interference with concentration while at work, etc.).

Work Factors. The specific workplace factors that contribute to work/family conflict vary somewhat among blue collar and white collar workers. However, the major factors that have been identified to date are: the total number of hours worked including overtime, the scheduling of work hours, control over work hours and work tasks, specific job demands, health and safety conditions, co-worker conflict, and the supervisor's competence and sensitivity to employees' family responsibilities.

According to a study conducted for the Conference Board of Canada, while actual weekly hours worked by employees has declined over the last 20 years to an average of 34.8 hours, only 70% of full-time workers in the non-agricultural sector work 40 hours or less per week. One out of every five full-time workers actually worked more than 50 hours per week in 1985 (Benimadhu, 1987).

The scheduling of work hours has received a considerable amount of attention, with research indicating that non-day shift work has specific negative consequences, both for individual workers and for their families (Finn, 1981). While some dual earner families deliberately off-shift their hours in order to avoid using non-parental child care, the cost is in the amount of time a couple has together and in the rarity of "whole family time." Evening or night work also disrupts normal family routines and can affect workers' physical health if they have difficulty sleeping during the day. Current studies suggest that 15–30% of full-time workers who are parents work either a non-standard or rotating shift (Johnson & Abramovitch, 1987; Lero, Pence, Goelman & Brockman, 1985).

Even workers who work a normal daytime shift (e.g. 9 am to 5 pm) can experience work/family conflict due to scheduling and logistical problems that could be improved if their work hours were more flexible.

Family Factors. Less research has been done on the characteristics of families that contribute to or exacerbate work/family interference; however, those populations most at risk for experiencing work/family conflict are mothers of children younger than 12 years of age, single parents, and parents of infants.

The literature confirms that women are particularly affected by family and child factors (Crouter, 1984; Emlen & Koren, 1986), although some have suggested that it is not gender per se that is the factor but the degree of family responsibility attributed to mothers. Burden & Googins (1985) have reported that men with high family responsibility and low salaries react exactly the same as women, with reduced physical and emotional well-being. Regardless, it is women who are more likely to be absent from work when a child is sick, when care arrangements break down, or when a spouse or family member is ill or needs attention. Englander-Golden and Barton (1983) have pointed out that earlier research studies that suggested that women lose more work days due to personal illness than men actually masked the fact that women were bearing the brunt of child care responsibilities. Since it is not "acceptable" for women (or men) to admit that they need days off to attend to sick children or family problems, personal illness is most often given as the excuse for staying home. Besides perpetuating the lie that child care and family problems are not affecting absenteeism, this practice actually places parents (especially women) at risk of ill health, since they may refrain from taking off sick days when they, themselves, are legitimately ill. Women are also more likely to feel that their jobs are being jeopardized under such circumstances, since meeting family and child care responsibilities may put them in the position of possibly losing their jobs, missing promotions, and feeling overloaded and anxious about work projects that are not completed on time or done well.

One factor that can help or hinder parents in coping with work/family conflict is a more equitable distribution of labour in the home. The perception that a spouse is not doing his/her fair share of housework and child care appears to be correlated with depression, anxiety, parenting stress, and marital dissatisfaction among women in dual earner couples (Hughes & Galinsky, 1988). Employed mothers who attempt to maintain a full double work load inevitably feel overloaded, guilty, and inadequate. Husbands who feel that their wives are not doing their share of the housework may be unhappy, but this does not seem to be a statistically significant contributor to reported work/family interference.

Child Care Factors. Several studies have explicitly demonstrated the ways in which child care difficulties affect parents' work performance. Emlen & Koren (1984) have verified that working parents can have major difficulties with any or all the following:

- Finding suitable child care,
- Managing the cost of high quality child care,

- Caring for sick children, and
- Coping with instances when the care arrangement breaks down.

Friedman (1985) has described the logistics of parenting and working as resembling a Rubik's Cube. Just when all the pieces are about to mesh, some new twist comes along to disrupt the order—a work shift changes, an in-home provider gives notice, a child is sick, one parent has to go out of town, the school year is ending, etc. Nor should one assume that the task is as simple as finding and maintaining only one care arrangement per child. Current research suggests that combinations of two or more arrangements are common, even for one child (Lero, Pence, Goelman & Brockman, 1985).

Several research studies suggest that difficulty in finding child care is one of the most significant predictors of absenteeism. Emlen & Koren found that, "overall, 59% of women and 40% of men employees reported difficulty finding child care" in their survey of 8,121 employees in the Portland area (1984: 5). The nature of the difficulties include a) not having an adequate selection of options to choose from, b) difficulty locating high quality care, c) difficulties finding out about available caregivers, and d) not being able to afford the care arrangement that parents would most prefer and feel their child(ren) deserve(s). Galinsky quoted one parent who described the task of finding out about available sources of child care as comparable to "learning the rules of a hidden, somewhat secret society" (1986: 116). In addition to the stress that difficulties finding appropriate child care produce, this problem also impacts on the workplace by causing absenteeism, interference with concentration on work tasks, and taking time from work to deal with child care issues. A promotional brochure for an in-house child care information and referral service makes the claim that finding each new child care arrangement consumes an average of 10 hours of work time. While finding appropriate care is a concern to parents of children of all ages, it is a particularly acute problem for parents with infants, in part because of the limited number of licensed spaces for this age group, and the lack of trained in-home caregivers whose rates are affordable.

At this time there is no accurate information about how much Canadian parents are paying in out-of-pocket costs for child care. An American estimate is that child care is often the third to fourth most costly item in the family budget (Hughes & Galinsky, 1988). If it is perceived as a woman's expense, the financial cost may not be justified by the income she can earn. Ultimately, the lack of available, affordable, high quality child care can act as a real constraint on women's employment, as well as a contributing factor to work/family interference and reduced productivity. Equally important, it can have major effects on children's development, especially if their early lives are spent in a succession of short-lived, non-stimulating arrangements with people who are not particularly committed to their care.

How working parents manage caring for sick children has been described as the issue that is the most stressful and difficult for them to deal with. Fernandez (1986) reports that providing care for sick children was at the top of the list of 15 possible child care problems that working parents experience. According to Friendly (1989), parents can expect their infants to be sick 9 to 10 times a year with respiratory illnesses and digestive upsets; preschool children may be sick as often as 6 or 7 times each year. Regulated child care programs and schools are likely to exclude sick children from attending, and parents recognize that parental care is needed to comfort a sick child, even if the workplace doesn't, resulting in a significant amount of absenteeism. Fernandez found that caring for a sick child was the reason given for missed work by 56% of women employees who had missed 1 to 3 days of work in the last year, 78% of women who had between 4 and 6 absences, and 82% of those who had missed more than 6 days of work in the previous year.

Even when parents are lucky enough to find good quality care that fits their family needs, breakdowns in the arrangement occur. Instances when children are sick constitute one specific cause of arrangement breakdown. Other instances occur because a caregiver is sick, wants to take a vacation or decides to take another job; or when day care or schools close for vacations, snow storms, or professional development days. Emlen & Koren found that women whose children were cared for outside the home, and those who relied on care by a child (self care or care by an older sibling) were most likely to miss full days of work, arrive late for work, and be interrupted while at work. In that study, 15% of fathers and 28% of mothers said they used care by a child as their main form of child care for a child younger than 12 years of age. Their reasons for using this form of care included its low cost, convenience, and the fact that it is "the path of least resistance." It is also true that spaces in licensed programs for school-aged children are almost as rare as those for infants.

This summary of the research literature has focused on the factors that can contribute to parents' stress and conflict when attempting to fulfil both work and parenting functions. It is interesting to compare those results with Frankel's findings of differences between workers with high and low work/family fit. Frankel (1988) found that employees with high self-reported work/family fit had the following characteristics: at work, these individuals reported more control over their work hours and over the timing of their work tasks. They had flexible supervisors who were sympathetic and sensitive when family emergencies arose. At home, their family life was characterized by high adaptability, cohesiveness, and support. Families responded "creatively and productively to changing circumstances and new problems" and generally manifested a positive "can do" attitude. The most popular form of child care utilized, especially for children under 3 years of age, was care by a relative (often a grandparent) in the child's home. High fit employees had lower absenteeism rates than other workers in the same firm with low work/family conflict. They also scored higher on measures of job satisfaction and family satisfaction. In effect, Frankel's findings are entirely consistent with the literature on work/family conflict.

Consequences of Work/Family Conflict

The effects of work/family conflict on the workplace have been documented throughout this review. The most direct consequences are absenteeism, worry and reduced concentration while at work, spending time while at work on child care issues, tardiness, and having to leave work suddenly. Other effects may include friction between workers and their supervisors, difficulties experienced by co-workers when work is not completed or when they must take on more work to cover for their colleagues, and reduced job satisfaction and morale. The more obvious indicators of lost productivity have been studied. No research to date, however, has considered the cost of work/family conflict in terms of actual resignations, a reduced commitment to one's job, lost accounts or contracts, or the cost of replacing "burned out" employees. Certainly, all these factors have tremendous implications for lost productivity and increased costs to employers.

The consequences for individual workers and their families have been noted. These consequences include a considerable amount of tension, stress, and fatigue, as well as generally lower levels of marital satisfaction and life satisfaction. In addition, Hughes & Galinsky (1988) have noted the relationship between both work/family interference and the frequency of child care breakdown with their respondents' reported incidence of stress-related health problems, including depression, back and neck pains, overeating, drinking problems, physical symptoms of anxiety, etc.

An important omission in the research literature on work/family conflict is the lack of research focused on children. While the consequences of high levels of work/family interference are likely to be mediated by the quality and reliability of child care arrangements and by the ways parents arrange their lives and provide support to each other, one can speculate that in such cases it is more likely that:

- Children would be constantly rushed in order to accommodate rigid time schedules at work or at child care settings;
- For some children, there would be few opportunities to spend time with one of their parents during the week or on a weekend work day, or with both parents in a relaxed, comfortable fashion;
- Instability in care arrangements, which could disrupt normal patterns of attachment both to adults and to other children, and may result in withdrawn or aggressive modes of interacting with others;
- Children may be sent to school or to day care settings when they are mildly ill because parents can't afford to take any more time off (resulting in a higher level of illness in the child population in general). In other situations, a child who is ill may be cared for by a parent who is anxious, or by a caregiver who is called in at the last moment and has little real concern about the child;
- Disturbances in parent-child relationships, fed by ambivalence, tension, and parents' unresolved concerns about their adequacy as parents and as workers may be more common.

In summary, a significant percentage of women and men in the work force are experiencing considerable difficulty reconciling their work and family roles. In large part, their difficulties stem from role overload, lack of family responsive policies and practices in the workplace, insufficient child care services to support working families, and the unavailability of real choices or options that would allow harmonization of both roles. The next section will examine the range of policies and workplace supports that would better serve children, parents, and employers.

Policies, Practices and Benefits: Steps Towards Reconciliation

There are a variety of changes and innovations that could be introduced to help families achieve a better balance between work and family life. Much of the writing on this subject has been focused on changes that could be made in the workplace by employers (Axel, 1985; Galinsky, 1986). However, not all work-places are as capable of creative innovations, and some workplace changes depend upon policies and incentives at the provincial and/or federal level. The major changes that have been suggested to date can be grouped in several ways. In brief, we can examine steps that would ease time constraints, provide benefits, and/or offer family-responsive services to employees and to the community at large.

Easing Time Constraints

There are a number of policies and practices which could ease the time constraints that parents frequently feel drive or control the quality of their lives. Some (such as leave policies) provide time to parents when personal or family circumstances are such that continuing to work on a daily basis constitutes a hardship, or interferes with care giving. Others (such as flexitime, and part-time work) could be used on a continuing or long-term basis to enable parents to more easily orchestrate their work hours or work schedules in concert with their own needs, the needs of their families, and practical realities (e.g. commuting schedules or the hours of operation of child care centres).

Leave Policies. Policies that are critical to women and to families include maternity and paternity leave, adoption leave, extended parental leave, and leave to care for sick children or for other family-related reasons. A statutory leave policy or employer-generated leave policy sets out the conditions under which an employee is entitled to a period of leave, and normally specifies the extent to which seniority and other benefits will be maintained during the leave. The understanding is that the employee's job or one equivalent to it will be held for that person, and that taking such a leave does not put the employee in jeopardy of losing his/her position. A leave may be granted on a paid or unpaid basis, and indeed, that may be the factor that determines whether the leave option is a real one for some parents.

Leave policies are an important instance in which one can analyze the differential effects of providing a leave as a legislated, universal benefit or as an option provided at the discretion of individual employers. When enacted through legislation, leave policies generally convey a policy goal and are intended to make the benefit a "right" available to all eligible recipients. For example, Sweden and West Germany view maternity and parental leave policies as desirable instruments for encouraging women's fertility, while enabling women and men to share some of the responsibility and joy of child-rearing. Other governments may see maternity leave as a way of preventing overt discrimination against women in hiring and promotional practices. In the United States, there is no federal statute, but states and employers are being encouraged to enact legislation and/or provide maternity benefits to offset this form of "worker disability," under the *Pregnancy Discrimination Act* of 1978. In Canada, the original intent of maternity leave policies was to minimize the extent of earnings interruption caused by the mother's incapacity to work or look for work during the period surrounding a birth. In practical terms, however, it is considered a reasonable means of allowing mothers to care for their babies in the first few months of life. Zigler and Muenchow (1983) have argued strongly that infant care leaves are critical means of supporting infant and family health, and are much more appropriate and cost effective than expensive infant day care services.

Maternity leave provisions are provided to most Canadian women under their province's employment standards legislation. Some federal employees are covered under the *Canada Labour Code*. Unfortunately, there is no standard set of eligibility requirements across the provinces, resulting in differential rules on who is excluded from coverage, the length of the qualifying period, and the period of maximum basic leave. Thus, for example, workers covered under the *Canada Labour Code* are entitled to 17 weeks of maternity leave and up to 24 weeks of child care leave that may be taken by either the mother or father. The qualifying period is 6 months of continuous employment with the same employer.

Most workers in Ontario are covered under the province's *Employment Standards Act* (1988), under which rights to maternity leave are provided to women who have been employed for a period of 12 months and 11 weeks with the same employer prior to the expected date of birth. This is the longest qualifying period of any of the provinces. It penalizes any female worker who changed jobs or did not work continuously within that period. The Ontario legislation presently includes no provisions for paternity leave, adoption leave, or extended child care leave. Furthermore, the lengthy qualifying period is out of step with the qualifying period for maternity leave benefits provided under the federal *Unemployment Insurance Act*. Under current UIC provisions, as amended in 1984, maternity benefits are available to mothers who had worked for only 20 weeks in the previous year, and benefits may be provided to mothers or fathers of newly adopted children.

The amount and duration of UIC Maternity Leave Benefits have been criticized both by the Federal Task Force on Child Care and the Special Parliamentary Committee on Child Care. The reports of both of these groups and others recommended that the level of payment be increased and that the obligatory two-week period be abolished, since it effectively reduces the benefit to only 53% of insurable earnings. Proposed changes to UIC legislation would provide for more flexible leave provisions for both mothers and fathers. Regardless of the changes introduced at the federal level, the restrictiveness of current provisions in Ontario's employment standards legislation constitutes a serious form of discrimination against women. One would hope that its lack of inclusion of paternity leave and adoption leave rights, as well as provisions for leave for family responsibilities, will be addressed in order to allow Ontario families greater flexibility in reconciling work and family roles.

It should be recognized, of course, that individual employers are free to provide more generous or flexible leave options and benefits than those found in statutory provisions. These may be provided as part of an employer's benefits plan or may be negotiated in collective agreements. In general, workers employed in the public service and in larger corporations are more likely to have access to extended leave options and to enhanced benefits.

Reduced Work Hours. One of the obvious ways in which parents can reconcile work and family roles is to limit the number of work hours. Part-time work has been an option women have utilized over the years. This category includes both regular part-time work (for fewer than 30 hours per week), casual part-time work, and job-sharing. Job-sharing is a relatively recent introduction. Under this scheme, two people (almost always women) share one job, usually with a reduction in benefits. Research to date suggests that this option often is employee-initiated, and may only be extended to workers who are highly skilled and difficult to replace. It seems to be particularly attractive to professional women with babies and very young children, who can afford the reduction in income for at least a few years.

Women have constituted about 70% of the part-time work force consistently since 1976 (Dumas, 1986). Presently, about 28% of married women work part-time, in comparison to 3% of employed, married men. Some of the current literature, including a recent study conducted by the Conference Board of Canada (Benimadhu, 1987), suggests that many workers would be interested in reducing the number of hours they currently work. This option seems to be particularly attractive to women with children under the age of 5, and to many full-time workers in managerial and professional positions. However, the positive view of part-time work that full-time managers and professionals have is quite removed from the realities of part-time work as women have experienced it over the years. A recent report on the subject commissioned by the Canadian Advisory Council on the Status of Women concluded that, "Part-time work carries a heavy cost. Most part-time work is available only in the clerical, service and sales sectors and at the lowest levels, with rarely any opportunity for change or advancement. This type of work is predominantly low-paid, with few benefits and little security, and the low rate of unionization among part-time workers inhibits improvement in these conditions" (1987: 3). While changes in the labour force may encourage employers to provide additional benefits to regular part-time workers in order to maintain a stable work force, they are under no obligation to do so. Instead, amendments to the *Employment Standards Act* (1988) of Ontario could insure equal treatment and pay equity for part-time workers on a par with their full-time counterparts.

There are several barriers to the introduction of significantly more part-time work. Employers are concerned about the cost and about lost productivity. Trade unions have been opposed, in large measure arguing that it is a way of cutting full-time jobs and benefits. In sum, large-scale changes in the proportion of part-time workers will not happen easily, resulting in individual families continuing to make their own accommodations as best they can. As a footnote, however, one should not assume that the solution is necessarily more part-time work opportunities, since single parents and low-income families would often prefer to work more hours, as would others who would consider doing so if reliable and affordable child care were available.

Flexible Work Scheduling. Another way of easing time constraints is to provide some flexibility, either through flexitime or variable work scheduling options. Flexitime allows workers to choose their own arrival and departure times within limits set by an employer. For example, some workers might work an early schedule, so that they could finish by 3:00 in order to be home at the end of the school day. Flexitime could also be used to allow workers to attend classes or be involved in other activities. Some workers might be interested in a compressed work week (full-time work in less than five days). One of the most innovative options is that of a "time bank" in which employees have a number of available paid hours or paid days that can be shifted to suit their personal and family needs. These options generally are not costly for employers, and can reduce some of the strain that workers might otherwise experience in locked-in, arbitrary schedules. Finally, we should also mention that improvements in shift work and overtime policies could be made so that families with children are not unduly penalized if they refuse either one. Scheduling overtime and shift work changes in advance would also be helpful so that parents can arrange for child care.

Benefit Plans

There are a number of financial benefits and benefit policies that could help families. Many larger companies already have fairly comprehensive benefit programs, but they are generally inflexible. Flexible or "cafeteria" benefit programs allow employees some choices among specific alternatives. Given the choice, for example, some parents might choose a dental plan over life insurance or opt for complementary benefits when both parents are employed. One suggestion appearing in the American literature is the option of flexible savings accounts, whereby employees can reduce their pre-tax salaries by a certain amount and be reimbursed for predetermined expenses such as child care. Voucher plans, in which the employer reimburses the employee for all or part of his/her child care expenses have also been suggested. According to the Special Parliamentary Committee's report, these types of plans are rare in Canada and their tax implications are not yet clarified. Until they are, employers are unlikely to introduce significant child care benefits in their benefit packages.

Family-Responsive Services

Three examples of these types of services are information and referral services, the provision of on-site or near-site child care, and seminars and discussion groups related to family life.

Information and Referral Services. Friedman (1985) has named child care resource and referral services as the fastest growing child care initiative in the U.S., and assistance with child care, more broadly, as "*the* benefit of the 1990s." Information and referral services vary in their operation, but generally consist of counselling and information services that all employees can use in order to find appropriate child care. The services range from simple lists that are updated regularly, to more in-depth, personal counselling that helps parents evaluate their own needs and be better consumers of existing child care services. Some information and referral services have recently extended their operation to include information and support related to elder care, enabling them to serve a wider range of employees within any given company.

On-Site Day Care. The issue of workplace day care is a complex one. On the one hand, it provides many advantages to families with very young children for whom other options are decidedly inferior. On the other hand, on-site day care may not be advisable if the centre is located in an industrial area, if the employee works shifts or extended hours, or if the child is four or five years old and is starting to attend junior or senior kindergarten. Employers seem concerned about the long-term costs and benefits, and in the end, while conveniently available, on-site day care may still be too expensive for many working parents. As of October, 1988, there were 49 on-site child care centres in Ontario. One quarter are provided by the Ontario Public Service, one quarter are in the private sector, and the remainder are provided by other public service or non-profit organizations, such as hospitals, school boards, and colleges and universities. Three particularly interesting examples in the Toronto area are the Global Playhouse Child Care Centre—the first child care facility in Ontario sponsored by a consortium of employers; the Fashion District Day Care Centre, which derives from a creative partnership between all three levels of government and union, management, and community representatives to serve Spadina Avenue's garment workers; and an organized network of family day care arrangements designed to provide child care to members of the Metropolitan Toronto Police Force. While workplace-sponsored child care is a welcome form of family-responsive services that increases the supply of child care spaces, it is no panacea, and does not replace other, more systematic means to ensure that all families have access to affordable, high quality child care services.

Seminars and Discussion Groups on Balancing Work and Family Responsibilities. These can be held at lunchtime and are another family-responsive service that companies can offer. A variety of professionals from the community can provide information and advice, and more supportive relationships among co-workers often result. Such seminars are an example of an arena in which parents can learn from one another as well as from professionals, and out of which other creative suggestions for harmonizing work and family life may blossom.

How Available Are Such Benefits and Services?

Two recent studies, one undertaken for the Special Parliamentary Committee (SPR Associates Inc., 1986), and one conducted as part of the Working Families Project by the Social Planning Council of Metropolitan Toronto (Johnson, 1986), indicate that workplace supports are still very limited. Both studies found that relatively few employers provide alternative work arrangements, benefits, or child care services of the kinds listed in this chapter. Both surveys indicate that alternative scheduling (flexitime and part-time work) is far more common than job sharing, work at home, or workplace day care services; alternative work arrangements, when available, may only be extended to a limited range of employees; and relatively few employers see themselves as likely to be strong innovators in the immediate future. Most employers would prefer to handle these matters on an ad hoc basis, retaining flexibility in response to individual employees' needs, rather than having legislation imposed on them, e.g. having to provide a minimum number of paid or unpaid leave days for family-related reasons. It seems then, that other than those large employers who have an interest in providing such benefits and services to a unique (or largely female dominated) work force, most employers are content to leave working parents with the full responsibility for juggling, rather than harmonizing, their work and family roles. While credit should be given to the Child Care Branch within Ontario's Ministry of Community and Social Services and the Ontario Women's Directorate for providing information and support designed to encourage employer-sponsored benefits and services, additional leadership, especially at the federal level, is needed.

A Policy-Relevant Research Agenda on Reconciling Work and Family Life

Clearly, there are now many studies that illustrate how workplace, family, and child care variables can operate to enhance or impede family relationships, children's and parents' well-being, and productivity and morale in the workplace. The challenge that remains is to utilize that information in creative ways to develop and evaluate alternative policies and benefits. Researchers who are skilled in program evaluation methodology and in family-impact analyses could provide useful information to employers, parents, and policy makers. As yet, few rigorous evaluations of the effects of workplace supports have been conducted. Several more anecdotal studies suggest that the provision of on-site child care has positive effects for employers. These services seem to result in increased employee morale, lower absenteeism, and a recruitment advantage (Friedman, 1986). The introduction of flexitime and other alternative work schedules also seems to have some positive effects, but of a lower magnitude. What is needed, however is more systematic analysis that addresses the following questions:

- Who benefits most from specific workplace supports, and in what ways? What effects do such policies, benefits, and services have on individual families and on their children, in addition to those that may be observed at the corporate level? Who does *not* benefit, and why not?
- What are the effects of changes in statutory provisions related to parental leave policies for employers, for employees and for families?
- What are the long-term effects of such services as workplace day care? How does it relate to community-based child care services? Does it fill a complementary role or does it create a two-tiered system in which employees of large corporations benefit at the expense of other families?
- What will be the long-term effects of corporate policies that are designed to support families? Under what circumstances do alternative leave policies and work schedules result in a true harmonization of work and family life for both men and women, as opposed to a further ghettoization of women into low paying, low advancement jobs?
- How can policies and benefits be distributed in an equitable manner so that employers and workers in small businesses are not unduly penalized?

These and other questions can be addressed in Ontario, in Canada, and in comparative studies across countries with different family policies, child care provisions, and levels of employer support. The results may ultimately lead to family-responsive policies, not only in the workplace, but in society at large.

Thus far, this review has indicated that a considerable proportion of parents are having difficulty balancing work and family responsibilities. Ecological studies of the complex ways in which work, family, and other variables interact suggest that a critical factor that influences the degree of difficulty parents have in this règard is the quality and responsiveness of their support systems (Abramovitch & Johnson, 1989, Frankel, 1988). An essential element in those support systems, especially for families with very young children, is their child care arrangements. Current child care policies and programs in Ontario, therefore, provide the context in which such efforts occur. Ultimately, they can facilitate or inhibit parents' capacities to provide for the economic and psychological well-being of their children, and their capacity to reconcile work and family life.

IV. CHILD CARE SERVICES IN ONTARIO

A Description of Ontario's Child Care Programs

Ontario's child care programs currently fall into two major categories: those that are recognized and funded under the *Day Nurseries Act 1983* and related regulations, and those that have been developed more recently and are funded under other acts, such as the *Ministry of Community and Social Services Act 1980.*

Day Nurseries Act

The *Day Nurseries Act 1983* recognizes two basic types of services: group centre care and private home day care (PHDC). Group centre care is defined as temporary care and guidance for more than five children, aged ten and under (except for developmentally handicapped children). Private home day care is temporary care for five or fewer children under ten years of age, provided in a private residence.

The *Act* allows the ministry to establish standards for the operation of these programs, including requirements regarding the physical setting, nutrition and safety, staff qualifications, and staff-child ratios, as well as organization and management. In Ontario, unlike other provinces, legislation requires that agencies which supervise home caregivers be licensed, not the caregivers themselves. Standards for PHDC, therefore, focus on the nature and extent of supervision required by agencies, in addition to the agencies' responsibility to ensure that homes and caregivers meet certain basic requirements. Home day care providers who are not affiliated with an agency are not expected to meet any requirements, beyond that of caring for fewer than six children.

As a consequence of this policy, Ontario has, in effect, created two family day care systems: one in which caregivers are supervised by agencies and are required to meet certain standards, in return for which they are eligible for direct grants, subsidies and other resources; and the other, often referred to as "the informal system," for which there is no funding, no minimum standards, and only very limited support. The more common practice in other jurisdictions across Canada and the U.S. is to require individual caregivers to be licensed, regardless of whether they are attached to an agency or network that provides training and other support services.

Both group and private home day care services are operated on a full and/or part-time basis, and variously provide care for infants, toddlers, pre-schoolers and school-aged children. They can be offered under a variety of auspices, including municipal governments, non-profit and for-profit organizations, Indian Bands, and employers in the workplace. Some programs extend care to children with special needs (i.e. developmental and physical handicaps). Others are highly specialized and serve *only* children with severe handicaps. More recently,

Table 2–1: Age of Children Enroled in Group Care

Age Group	Central	East	North	West	Total	%
Infant	1,442	424	28	659	2,554	2.3
Toddler	4,326	1,383	375	2,550	8,634	7.7
Preschool	41,350	14,995	4,421	27,183	87,949	78.1
School-Age	9,435	1,647	507	1,658	13,247	11.8
Over Ten	26	23	8	25	82	0.1
Total	**56,579**	**18,472**	**5,340**	**32,075**	**112,466**	**100.0**

Source: DNIS request # A880083.

however, efforts are being made to integrate children with handicapping conditions into regular day care programs within their local community.

Availability of Care. Because of complex problems associated with the collection and organization of information about child care services, it is virtually impossible to obtain reliable statistical information about the numbers and ages of children enroled in the various kinds of day care programs currently being provided in Ontario. The MCSS *Report on Year One* (1988) of the New Directions for Child Care, states that, "between March, 1987 and March, 1988, the licensed child care centre system in Ontario grew by 8%, from 85,663 to 92,531 spaces" (p. 4).

The National Council on Welfare's Report, *Child Care, A Better Alternative* (1988), reports that as of December of 1987, Ontario had 94,018 licensed child care spaces based on information from the National Day Care Information Centre. It also noted that there were, at the same time, 766,751 Ontario children under 13 years of age whose parents were working or studying, suggesting that overall, 12% of children were placed in licensed child care—slightly less than the national average of 13% (p. 4).

As of October 31, 1988, however, the Day Nurseries Information System (DNIS) reported a *total enrolment* of 112,466 in group centre care. Table 2–1 shows the following age distribution by region. These statistics from DNIS are problematic because the categories are not discrete, and because they include children enroled in part-day as well as full-day programs. Within the limitations of the available data, care for preschool children (approximately 3–5 years of age, including those in junior and senior kindergarten categories) clearly predominates, accounting for about 78% of all child care. School-aged care is more limited, accounting for 11.8% of care, toddler care is approximately 7.7%; while infant care is even more scarce, at 2.3% of licensed spaces. Care for children over 10 would be confined to children with very specific special needs or handicapping conditions.

The DNIS has never collected information about private home day care, so that any existing information about this program has been gathered on an ad hoc

Table 2–2: Per Capita Distribution of Group Care in Ontario

Region	Enrolment	Child Population (0-9 years)	Distribution %
Central	56,579	414,560	13.7
East	18,472	236,405	7.8
North	5,340	135,634	3.9
West	32,075	424,010	7.6
Total	**112,466**	**1,210,609**	(Average) **9.3**

Source: DNIS request # A880083.

basis and from occasional surveys. In 1988, the Norpark *Survey of Private Home Day Care Services in Ontario, 1988* reported that as of March 31, there were approximately 10,274 children being cared for by about 4,371 providers, who were supervised by 78 licensed private home day care agencies. About 18% of the children enroled were infants, 15% toddlers, 29% were preschoolers, 13% were in kindergarten (over 5 years but under 6 years), 22% were school-aged, and 3% were over 10 years of age. About 80% of the children enroled were subsidized (Norpark 1988: 9, 55).

Distribution of Care. If the DNIS figures on enrolment in group care are compared with the numbers of children 0–9 years of age by Ontario region, as recorded in the 1981 Census, the per capita distribution of care is as shown in Table 2–2.

Auspices. Apart from Alberta, Ontario is the only province in Canada in which child care programs are operated directly by municipal governments. In 1987, the national *Status of Day Care in Canada* report (National Day Care Information Centre, 1987) noted that there were 9,510 day care spaces in Ontario operated by municipalities (p. 2).

Ontario also has a significant number of commercially-operated programs. Information from the MCSS Direct Operating Grants (DOG) Data Base indicates that commercial programs currently constitute approximately 35.6% of licensed centre capacity, with non-profit programs providing 64.4% of the total capacity. Table 2–3 compares the capacity of commercial and non-profit programs by age category of children enroled.

Child Care Initiatives (Ministry of Community and Social Services Act)

Beginning in 1980–81, the Day Care Initiatives Program and subsequent Child Care Initiatives were introduced to "stimulate the development of support services to enhance the quality of informal child care" arrangements. "Child care support services" and, in particular, child care resource centres are the terms that have come to be used to define the groups that provide the fairly wide range of

**Table 2–3: Capacity of Commercial and Non-profit Programs
January 1989**

Age Group	Commercial*	Non-Profit
Infant	1,123	1,632
Toddler	3,805	4,932
Preschool	24,374	37,644
Kinderegarten	1,267	2,115
School-age	2,145	11,463
Handicapped	99	1,667
Total	**32,813**	**59,453**

Source: Direct Operating Grant Data Base, January 13, 1989.

*Note: The DG Data Base does not include the capacity of new or expanded commercial programs after December 1987; it does include closures of commercial programs during 1988. As a consequence, the total capacity of commercially-operated programs is slightly underestimated.

services that have sprung up to support unsupervised caregivers and parents who use informal arrangements. In practice, these services have also been widely used by non-working parents.

In July 1987, the MCSS *Survey of Child Care Support Services*, which reported on 115 programs, found that there were about 15 different (but related) kinds of services provided through resource centres. The most frequently reported program components were workshops and discussion groups (88%), followed by play groups/drop-ins with parent or caregiver in attendance (75%), and toy libraries (58%). In addition, 37% of the centres provided community linkage and outreach services, 35% provided information about child care, 20% provided parent relief, 19% conducted home visits, and 16% offered a food and clothing depot (Doherty, p. 8).

The number of resource services were distributed as follows: 41 in Central region, 23 in the East, 31 in the West, and 20 in the North (Doherty, 1987, p. 4). Fifty-nine percent of them serve rural communities (p. 61). The Survey also found that among the 109 programs that participated, the average annual operating cost was $56,527 in 1985–1986, ranging from a low of $8,700 to $325,368, with just over 72% of their funding coming from the Child Care Incentive Fund (p. 67).

Expenditure on Child Care Services: 1977–87

The following is a summary of expenditures for child care services over the last decade. Except for the fiscal years 1978–79, expenditures for child care services have been growing steadily over the last decade. Changes in specific years have been due to the following:

Table 2–4: Expenditure on Child Care, 1977–87

Day Care Expenditures				
Year	Day Care (In M's)	Day Care as % of MCSS Expend	In Constant $'s (1981 = 100)	% Change
76/77	29	2.8	46,104,928	-
77/78	35	3.1	51,546,391	11.8
78/79	38	3.1	51,420,838	-0.2
79/80	42	3.1	52,044,609	1.2
80/81	50	3.3	56,242,969	8.1
81/82	60	3.4	60,000,000	6.7
82/83	74	3.5	66,787,003	11.3
83/84	81	3.4	69,112,627	3.5
84/85	87	3.3	71,135,549	2.9
85/86	106	3.7	83,333,333	17.1
86/87	143	4.7	108,006,042	29.6

Source: Select Committee on Health, p. 57, Table 7. Compiled from MCSS Estimates and Briefing Books, and Treasury and Economics, Public Accounts, 1977/78 to 1985/86.

- The 1977–78 increase resulted from legislative changes which introduced funding for day care services to handicapped children.
- 1978–80 was the beginning of a period of major cutbacks in Ontario social services funding. Programs were given 4–5% increases at the same time that inflation was in the double digit range.
- The 1982–83 increase was a result of the Day Care Initiatives program coming on stream.
- The 1985–87 increase reflects the expansion of day care subsidies, as well as the introduction of a variety of the new Child Care Initiatives announced under Enterprise Ontario and continued by the Liberal government.

The child care portion of MCSS expenditure has increased only very gradually over the last decade, averaging 3.4% of total MCSS expenditures. With the introduction of the new funding policies in *New Directions*, it should continue to increase.

While there is no data about what parents pay towards the cost of child care, there is no question that at present they pay the bulk of costs. For example, the National Council of Welfare (1988) reports that in 1987, only 10% of the children eligible for either a full or partial subsidy in Ontario received it (1988: 11). In *Child Care: Annual Statistics* (1987), it was estimated that there were 30,068 full-time subsidized spaces [September 1986], compared with a group care capacity of 78,218 [March 1986], plus approximately 6,400 children in PHDC (Table 9, p. 7, Table 20, p. 17). This would suggest that in 1986, parents were paying about two-thirds of the cost of licensed care (before child care tax deductions).

The Current Status of Child Care Policy In Ontario

Historical Background

The need to provide supplemental care for children while parents are away from home at work has been recognized as one of the critical social issues to be addressed by families and public policy. The history of how this need for non-parental care and support has come to be recognized and how it has been defined in Ontario over the last century is a complex one. In reviewing the historical development of child care services in the province, it is also possible to trace a considerable evolution in values concerning family lifestyles, parental roles, children's development and ultimately, the changing definition of public responsibility regarding the provision of support to families.

Child care policy development in Ontario has gone through several major philosophical policy periods marked by: (1) the initial organization of creches and nurseries by church groups, voluntary social agencies, and women's organizations, [1870's to 1945]; (2) the introduction of government support, which viewed day care narrowly as a welfare service, or as a form of social assistance to low-income families and children with special needs [1946 to 1984]; and (3) the beginning recognition of child care as a necessary and more comprehensive service: more recently, with political rhetoric that has promised a public service, but with funding and service delivery mechanisms that perpetuate the welfare tradition [1985 to the present].

Figure 2–1 presents the key federal and provincial government policy positions gathered from legislation or major policy documents developed during each period. The legislation and policy statements have been examined with a view to understanding how the following basic factors were addressed: (1) what is the stated purpose of the program and how is need defined; (2) under what auspices are services provided, using what kinds of program models; (3) what funding is provided and what mechanisms are used; and (4) what mechanisms and/or supports have been provided to assure quality.

Current Child Care Policy: New Directions—1987

In June 1987, the Honourable John Sweeney announced *New Directions for Child Care*, the first major policy statement in many years. Although the *Day Care Policy White Paper* had been released in 1980, it did not make a clear policy statement, but rather suggested that "licensed day nurseries in Ontario do not constitute a single, clearly defined program, but a complex series of programs with differing and somewhat conflicting goals" (p. 15). *New Directions*,

Figure 2–1: Summary of Key Federal/Provincial Child Care Policy Positions

Summary of Policy Positions

Legislation	Purpose	Auspices/ Services	Funding	Quality Assurance
I. Charitable and Employment Services				
No provincial legislation 1870's–1945 Dominion-Prov. War-time Agreement 1942	Service for neglected, unsupervised children; mothers should be at home, except under extraordinary circumstances	Charitable and voluntary agencies; employment service for domestic helpers; day care and nursery schools	Very limited except for war years, when some federal funds for women working in "essential industries"	No standards or monitoring; Care custodial, often very poor quality; Nursery school movement emphasized child development.
II. Day Care As A Welfare Service				
Day Nurseries Act 1946	"Care and guidance" of young children for "families in need" for children under six years of age	Charitable and voluntary agencies. Municipally-operated programs	50% provincial cost-sharing of municipal expenditures and some purchase of service	Centres required to be licensed, meet minimum standards; Funding inadequate to support regulations.
Canada Assistance Plan 1966	Welfare-oriented; For families "in need" or "likely to become in need"	Municipalities, Indian Bands, Purchase of service from community programs	"Needs-tested" subsidies; Cost-sharing: 50% federal (open-ended), 30% provincial, 20% municipal	No national guidelines or standards set; legislation, monitoring seen as a provincial responsibility.
Birch White Paper 1974	Welfare service; Complement kindergarten and provide children with "ancillary care and informal education;" Inclusion of "special needs," "handicapped" children	Stressed diversity of auspices, i.e., Municipalities, Indian Bands, Purchase of service	"Needs-tested" subsidies, as above; proposed expansion of subsidies and some capital $'s	Proposed reduction of number of staff caring for children, also of training requirements; Parent responsibility and involvement stressed.

Legislation	Purpose	Auspices/Services	Funding	Quality Assurance
Advisory Council Report 1975	Proposed objectives: Day care is a developmental service for children; surrogate care for working parents; community service network to enhance the general welfare	As above, but proposed the inclusion of a new service model: "private home day care services"	"Needs-tested" subsidies, as above; Proposals implied need for expansion of subsidy and capital $'s	Reaffirmed need for good ratios, staff training, and stressed quality; Recognized preventive role of care. Identified need for planning for service development
Day Care Policy White Paper 1980	No clear statement of purpose; only consideration of a range of service possibilities: welfare, child development, child welfare, special needs, assist working parents	As above, but introduced support for "informal care;" i.e., child care resource services, other "Day Care Initiatives."	As above, but identified problems with the subsidy system: equity, supply, ineffective use of existing resources; Initiatives funding generally not cost-shared under CAP	Public consultation on standards underway. Support for parent education, programs to improve the quality of care in informal arrangements. Start to plan, and to test out new models: "family group care" and workplace day care

III. Emerging View of Child Care As A Necessary, Comprehensive Service

Legislation	Purpose	Auspices/Services	Funding	Quality Assurance
Standing Committee on Social Development 1985	Day care essential to permit parents, particularly women, to achieve full and equal employment opportunities	Diversity of auspices. Noted controversy of whether welfare or education: profit or non-profit. Stressed better coordination of Ministries in Social Policy Field, Health, Education	Raised issues re: "needs test," equity of subsidies; concerned with low staff salaries. Suggested need to renegotiate federal cost-sharing and child care tax deductions.	Suggested standards should be reviewed to allow more flexible interpretation. Endorsed variety of programs to support informal care.
Select Committee on Health 1986–87	Child care necessary to allow women equal participation in society; Benefits: provide children with good quality developmental care, integrate special needs children, assist parents to work or retrain.	Diversity of auspices. Support for commercial role. Also noted need for emergency temporary child care, more flexible service models.	Proposed move to "income-testing;" Ontario should take full advantage of CAP income levels to expand subsidies. Direct grants should be made available to both profit and non-profit groups.	Recommended better monitoring to ensure compliance with minimum standards. Also suggested requiring parent involvement in programs, better parent education and information. Incentives for commercial centres to convert to non-profit should be provided

Figure 2–1: Summary of Key Federal/Provincial Child Care Policy Positions—Continued

Legislation	Purpose	Auspices/ Services	Funding	Quality Assurance
New Directions June 1987	Commitment to build a comprehensive child care system; move from a welfare connotation to "public service." Principles included: reasonable access, responsive services, high quality care to promote child development, informed parents, community-based programs, improved employment leave, affordable child care	Diversity of auspices. Including for-profit. Further experimentation, expansion of service models, e.g., rural child care, temporary and emergency care: workplace, etc. Coordination with Ministry of Eudcation, joint sponsorship of school-based, school-aged programs	Need to negotiate with federal government to improve cost-sharing. Introduction of direct grant; expanded capital funding and subsidy dollars; explore move to income testing	Day Nurseries Act to be revised. Promote parent particapation, better education and information. Plan to review enforcement and licensing policies. Review of staff training needs, beginning development of multi-cultural resources. Support for research.
Proposed Canada Child Care Act Bill C-144 1988	Commitment to increase child care spaces by 200,000 by March 1995. Recognized need to improve availability, affordability, access, and quality of services	Diversity of auspices, including for-profit. Child Care Special Initiatives Fund to support research, development, and public education	$3.B to expand spaces: ($100.M. for Special Initiatives). Cost-sharing of operating grants, capital expenditures. Set ceilings on amount of cost-sharing—may limit provincial expansion	No principles or national standards. Special Initiatives Fund will indirectly improve quality through research, program development and public education

however, reaffirmed earlier statements in the Liberal-NDP "Accord" (which was the contract that had brought the government to power) and in the Throne Speech, which reaffirmed the government's "...commitment to building a comprehensive child care system that will meet the needs of all citizens; a system that would move child care from a welfare connotation toward one of public service" (p. i).

The policy which sets out the present framework for the development and operation of child care services in Ontario is based on the "guiding principles" of reasonable access to a range of appropriate and affordable services; high quality programs that support children's health, safety and development and are responsive to individual cultural and regional needs; local coordination of programs; informed parental choice; and flexible employment leaves and benefits to assist parents with work responsibilities (p. i).

The announcement of *New Directions* also marked the beginning of a three-year plan to provide an additional $26 million in fiscal 1987, and an overall increase of $165 million over the balance of the three-year period, to a total of $325 million (gross) by 1990.

New Directions included new allocations and funding approaches to support the existing child care system and its expansion. It proposed that the MCSS work cooperatively with the Ministry of Education and with municipal governments in the planning and delivery of child care services. It also proposed to negotiate better federal cost-sharing. The development of a comprehensive child care system would be encouraged through providing funding to develop new models of care; the policy statement also set out a number of strategies to promote better quality.

New Directions—Progressive Policies

The *New Directions* "guiding principles" and stated policy, taken together with the proposed funding and service provisions, place Ontario in the forefront of child care policy in North America. Implicit in these policy proposals is also a changed perception of women's role in the labour force, as well as a growing acceptance of the fact that families require social support to manage work and child-rearing responsibilities. The *New Directions* paper contains a number of elements that are significantly different from earlier policy statements which, if fully implemented, would lead to major changes in the development and operation of Ontario's child care system. In summary, they are as follows:

Purpose. The "commitment to build a comprehensive child care system that will meet the needs of all citizens" (p.i) signifies a major shift in thinking. It moves child care policy from the earlier debates about whether day care is a welfare service for children and families with special needs or a child development service, or a service for working parents, and so forth, to a more ecological or comprehensive approach that views child care services as including all of these purposes and as being designed to meet the needs of all children and families.

Auspices/Service Models. The *New Directions* policy has also redefined the scope of the child care system, thereby legitimizing the alternative child care and family support services that have been introduced since the early 1980s through the various Child Care (Day Care) Initiatives. The child care system is no longer defined solely by the collection of licensed and funded group and private home day care services, it now includes child care resource centres to support unsupervised (informal) caregivers and parents, who don't have access to formal services. The government's interest in testing out flexible new service models for shift work and emergency care, for integrating children with special needs, and for rural child care will further broaden the service spectrum and could, in the longer term, result in a more responsive system that gives families a greater number of service options from which to choose. The move towards improving "partnerships" with education, labour, municipalities and employers reflects recognition of the need for greater coordination, joint planning, and collaboration among the major stakeholders in the child care system, and has resulted in some initial strategies that have been proposed to begin the process.

Funding. The introduction of the direct operating grant to licensed programs was also a significant change, for it is the first time the Ontario government has recognized the fact that the costs of operating day care programs cannot be fully supported by parents' fees and subsidy payments. The intent of the direct grant (to provide funding to improve the salaries of day care workers and providers) over time may help to address some of the problems experienced in attracting and retaining trained staff, and help to bring more stability to programs, thus indirectly assisting in improving their quality. This move, which broadens the scope of the provincial funding commitment, is progressive, given that it is not known to what extent the costs of providing direct grants will be shared under CAP or the proposed *Canada Child Care Act.*

The commitment to expand capital funding, and to increase the amount of cost-sharing from 50 to 80%, is also a significant shift, because it recognizes that if the child care system is to expand, local groups will require funding to renovate or construct new centres and to start-up their operation. Again, under the current CAP provisions these expenditures are not cost-sharable.

Finally, the proposed move to "income-testing," although still a welfare-oriented test for eligibility, if adopted, would be less intrusive, simpler to administer, and would provide greater equity by using standardized guidelines.

Quality Assurance. The initiative to bring MCSS and the Ministry of Colleges and Universities together to plan for human resource training and development is an important new addition. This move is essential if the problems resulting from the serious shortages of trained staff in certain areas of the province are to be addressed, and if the educational resources needed to support an expanding child care system are to be developed. The commitment to revise the *Day Nurseries Act* and to review enforcement and licensing policies and procedures is important work that is long overdue.

What Problems/Issues Remain?

Notwithstanding the progressiveness of the new policy and funding provisions, many fundamental issues remain to be addressed. Some of these issues arise from inconsistencies between the declared policy and its implementation (or alternatively, from the lack of follow-through); other issues remain because the *New Directions* policy statement did not consider them in the first place. Finally, the proposed *Canada Child Care Act* has had a negative effect on Ontario developments because of its introduction of new ceilings on cost-sharing.

Purpose

No definition of "public service." While the Accord, the Throne Speech and the *New Directions* (1987) policy paper all make commitments to move "child care from a welfare connotation toward one of public service," what is meant by this phrase is never defined. In fact, decisions to support the payment of direct grants to for-profit operators (whose efforts to earn profits drain needed dollars from subsidy and direct grant funds); the continuing use of an eligibility test; and, *in particular* the lack of sufficient funding to ensure that services are available and affordable across the province, together continue to perpetuate the welfare orientation of child care services and undermine the progressive promises.

An example: although *New Directions* (MCSS 1987) promised that "by 1990, provincial resources directed toward child care will have increased three-fold over five years..." (p. 5), thereby addressing the problems of availability and affordability, since August of 1988, Metro Toronto has been experiencing its most severe day care funding crisis in recent years:

> In 1988, Metropolitan Toronto had already implemented 1,552 new purchased group child care spaces when the Ministry announced it would cost share only 700 expansion spaces. Executive Committee approved the establishment of a $2.3 million emergency fund to preserve the level of subsidized child care implemented in 1988...Written provincial budget approval was officially received November 14, 1988. The level approved for provincial cost sharing falls $5.3 million short of the per diem rates paid for 1988 in the purchased group program. And the anticipated economic adjustment level of 4% will mean that cost-sharing could fall still further behind in 1989 (Picherack, 1989: 1–2).

With an estimated 4,500 children on the waiting list who have already been assessed as eligible for subsidy, the problem facing Toronto is acute. Further, Metro's move to a public service approach is now under attack:

> Service priorities have clearly become an issue within the Metropolitan community. This municipality, after a prolonged community consultation process in 1984, deliberately moved to a "first come, first served" approach to reflect its belief that child care is a public service and not a welfare service and that all who are eligible under the provincially-approved needs test are equally deserving of care. In the current climate of limited subsidy spaces, no subsidy growth and long waiting lists, the Ministry has criticized this municipality for not serving the most needy first...(Picherack, 1989: 2).

The provincial commitment to support a public service seems to have rapidly disappeared, along with the principles of affordability and reasonable accessibility. There does not seem to be an over-riding view of what a fully-developed public service might look like—such as one might find in France or Sweden— but rather a continuation of the patchwork of funding approaches and service models.

Related to this problem is the issue of the municipal role. Municipalities in Ontario are currently involved in the provision of child care in a number of ways. They administer and share 20% of the cost of day care subsidies—either through their directly operated programs, or through purchasing services from community programs. In some parts of Ontario, municipalities monitor and inspect the operation of the programs from which they purchase services. In the larger urban areas such as Windsor, Hamilton, Toronto, and Ottawa municipalities also take a leadership role in planning for the delivery of local child care services. However, because municipal involvement is discretionary, there are also areas of the province where municipal governments have been unwilling or financially unable to cover 20% of the subsidy costs. As a consequence, the lack of municipal involvement in certain areas has become a major obstacle to the equitable development and expansion of day care services across the province.

The *New Directions* policy paper announced that a review of the municipal role—both in the provision of child care and other social services—would be conducted (1987: 10). This review is currently under way, but to date, no decision has been reached. The discussions are complex because they also involve a consideration of cost sharing for social assistance and other social service programs.

One of the options proposed by the Social Assistance Review Committee (SARC) is that the provincial government assume all costs of funding social assistance programs currently provided by municipal governments. In return, the municipalities would take on the full 50% of cost sharing of child care. If this approach were to be adopted, given the uncertainty of federal funding and the proposed ceilings on cost sharing under Bill C–144, many municipalities would be in the position of either having to limit future expansion, or of having to absorb 100% of the costs of expansion. Neither alternative bodes well for achieving an equitable provision of child care services across the province.

Lack of Definition of Need/Demand for Services. Apart from a few generalized comments, the *New Directions* paper never considers the question of actual need/demand for child care services across the province, nor does it present a provincial plan detailing future expansion.

The document commits $7.4 million to new subsidies (fiscal 1987–88), which it estimates should provide assistance to about 13,000 more children over the next three years (p. 8). The 1988 Status Report notes that "nearly 5,000 new subsidies were introduced" in the first year, with an expenditure of $6.7 million—and at a much higher cost than originally projected (1988: 1).

It is also not clear how the proposed 13,000 new subsidies relate to the overall provincial need, nor what is planned in future years. While there is no question that Ontario has expanded the number of child care spaces and subsidies to a considerable degree over the last several years (estimated increase in subsidies between 1985–87: 10,600 [New Directions, MCSS 1987: 6]), it is interesting to note the National Council on Welfare (1988) finding that in 1987, only 12% of children whose parents were working or studying were placed in licensed day care—slightly less than the national average of 13% (p.4). The Council also noted that only 10% of children eligible for either a full or partial subsidy received it (p. 11).

Location of Child Care Within MCSS. While perhaps an issue of somewhat lesser magnitude, the continuing location of child care services in the Family Support and Income Maintenance Division of the MCSS, rather than with other Children's Services (i.e. with prevention and community support programs), seems to perpetuate the traditional welfare and special needs approach to child care. In this Division, child care services are functioning alongside and sometimes in competition with social assistance programs and other family support services which have tended to operate from a strongly entrenched welfare/special needs perspective.

Auspices/Service Models

Continuation of Support for Commercial Programs. Although there appears to be some vacillation, the new policy seems to be taking a middle-of-the-road position by "grandfathering" existing for-profit programs and attempting to limit the development of new for-profit programs by making them ineligible for start-up and expansion dollars.

Under *New Directions* (MCSS 1987), direct grants were to be extended to the *existing* commercial sector provided current federal restrictions were removed; on April 1, 1988 they were extended to commercial programs, as the result of extensive lobbying by commercial operators. They were, however, set at half the level provided to non-profit programs because federal cost-sharing has not been negotiated.

The provincial government has been waiting to see what the federal position regarding funding for commercial programs would be when the *Canada Child Care Act* (Bill C–144) was finalized, and by doing so has succeeded in shifting the debate to the federal level. Although it was not passed, the draft *Act* proposed sharing the cost of operating grants to both commercial and non-profit programs.

In its response to the federal proposals, the National Council of Welfare (1988) has stated:

> We do not believe the profit motive should be a dominant or long-term feature of child care in Canada. Profits are made by keeping costs down—paying low salaries to caregivers, raising child-staff ratios or compromising health, safety or nutritional standards—all of which hurt children (p. 27).

Although research on the differences in quality between for-profit and non-profit programs is limited and largely American, the recent *Study on Compliance with the Day Nurseries Act at Full-Day Child Care Centres in Metropolitan Toronto* reiterated a number of the concerns regarding the quality of care offered by commercial programs. Among her findings, West (1988) noted that while compliance problems existed in a number of types of programs, generally commercially-operated centres:

... were less likely to meet the requirements of the *Day Nurseries Act* and consequently more likely to receive a more restrictive type of licence than non-commercially-operated centres;

... were more likely to have a complaint lodged against them than any other type of operator;

... were more likely to have a staff-child ratio violation than non-commercially-operated centres;

... were more likely to be short the required number of trained staff, over a longer period than non-commercial centres (p. 2–3).

While this one study cannot in any sense be taken as definitive, the issue of whether commercial programs are offering generally poorer quality care is clearly one that requires further research and evaluation.

A Question of Jurisdiction

The *New Directions* paper never directly addresses the fundamental question that had been raised by various groups in earlier legislative hearings and which continues to be the subject of much debate among advocates and planners: whether child care services should come under the jurisdiction of education or social services.

In supporting a change, it has been argued by some that if child care services are to become truly available and affordable, if issues of low staff salaries, professional recognition and limited funding are to be resolved, if child care is to become universally available, then jurisdiction for these programs should be transferred from Community and Social Services to Education (Grubb and Lazerson, 1982).

The elementary school system (with both junior and senior kindergartens) already has a network of facilities in place in many communities throughout the province. Under earlier efforts (both MCSS and MOE), a number of these same schools added before- and after-school programs, as well as some full-day programs for younger children. In rural areas, the transportation systems to bring children to classes are in operation and could be extended for use by day care children. Under *New Directions* (MCSS 1987), new schools will be required to provide child care spaces in their construction plans, and existing schools are being encouraged to make greater use of school facilities for day care services.

For many, however, there is a fundamental question about the nature or kind of child care system which should be built, including the question of whether the education system is the best repository for the increasingly complex range of child care services. Grubb and Lazerson have articulated this viewpoint:

Public school control would lead to child care following the more conventional concept of the state's relationship to the child: it would require traditional education-based credentials for child care workers; it would dilute parental control and new concepts of professionals working with parents; it would make child care bureaucratic and relatively less flexible; and it would almost certainly emphasize school-like activities, eliminating the more "utopian" and community-oriented concepts of child care and ignoring the variety of purposes and models which now characterize child care (1982: 221).

By default, Ontario seems to be creating a patchwork system, with different mixes of child care and primary education services being developed in different communities.

Further, although the mandate and purpose of these two major service streams has differed historically (i.e. care vs. education), in recent years these differences have been disappearing. Day care programs are placing an increased emphasis on child development and early learning, and education, in turn, has been examining its approach to teaching early primary children and has identified the need to establish better "communication links with day care, caregivers and others involved in the education of young children to ensure consistency and continuity in program" (Early Primary Education Report, Ministry of Education, 1985: 34).

The problem remains, however, that there are now two major service systems in place in Ontario—child care and education—that are continuing to develop and expand services for essentially the same target group of young children.

Unresolved issues that arise from this overlap of mandate include:

Present and Potential Problems of Duplication of Services. In some areas of the province, full-day kindergarten programs have been introduced, resulting in the closing down of local day care or nursery school programs. If the proposal to permit flexible entry into kindergarten is adopted by Boards, it will also affect the demand for day care services (similar to the dual entry system in B.C.). Because of the kind and extent of funding available, day care programs are in no position to compete with kindergartens, irrespective of whether or not they may be the most appropriate service for the community.

The Need to Reconcile Different Standards of Operating. Reconciliation of standards is needed to avoid having different requirements for staff training, staff/child ratios, staff salaries, and the set up and organization of facilities—washrooms, kitchens, playgrounds, etc., in child care and kindergarten settings.

The *New Directions* (MCSS, 1987), policy promised a "joint consultation on kindergarten and school-aged child care needs and solutions" (p. 9); to date, this has only begun to take place and with a very limited scope.

Flexible Services/New Models

The move to support the development and testing of new, more flexible service models to begin to address needs not currently met by group and private home day care programs is a progressive one. The ministry has identified four specific categories of programs: shift work and emergency care, integration of children with special needs, new models for school-aged child care, and care for children in rural and isolated communities, in addition to child care resource centres. There are, however, some policy issues which need to be considered regarding these developments.

Shift Work and Emergency Care. While it is clearly useful to explore how services for parents working irregular hours or coping with emergencies and illness can be developed, the implementation of such services raises certain fundamental policy questions. For example, in the case of emergency and sick child care, is it good practice to have children who are ill, or experiencing a family crisis, taken care of by strange caregivers, often in a strange situation—or should working parents be given more leave to care for their children themselves? As an alternative, should Ontario be exploring different approaches to parental leave, such as those used in Sweden, which allow young parents to take extended leave or to work shorter hours when their children are very young? By funding and supporting these new programs is government essentially allowing employers to continue to ignore the family responsibilities of workers?

Integration of Children with Special Needs. The MCSS background paper, *Integrating Children Experiencing Special Needs in Day Nurseries* (1988), reported on a survey of programs carried out in 1983–84 and identified a number of service and funding issues. For some time now, there has been considerable agreement that many children with special needs can and should be integrated into "regular" day care programs, and that the "resource teacher combined with home-visits" model is too limited an approach for use in all settings. Beyond this general approach, however, there seems to be a policy vacuum and absence of a sense of direction at the provincial level. Although twenty five projects have been funded under *New Directions* (Status Report, 1988), there is no general plan to assist the hundreds of new child care centres that are being set up to include special needs children in their programs, nor to provide the special consultation and pre- and in-service training that would support a more serious move to integration.

Child Care Resource Services. The rationale behind the introduction of funding for child care resource services was to provide information and resources to "informal caregivers" and parents using these arrangements so that the general quality of informal child care arrangements might be improved. The *Survey of Child Care Support Services* (Doherty, 1987) reported that, in reality, many of the programs focus on supporting parents—middle class mothers seeking to strengthen their parenting skills and to provide socializing experiences for their child, or high risk mothers, e.g. teen mothers or those referred by child welfare authorities.

In practice, the distinction between parents and "informal caregivers" is a somewhat artificial one. While a parent may come to a resource centre for support with her own children, many move to become "informal caregivers" through joining babysitting co-ops, taking part in drop-ins and other activities, or through the simple gesture of helping another parent whom they have befriended.

Perhaps, considered in the light of the movement to develop a more comprehensive child care system, it is time to re-evaluate the relatively narrow mandate prescribed for child care resource programs and recognize the preventive and supportive role they can play in relation to all families, regardless of whether mothers are at home caring for young children or employed outside the home and dependent on alternative child care arrangements.

In other jurisdictions where these services have been in existence for a number of years, some child care resource centres have taken on the role of coordinating and helping to plan local child care services, bridging the gap between formal and informal child care, as well as between other children's and family services in the community (Weiss, 1983, Weissbourd, 1987).

Private Home Day Care Services

In recent years, the basis on which private home day care was developed has come into serious question. With the increased numbers of women participating in the labour force, the pool of caregivers remaining at home to care for children has been diminishing. Originally, funding for private home day care was based on a view that providers who were already at home caring for their own children could take in a few extra children—as company for their own youngsters, and earn a few extra dollars on the side.

With the move to licensing agencies and setting standards for private day care homes, with increased reporting and training requirements, and with more progressive labour legislation, private home day care services have become more professionalised and the employment status of providers (employee or independent contractor) has come into question. Because of these changes, the overall costs of private home day care have increased dramatically, so that what was once thought to be an inexpensive service is now equal to and in some cases more costly than group care.

As a result, it has become necessary to rethink the whole approach to private home day care, and MCSS is in the process of conducting a fundamental review of the service. In addition to the problems associated with this service model, there is also a problem of inequity if private home day care services are viewed within the context of a more comprehensive child care system. By setting standards which only apply to homes supervised by licensed agencies, government has, in effect, created a two-tiered system of home care. A small number of homes, those supervised by licensed agencies, are required to meet operating standards, and in turn, receive regular support and access to a variety of resources and training opportunities. The majority of homes—operated by informal caregivers—are not required to meet any standards beyond that of having fewer than six children, and do not have access to subsidized children, nor, depending on their community, to child care resource programs. Most other jurisdictions require that all home caregivers be licensed or registered and meet certain minimum standards.

Funding

At its simplest, the amount of funding presently available for child care services, however managed, is inadequate to meet all the commitments made in the *New Directions* (MCSS, 1987) policy and to support the full development of a public service. Even the initial commitment almost to double the amount of funding—bringing the total expenditure to $325 million by 1990—may be threatened. Apart from the general impact of larger economic conditions, the dollars available to support child care have been threatened by two significant factors: (1) the proposed *Canada Child Care Act* and the uncertainty of future federal funding, and (2) the growing pressure for the Ontario government to increase funding for other social and public service programs.

The National Strategy on Child Care

Ontario has not been alone in reviewing child care policies. At the national level, the Royal Commission on Equality in Employment, 1984, the Task Force on Child Care, 1985, and the Special Committee on Child Care, 1987, have all issued reports considering the need for child care and parental support, and the role that the federal government should play in bringing this about.

In December of 1987, the federal government announced a "National Strategy on Child Care," the first part of which took the form of tax assistance—doubling the child care expense deduction and increasing the refundable child tax credit (by up to $100 per child in 1988, $200 in subsequent years) at an estimated total cost of $2.3 billion. It also included the creation of the "Child Care Special Initiatives Fund" which will provide $100 million over the next seven years for innovative research and development projects and for public education.

In July 1988, the second component, the proposed *Canada Child Care Act*, was introduced into Parliament, but failed to be approved by the Senate before a federal election was called in November 1988. The new *Act* was to replace the day care provisions in CAP; its goal was to increase "the number of child care spaces throughout Canada by at least two hundred thousand" over the next seven years at a maximum cost of $4 billion (Bill C–144, p.1). In addition, operating grants would be provided to both non-profit and commercial programs, capital grants would only be provided to non-profit programs, and cost-sharing would be on a 75 (federal): 25 (provincial) basis. Less wealthy provinces could also negotiate "top-up" grants to help develop their programs to bring them more in line with those in other provinces (Bill C–144; National Council of Welfare, 1988).

Although never passed, the proposed *Canada Child Care Act* suggested fundamental changes to the nature and extent of cost-sharing arrangements as they had existed under CAP and signalled the general intent of the federal government towards future funding for child care. While containing some innovative measures, Bill C–144 was not well received by child care, social service and women's groups who have lobbied strenuously against it. The proposed *Act* was criticized for its lack of innovation and vision; for the absence of any statement of national objectives or principles (such as can be found in the *Canada Health Act*); for allowing profit-making programs to receive funding; and for not including much needed changes in maternity benefits provisions under unemployment insurance.

Most importantly, from the perspective of the Ontario government, the new *Act* proposed to eliminate the open-ended nature of cost-sharing that exists in CAP and set ceilings on the amount of federal cost-sharing. At this time, there is concern that if the new *Act* were to be re-introduced and passed, provincial governments would be in serious difficulty in future years when the full cost of the newly expanded programs are realized. The National Council on Welfare (1988) also comments on the detrimental effect that ceilings would have on the problem of low staff salaries and on the poor staff/child ratios that exist in some provinces. "Putting a lid on expenditures could make it more difficult to get decent pay for child care workers, because wages account for about 75% of child care operating costs...Much the same can be said about the ratios of children to staff. If we want better ratios, we have to be prepared to hire more staff and pay them decent wages" (p. 24–25). Overall, the general lack of clarity about future federal cost-sharing arrangements, together with the threat of funding restrictions makes it difficult for Ontario to plan, and has resulted in a very cautious and conservative stance regarding any future financial commitments to child care.

Competition for Funding

Historically, child care programs have been, and continue to be in competition for funding with basic social service "safety-net" programs such as social assistance, child welfare, and services to the elderly and the handicapped. This problem is currently acute, for the Ontario government is caught with a major funding commitment to expand child care at the same time that there is considerable community and political pressure to fund proposals to reform social assistance programs estimated at an overall cost of over $2 billion.

In addition, there are growing demands for funding for seniors to support the development of community-based services, as well as for other children's services (such as the need for more salary dollars for group homes). These social services funding requirements are also in competition in the larger Ontario context with the need for increased funding in the housing, education, and health care systems.

Quality Assurance

Deficiencies in the Licensing and Monitoring System

Recently, the Globe and Mail carried a five-part series entitled *"Who's Minding the Children?"* It began as follows:

Nearly 40 percent of inspected day-care centres and nursery schools in Ontario fall short of the province's regulations on safety, cleanliness or quality, a review of hundreds of inspection reports show. An examination of more than 1,600 inspection reports, obtained by The Globe and Mail, reveals a day-care centre where 50 children were fed lunch with 3 1/2 pounds of chicken, another where children exercised on rotting equipment and many others where very young children played near uncovered electrical outlets, exposed wiring and unlocked drugs and cleaning supplies...what emerged after a review of reports was a picture of a child-care network whose quality and safety would shock parents, and a licensing and enforcement system that is straining, often unsuccessfully, to meet the demands of a growing social service...(McIntosh and Rauhala, Feb. 3, 1989, p. 1).

These articles have brought to public attention a problem that has been developing over a number of years. As the child care system has expanded, the number of Ministry staff who are available to support and monitor programs has not, and in some areas of the province they are carrying impossible workloads. As the authors report, there is also a lack of standardized policies and procedures in place across the province, resulting in widely different interpretations about what standards of care are acceptable. While some flexibility of interpretation is desirable because of the diversity of programs and settings, there is no centralized tracking of the kinds of accommodations or adjustments that are made, nor any analysis of them. To aggravate the situation further, in many areas the demand for more child care is so great that borderline programs are often left to continue operating (albeit with increased supervision and support) because most of the families using them have no access to alternative arrangements.

The *New Directions* (MCSS, 1987) policy identified the need to review current enforcement and licensing policies and procedures and to assess their effectiveness and consistency (p. 16). Although slow to begin the review, the publication of these articles may help to insure that it will be carried out.

Lack of Sufficient Training Opportunities at All Levels

The expansion of the child care system has also resulted in severe shortages of trained staff in some areas of the province. This, in turn, has been the result of insufficient training opportunities, both at the community college level to train early childhood educators, and at the university level, to train administrators, planners and policy analysts. There is also a general lack of opportunities and resources to support in-service training and to allow untrained or partially-trained workers to upgrade their knowledge and skills. A joint committee on Human Resources Planning and Training with representation from MCSS and the Ministry of Colleges and Universities has been set up and a study has been commissioned to review training programs and clarify the qualifications required for persons working in child care, as well as to present options for training standards and for assessing the competency of workers. A second project is planned to survey the supply and demand for early childhood educators, to explore factors related to the retention and attrition of trained staff, and to examine factors that affect the development of a career path in an expanded child care system.

Limited Support for Research

Although the *Status Report on Year One* noted that $340,000 was spent in 1987–88 on 12 research/data gathering projects, the emphasis to date seems to be on information-gathering or surveys. There does not appear to be enough support for more basic research on child development or for examining such issues as the longitudinal effects of child care on children's development and later success.

A Policy-Relevant Research Agenda on Child Care

A policy-relevant research agenda on child care issues could address many questions that could help shape and modify Ontario's policies and programs. On the most fundamental level, research could provide reliable information on the number, ages, characteristics, and distribution of children and families using alternative forms (and combinations) of child care arrangements. Basic estimates of the supply and demand for various child care services, for subsidized child care, and for support programs are all necessary for responsible and responsive social planning.

Second, research should address the effects of child care arrangements (and the lack of them) on children and families. What are the effects of group care, private home day care, informal care, and combinations of various care arrangements under present circumstances (e.g., is infant group care or extended parental leave better for babies, more cost-effective)? What are the effects of introducing new care options (e.g., junior kindergarten or workplace day care) or services (e.g. child care support programs) on children, families and communities?

Third, systematic research is also needed on the actual effects of different child care policies (operating grants, capital grants, changes in regulations, enhanced or restricted availability of subsidies) on child care availability and the quality of care that is provided. Similarly, research is needed on the effects of child care policies on men and women's ability to enter and progress in the labour force in order to improve their incomes and economic status, and to provide stable, nurturing care for their children.

Fourth, further research is needed on the interrelationship of child care quality and family variables on children's development. Suggestions in the literature that children from low income families are most adversely affected by poor quality care should be tested further. Other studies indicate that day care and family resource programs can play an important role in primary prevention by supporting parents and providing opportunities for children's learning and development. However, considerably more work is required to understand what specific kinds of programs and combinations of services are most effective and cost efficient. The results of such research would also be relevant for provincial plans for new primary prevention initiatives.

Finally, we would suggest that researchers study such policy-relevant issues as the factors that can support or undermine quality in child care settings, including the relative and cumulative effects of such factors as sponsorship (for-profit or non-profit centres), various program approaches, the level and kind of staff training, the degree of parental involvement, and changes in funding and program policies at the municipal, provincial, and federal levels.

V. CONCLUSIONS

This chapter has described the need for a variety of policies, benefits and services that can support parents and children. There are, undoubtedly, families in Ontario who are well served by the combination of government policies, workplace benefits, and child care services that are available to them. There are many others, however, whose daily lives are marked by continual frustration and distress as they try to ensure the economic and psychological well-being of their children. While there are signs that many new and creative efforts are being made, and that leadership is being demonstrated, the challenge of providing equitable access to necessary services and benefits that support families remains.

A complementary challenge is present for those interested in research on social policies in this area. Research is needed on all fronts, including basic descriptive research, comparative policy analysis, and evaluation research that considers child, family, and community variables and their interactions. We hope that this chapter provides some encouragement for that research, as well as for the policies that are needed in Ontario for the 1990s and beyond.

3

CHILDREN'S MENTAL HEALTH ISSUES
Prevention and Treatment

Michael H. Boyle

Prevention and effective treatment of mental health problems in children are major objectives of health and social welfare systems in developed countries. Governments pursue these objectives by developing policies and by sponsoring programs to: (1) promote positive mental health and adjustment among children in the general population; and (2) manage calls for help to resolve potential or existing mental health problems in individual children. This latter focus, though not necessarily the most desirable, is the most common, visible and direct means available to governments for reducing the burden of mental health problems among the young.

Ontario possesses a vast array of services, agencies, and practitioners to assist children and adolescents who have elicited mental health concerns. The Ministries of Community and Social Services, Health and Education, in addition to voluntary and self-help groups, all sponsor programs aimed at children's mental health. The most focused services are provided by Children's Mental Health Centres (CMHC's). CMHC's provide child treatment (and family intervention) for children exhibiting signs of mental or psychiatric disorder. There are 95 of these centres in Ontario; they are funded and licensed by the Ministry of Community and Social Services (MCSS) and operate under the provisions of the Child and Family Services Act, 1984 (Government of Ontario, 1987). In addition to the 95 CMHC's sponsored by MCSS, there are child treatment centres jointly funded by MCSS and the Ministry of Health, and a number of outpatient, inpatient and community mental health programs for children and adolescents sponsored solely by the Ministry of Health.

The objective of this chapter is to draw attention to a limited number of questions and mental health issues that might be addressed to advance the life quality of Ontario children. It is assumed that concern for child mental health should be broadly focused so that the relevant constituents for policy and research are not only children who find their way to mental health services but also children in the general population who experience mental health problems and related distress or impairment. In a strict sense, the chapter is about a central component of mental health, namely, childhood mental disorder. This circumscribed view follows the existing research base which concentrates on mental disorder.

This chapter is divided into five major sections and a discussion. Section I focuses on issues related to the definition, classification and measurement of childhood mental disorder. What does it mean to be diagnosed with a mental or psychiatric disorder? Do our classifications of disorder serve useful purposes? Should our focus on mental disorder be enlarged to include other characteristics of the child and his/her environment? Section II examines the frequency and seriousness of child mental disorders in the general population. What do we know about the scope and magnitude of these disorders? Are there perceptible trends that childhood mental disorders are increasing or decreasing? Section III discusses the provision of mental health services to children. We would like to believe that mental health services are available to and used by children in need who would benefit from help. What evidence do we have that this is the case? Section IV looks at the effectiveness of mental health interventions for children who use services. It is the attainment of preventive and therapeutic objectives that should stimulate our activities to improve child mental health. What do we know about the usefulness of these activities? Section V discusses the organization and provision of mental health services to children. A recent discussion paper sponsored by MCSS (Sullivan, 1988) points out that structural problems exist in the distribution, flexibility and responsiveness of services for child mental health. What are the origins of these problems? Are government initiatives to shift the focus of funding from an agency to a service basis and to decentralize responsibility for children's services (Ontario Ministry of Community and Social Services, 1979; 1987a; 1987b) effective responses to the structural problems that have been identified?

Ultimately, the central issue for children's mental health bears on the usefulness of activities to promote mental health and to prevent and to treat child mental health problems. Do these activities do more good than harm? Are they provided at reasonable cost? What changes are required to make them more effective, efficient and fairly distributed? Answers to these global questions will continue to elude us until we address a number of fundamental questions—some of which will become apparent in the remainder of the chapter.

Child, for purposes of this chapter, is someone under 18 years of age. This boundary coincides with the one used by the Child and Family Services Act, 1984 (Government of Ontario, 1987) to restrict child mental health services provided by agencies funded through MCSS. Because of its scope, recency and relevance, the Ontario Child Health Study (OCHS) will provide the core data for analyzing childhood disorder in the general population (Offord et al., 1987). Information from other epidemiologic studies will be included, when available, to complement, extend or challenge inferences that arise from the OCHS. Details of the OCHS methodology appear elsewhere (Boyle et al., 1987); a brief summary is included as Appendix 1.

I. CLASSIFICATION AND MEASUREMENT OF CHILDHOOD MENTAL DISORDER

The features that distinguish mental disorders from mental health problems are complexity and severity. Childhood mental disorders encompass complex, serious and persistent difficulties of cognitive functioning, emotional control and behavioural expression. In the present context, the term mental disorder is used generically and not restricted to disorders thought to have a biological basis.

Definition of Mental Disorder

Consensus has emerged that childhood mental disorder, as a general category, possesses two defining characteristics: (1) the presence of symptoms; and (2) co-existing distress, impairment or disadvantage (Rutter and Graham, 1968, Rutter, 1975, pp. 18–24; Cantwell, 1980; Kazdin, 1983; Knopf, 1984 pp. 23–28; Hersov, 1985). Symptoms are signs of abnormality tied to psychological processes; they should be developmentally inappropriate and signal maladaptation in the child. Symptoms come in a variety of forms and may be expressed as an abnormality of overt behaviour (aggressive act), affect (depressed mood), cognition (irrational belief) or perception (hallucination) (Kazdin, 1983).

Distress, impairment or disadvantage may be viewed as the negative consequences of symptoms, indexed by suffering or personal discomfort, interference with development, social relationships or role performance; or limitations in attaining socially desirable objectives. Although a single "cardinal" symptom in conjunction with distress, impairment or disadvantage may constitute evidence of mental disorder, it is customary to require the presence of a cohesive group of symptoms that "run together" within a limited time period.

Attempts to refine our understanding of childhood mental disorder have prompted clinicians and researchers to look for children with distinctive symptom patterns that might be used to delineate specific childhood disorders for classification. These efforts are founded on the belief that mental disorder subserves multiple categories, nested hierarchically. Figure 3–1 illustrates this view. Additional categories might be defined to broaden or deepen coverage.

The dominant psychiatric perspective on mental disorder is that it is a property of individuals or exists "within the skin." As a result, persons are classified as exhibiting mental disorder when they meet predetermined criteria based on verbal or written reports and/or observation. At present, the criteria for classifying disorder attempt to be atheoretical; they rest on currently accessible descriptive information, namely symptoms and associated features of individuals.

A narrow view of mental disorder was adopted in psychiatry to unify approaches to classification and to make the descriptions of disorders more objective (Spitzer and Cantwell, 1980). In 1980, this perspective on mental disorder seemed like an effective way to break down barriers among mental health professionals from different backgrounds and to provide a common nosology for studying the etiology, course and response to intervention of children with differ-

Figure 3–1

Categories for Classifying Childhood Psychiatric Disorder (example)

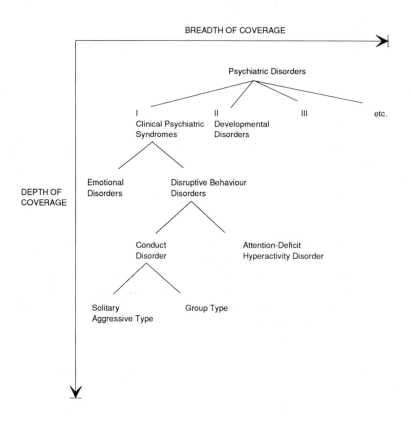

ent disorders. There are, however, some fundamental difficulties with our approaches to classifying and measuring childhood mental disorder. The central problems include the following:

1. Recognition of individual disorders
2. Use of thresholds to identify disturbance
3. Validity of classification
4. Limited conceptualization

Recognition of Individual Disorders

The classification of childhood mental disorder in North America is dominated by the Diagnostic and Statistical Manual (DSM) produced by the American Psychiatric Association. The most recent version of the DSM, called

DSM-III-R (American Psychiatric Association, 1987), lists 12 general categories of mental disorder arising by adolescence, and within these categories specifies 46 subcategories. Critics have argued convincingly that many of these categories are not justified. These arguments come from clinicians who feel that some categories are nonexistent and from researchers who are unable to identify empirically, many of the symptom patterns outlined in DSM-III (American Psychiatric Association, 1980).

Use of Thresholds to Identify Disturbance

DSM-III is essentially a multicategory classification system in which childhood mental disorders are defined dichotomously (as present or absent). Using categories to describe disorder enable us to talk about cases and this serves research, clinical and administrative needs (Vaillant and Schnurr, 1988). Unfortunately, our methods for defining disorder admit some ambiguity that needs to be acknowledged.

To define each category of childhood mental disorder, DSM-III-R provides a list of symptoms plus a cutoff that specifies the number of symptoms that must be present to identify a particular type of disorder. The usefulness of this approach rests on demonstrating that the major divisions between disorder and normality are non-arbitrary. This means simply that some objective basis exists for grouping children together other than arbitrary judgments. Two examples are provided in Figure 3–2. The top diagram of Figure 3–2 illustrates a frequency distribution of symptoms defining a hypothetical disorder in the population. The distribution is bimodal. It would appear that individuals with five or more symptoms cluster together, providing some objective basis for identifying a threshold for categorization. The bottom diagram of Figure 3–2 shows the relationship between a variable that is expected to be associated with mental disorder (e.g. presence/absence of poor school performance) and a count of symptoms defining a hypothetical disorder. The percent of children with poor school performance remains low and constant until a count of five symptoms is reached. At this point, the percentage of children with school failure dramatically rises and remains constant for children with six or more symptoms. Although these examples distort what could be found empirically, they illustrate what we should look for to demonstrate that categorical representations of disorder are potentially applicable and useful for the purposes that they are intended to serve.

Discovering an objective basis for categorizing childhood psychiatric disorder is going to be a formidable task. First, there are virtually no examples in the research literature reminiscent of the patterns displayed in Figure 3–2. Disorders such as autism and schizophrenia, by virtue of their infrequency and seriousness, might be expected to exhibit these patterns, but this is unlikely to be the case for the more frequently occurring disorders listed on Axis I of DSM-III-R. Second, clinicians are being directed increasingly to use symptom counts above arbitrarily selected thresholds to identify disorder (American Psychiatric Association, 1987). This implicitly acknowledges that most mental disorders are represented

Figure 3–2
*Top: Hypothetical frequency distribution of symptoms defining
a childhood psychiatric disorder.
Bottom: Hypothetical relationship between percent of poor school performance and
number of symptoms defining a childhood psychiatric disorder.*

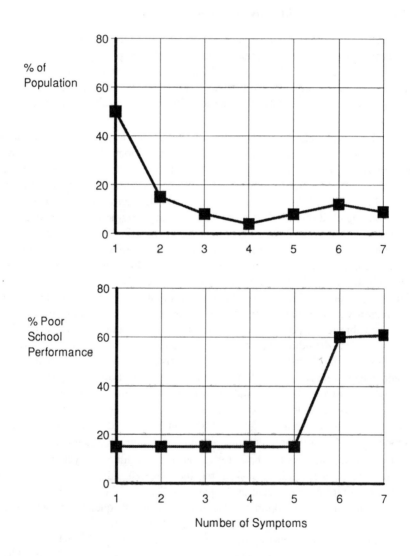

more usefully by dimensions than by categories and that distinctions between normal and abnormal rest on normative judgments. Third, the boundary problem—or where to draw the line between one disorder and another, and between disorder and normality—is as big a problem among adults as among children even though the study of adult mental disorder has had a much longer history (Kendell, 1988).

Validity of Classification

The need for and practical advantages of developing a classification system to describe childhood mental disorder are readily apparent. The concepts (disorders) used to classify children provide clinicians with a language for communication and patient management; administrators with a rationale for planning and resource allocation; and researchers with the opportunity to pursue scientific objectives. Further to this we have begun to consolidate our ideas about differentiating childhood psychopathology into a limited number of categories and have available to us instruments capable of reliable classification (Gutterman, O'Brien and Young, 1987).

Despite advances in the classification of childhood psychopathology, important questions persist about the informational value of such classifications beyond their defining characteristics. This is echoed in recent concern about the lack of validating criteria (Werry, Reeves and Elkind, 1987; Quay, Routh and Shaperio, 1987)—a concern that applies whether we measure disorder as a categorical phenomenon (i.e. present or absent) or a dimensional phenomenon (i.e. existing to various degrees). In plain terms, the lack of validating criteria refers to our inability to confirm empirically inferences that we would like to make about children classified with particular types of disorder. These inferences would focus on the origins of disorder, burden of suffering, untreated course and response to intervention. Inability to transcend the descriptive terminology (symptoms and other features) used in our classifications severely limits the clinical and scientific usefulness of our concepts.

The issues bearing on our attempts to discern mental disorder, particularly in children below age 14, are both complex and long-standing. In the first place, children rarely apply for help with mental health problems; rather parents, on their own or prompted by others, decide that help is needed. Our view of childhood disorder may be distorted by factors external to the child that influence parents to seek out child mental health services. Second, assessment of the young child poses special difficulty. Evaluation of standardized interviews to inquire about symptoms in children under the age of 11 years indicate that their replies are highly unreliable (Edelbrock, Costello, Dulcan, Kalas and Conover, 1985). Our response to problems of assessing young children has been to rely on the perceptions of informed adults, particularly parents and teachers. Unfortunately, these informants more often than not disagree with one another, and the reasons for this have not been investigated adequately (Achenbach, McConaughy and Howell, 1987). Third, the context for assessing children is one of rapid developmental change. Thus, symptoms must be evaluated against a shifting developmental background that enlarges the complexity of identifying disturbance. Fourth, the inner world of children poses special assessment problems. Informed adults or carefully trained observers may accurately describe a child's behaviour, but the link between child behaviour and his/her subjective state is not well understood. Furthermore, there is less agreement between raters (e.g. parents and teachers) on data pertaining to the inner state of the child than data on observable behaviour. Finally, unstandardized clinical assessments have been shown time and again to yield unreliable information (Kutchins and Kirk, 1986). This raises serious questions about our knowledge of childhood psychopathology that has been accumulating from experience with children and families requesting mental health services.

Limited Conceptualization

Although efforts to classify childhood mental disorder represent important activities, a danger exists that our vision of the child will become too restricted and negative. Until recently, mental disorder provided the frame of reference for discussing mental health. Current efforts to define mental health (Epp, 1988) remind us that our concern for children must be broadened.

Opportunities exist for developing measures of mental health that tap a full continuum of experience from positive to negative (e.g. Ware, 1988). Also, there are characteristics of children, distinct from, yet closely associated with mental health, that deserve attention. These would include the quality of interpersonal relationships, achievement of socially desirable goals, purposeful use of leisure time and the degree of support available in the environment. The preference here is to place these latter characteristics under the general heading "quality of life" and to distinguish them from the more direct measures of mental health that might be developed (e.g. psychological well-being, behavioural/emotional control, cognitive functioning).

Summary

A review of our approaches to classifying and measuring childhood mental disorder points out some difficult issues. First, the proliferation of categories for classifying childhood mental disorder has gone too far. Many of the categories listed in DSM-III-R are simply not recognizable in practice. Current efforts should focus on evaluating the usefulness (i.e. validity) of categories of disorder which seem meaningful to broad groups of mental health professionals.

Second, the absence of an objective basis for drawing the boundary between normal and abnormal creates problems for those attempting to estimate the magnitude and scope of mental disorder in the general population; for those seeking funds in support of mental health programs; and for those wishing to evaluate the extent to which existing mental health services are complying with their mandate to help the most troubled children and their families.

Third, preoccupation with childhood mental disorder has eclipsed concern for measuring aspects of child life quality that are separable from, yet related to, mental disorder. Axis IV (severity of psychosocial stressors) and Axis V (global assessment of functioning) on DSM-III-R represent somewhat crude attempts to broaden our perspective. Clearly, much more work needs to be done in this area.

II. FREQUENCY AND SERIOUSNESS OF CHILD MENTAL DISORDERS

A consensus has emerged on the usefulness of defining a limited number of childhood mental disorders. These disorders can be subdivided by their frequency of occurrence into two major groups: (1) very rare and severely debilitating conditions where suspicions exist that the brain is centrally involved; and (2) more frequently occurring disorders, subject to biological influences, but also closely associated with environmental forces including the family, schools, peers and social context. For most of these disorders, clinical recognition of symptom groupings is supported by empirical analyses (Achenbach, 1980; Quay, 1986; Achenbach, Conners, Quay, Verhulst and Howell, 1989; Edelbrock and Costello, 1988).

Scope and Magnitude

Among the disorders that would qualify for group (1), autism has received the most attention in community studies. Autism usually begins in the first two years of life and is characterized by severe impairment in social interactions, verbal and nonverbal communication, interests and activities. A population screening study done in a region of Nova Scotia estimated the prevalence of autism to be 10/10,000 (Bryson, Clark and Smith, 1988), somewhat higher than the 2–5/10,000 reported in earlier studies (Smalley, Asarnow and Spence, 1988). Notably, 75% of children designated autistic in Nova Scotia were also classified as mentally retarded.

There are a variety of other disorders (e.g. mental retardation, pervasive developmental disorders other than autism, schizophrenia etc.) that would qualify for group (1), but most of them occur too rarely in the general population for community study. Children with these disorders almost invariably grow up to become impaired adults. There is no controversy about the severity of these disorders and burden of suffering as evaluated by the adverse effects on the family and community, devaluation of life quality for the child and high economic costs to society for assessment and long-term care.

The mental disorders that have achieved a consensus and qualify for group (2) occur frequently enough in the general population to permit reliable study using existing survey methods. Although more frequent, these disorders are often as distressing and disabling as those classified in group (1).

It has been customary to subdivide the more common mental disorders into two major groupings: disruptive behaviour or externalizing disorders and emotional or internalizing disorders. Conduct disorder and hyperactivity (or attention-deficit hyperactivity disorder) have received the most attention in the behavioural category. Each of them are reported to affect from 2–10% of children depending on the population studied and methods of assessment (Costello, 1989). Rates for boys are frequently 2–3 times higher than rates for girls, and the disorders frequently co-exist in individual children. Typically, children presenting clinically with conduct disorder exhibit severe, persistent and unmanageable antisocial behaviour in which the basic rights of others and major age-appropriate social norms are violated. Common indicators of the disorder are physical aggression, destructiveness, lying, stealing and delinquent behaviour. The best available evidence indicates that about 50% of children clinically referred with conduct disorder will be physically violent or engage in illegal behaviour as adults (Robins, 1966; 1978). Hyperactivity is characterized by impulsiveness, motor over-activity and restless, hyperactive behaviour. Information on the sequelae of hyperactivity is less extensive. The best available data suggest that about 30% of children clinically referred with hyperactivity will exhibit features of the disorder in young adulthood and that about half these individuals will meet criteria for conduct and/or substance use disorders (Gittelman, Mannuzza, Shenker and Bonagura, 1985).

In the emotional category, depression and various forms of anxiety have received the most intensive study in the general population. Prevalence of depression has been reported to go from 1–2.7% in childhood to 3.7% in adolescence (Fleming, Offord and Boyle, 1989). As summarized by Costello (1989), the prevalence of anxiety varies by type: 3.5–5.4% for separation anxiety, 2.7–4.6% for overanxious disorder, and 2.3–9.2% for simple phobias. Rates for emotional or internalizing disorder tend to be higher in girls than in boys during adolescence but not childhood (Angold, 1988). Evidence is accumulating that over 50% of clinically referred children with a diagnosis of depression will experience relapses of the disorder within five years (Asarnow, Goldstein, Carlson, Perdue, Bates and Keller, 1988; Garber, Kriss, Koch and Lindholm, 1988; Kovacs, Feinberg, Crouse-Novak, Paulauskas, Pollock and Finkelstein, 1984). However, the psychiatric sequelae of childhood and adolescent anxiety disorders are not well documented (Gittelman, 1986).

Until recently, inclusive estimates of mental disorder among children in the general population varied enormously from 6.3–37.0% with a median rate of 11.9% (Gould, Wunsch-Hitzig and Dohrenwend, 1981). Studies of late have produced tighter estimates but they have all been high; for example, five community studies reviewed by Costello (1989) reported prevalence of one or more disorders to go from 17.0–22.0%. If the long-term profile of even half the children classified with mental disorder in the general population turns out to be similar to clinically referred children, then the burden of suffering associated with childhood mental disorder will be truly alarming.

In addition to the mental disorders that are recognized widely at present, there are a variety of other problems in childhood and adolescence that attract the concern of mental health professionals. Some of these problems occur frequently, such as alcohol and drug use in adolescence; some are rare, such as attempted suicide; others signify danger to the physical and emotional health of the child caused by poor parenting (e.g. abuse, neglect and abandonment) or life in poverty. Each of these problems and many more related to mental disorder deserve full examination. Space limitations rule out such analysis here.

Future Trends

To estimate future trends in childhood mental disorder, it would be necessary to have available longitudinal information on childhood mental health problems from successive groups of children born in different years. Even if this information were available, predicting levels of childhood psychopathology would be hazardous. Although some data suggest that maladjustment among adolescents is increasing, the evidence is not conclusive.

In a recent analysis, Klerman (1988) used data from a number of large-sample family studies and community epidemiological surveys to argue for increased rates of depression among adolescents and young adults born in the years after World War II. Although his arguments were impressive, measurement and sampling deficiencies in the studies cited could account for some of the results. Moreover, relevant Canadian data are not available.

Increases in adolescent suicide, particularly among white American males, also have raised concerns about future mental health problems in the young (Rosenberg, Smith, Davidson and Conn, 1987). To put these concerns in perspective, Klerman (1988) noted that these rates peaked in 1978–1980 and have been declining since. Canadian data on suicide among 15–19 year olds reveal alarming increases between 1966 and 1977 but an essentially flat pattern between 1977 and 1985 (National Task Force on Suicide in Canada, 1987, p. 82). Among 20–24 year olds, the highest rate of suicide since 1960 was 22.6/100,000 recorded in 1977; the rate in 1985 was 17.7/100,000.

Increased hard drug use among American youth, particularly use of cocaine (O'Malley, Bachman and Johnston, 1984) has stimulated concern about a drug epidemic. In Canada, this concern may not be as acute, at least among school attenders. Evidence from repeat surveys among Ontario students in grades 7–13 indicate that cocaine use has not varied appreciably between 1977 and 1985 (Ontario Ministry of Treasury and Economics, 1987). In addition, use of tobacco, alcohol, cannabis, barbiturates and LSD declined consistently and modestly from 1981. To place the Ontario survey data in perspective, it should be noted that for all age groups total drug offenses related to cocaine increased in Ontario from 371 in 1977 to 1,411 in 1984 (Ontario Ministry of Treasury and Economics, 1987, p. 69).

A recent analysis of young offenders in Ontario (Leschied, Jaffe, Suderman, Austin and Willis, 1988) raises some concern about severity of disturbance among children and adolescents in trouble with the law. Violent offenses (i.e. homicide, assault, sexual offenses, abduction and robbery) among 7–15 year olds increased from 3,015 in 1974 to 4,604 in 1983 despite a decline in the adolescent population by 14.6% (Leschied at al., 1988, pp. 15–16). However, the increase in violent offenses was not accompanied by increases in the overall number of charges, which remained stable at about 66.1/100,000 population aged 7–15.

Another position is that demographic, economic and technological changes may increase the risk of childhood mental disorder in the future. It is not clear how far to take this argument. For example, single parent families in Ontario as a percent of census families has increased from 8.9% in 1971 to 11.9% in 1986 (Statistics Canada, 1988). The emotional and economic burden normally associated with single parent status can be expected to affect the children in these families adversely. To place this in perspective, it should be noted that the percent of live births accounted for by teenage mothers (another "high-risk" group) has decreased from 10.9% in 1976 to 5.5% in 1985 (Province of Ontario, 1987). Further reductions in births to teenage mothers might be expected to reduce the risk of a variety of adverse outcomes for children. Of course, this must be weighted by the increased proportion of teenage mothers now keeping their babies.

On balance, the evidence available for predicting changes in levels of childhood psychopathology is weak. It would appear that the volume of child mental health problems will remain proportionate to population size. This is not to say that demand for child mental health services will follow the same course. Demand for service is driven by many factors in addition to health concerns (Richman, Boutilier and Harris, 1984). Increasing the visibility, accessibility and acceptability of child mental health services can be expected to increase demand even when levels of mental health remain constant.

Summary

Several points arise from a discussion of the scope and magnitude of childhood mental disorders. First, rare conditions such as autism, mental retardation and schizophrenia are severely debilitating and accompanied by enormous adverse consequences for affected children and their caretakers. Children with these disorders are likely to come to the attention of the mental health system and deserve high clinical and research priority. The low prevalence of these disorders makes it impractical to study them in the general population.

Second, the more frequently occurring disorders such as conduct disorder, hyperactivity (or attention-deficit hyperactivity disorder), depression and the anxiety disorders are reported to effect 15–20% of children in the general population. Research evidence suggests that anywhere from 30–70% of clinically referred children meeting the criteria for these disorders will experience recurrent difficulties in later life. It cannot be said that these outcomes will apply to children in the general population classified with these disorders. The clinical and social importance of estimated prevalences of childhood mental disorder in general populations awaits longitudinal study.

Third, predicting future trends in childhood mental disorder is a hazardous enterprise. Informal discussions with those who work in child welfare, child mental health and young offender settings would suggest that the problems experienced by children are becoming more complex and serious. The data needed to evaluate this perspective from a sound, empirical basis are simply lacking.

III. PROVISION OF CHILD MENTAL HEALTH SERVICES

In Ontario during 1983, the six-month prevalence of one or more disorders was 18.1% (Offord et al., 1987). Estimates for the four administrative regions of MCSS were not significantly different from one another, nor were the regional rates for any of the individual disorders.

The prevalences for the individual disorders subdivided by child age and identifying respondent are displayed in Table 3–1. Several points emerge. First, parent ratings exceed thresholds for disorder far less often than do teacher ratings in the 4–11 age group or youth ratings in the 12–16 age group. Although parents identify more 4–11 year olds with emotional disorder than do teachers (i.e. 6.0 vs. 4.7%), teacher ratings account for almost all the children identified with conduct disorder and hyperactivity. Second, pervasive disorder is extremely rare. In the 4–11 age group, the prevalence of disorder where ratings from both parents and teachers exceed the threshold (pervasive disorder) is only 1.6% (Table 3–1). Third, the prevalence of conduct disorder is higher in the 12–16 age group than the 4–11 age group, while the reverse is true for hyperactivity. Fourth, the internalizing disorders (i.e. emotional disorder and somatization) are more prevalent than the externalizing disorders (i.e. conduct disorder and hyperactivity).

Although the overall prevalence estimate of 18.1% in the OCHS seems inordinately high, it is within the range of 17.6 to 22.0% reported recently from other prevalence surveys done in community samples (e.g. Costello, 1989). The large magnitude of these estimates raises some fundamental questions about the need for, use and targeting of child mental health services in Ontario.

Need for Mental Health Interventions

Although 18.1% of children met the criteria for disorder, it cannot be assumed that all need or would benefit from existing mental health services. Concern has been expressed that prevalence surveys such as the OCHS are creating a myth about the need for mental health services by identifying so many individuals in the general population with mental disorder (Richman and Barry, 1985).

In the OCHS, inquiries were made about respondent perception (i.e. parent and teacher in the 4–11 age group; parent and adolescent in the 12–16 age group) of the child's need of professional help for emotional and behavioural problems. Need was defined as present when positive responses were given to two general questions. "During the past six months—that is, since August of last year—do you think that (name) has had any emotional or behavioural problems? Do you

Table 3–1: Six-Month Prevalence (per 100 Children) of Individual Psychiatric Disorders by Age and Informant

Age Group (No. of Children) Disorder	Prevalence per 100 Children			
	Parent Only	Teacher/Youth Only[a]	Both Informants	Total[b]
4 – 11 (N = 1442)				
Conduct Disorder	0.8	3.4	0.2	4.4
Hyperactivity	0.9	4.8	0.7	6.5
Emotional Disorder	6.0	4.7	0.4	11.1
> 1 Disorder	6.2[c]	9.4[c]	1.6[d]	17.1
12 – 16 (N = 1232)				
Conduct Disorder	1.8	4.0	1.0	6.7
Hyperactivity	2.1	2.7	0.2	4.9
Emotional Disorder	2.2	5.3	0.9	8.4
Somatization	2.1	5.0	0.8	7.9
> 1 Disorder	4.1[c]	11.1[c]	3.7[d]	18.9

[a] Teacher informant used in the 4–11 age group and youth informant used in the 12–16 age group.
[b] Totals in this column will not always equal the sum of the row estimates due to rounding errors.
[c] This prevalence will be less than the sum of prevalences for individual disorders because the latter are not mutually exclusive.
[d] This prevalence includes a few children where informants identified different disorders in the same child (e.g., parent identifies emotional disorder and teacher identifies conduct disorder).

think that (name) needs or needed any professional help with these problems?" The percent of children perceived to need professional help by the occurrence of individual disorders is shown in Table 3–2. The categories in Table 3–2 are mutually exclusive and collectively exhaustive, unlike Table 3–1 which allowed overlap among the individual disorders.

Table 3–2 shows that respondents rarely perceived the need for professional help among children not meeting criteria for disorder (none of the above). Among children meeting the criteria for disorder, there were large variations in the percent whom respondents reported needing help. In general, larger percentages of disordered children in the 4–11 age group than the 12–16 age group needed help. Proportionately more children with multiple disorders than single disorders in both age groups were reported needing help. In the 12–16 age group, only small percentages of children with hyperactivity (9.1%) and somatization (4.8%) in the absence of other disorders elicited the perception that professional help was warranted.

Table 3–2: Percent of Children Perceived to Need Professional Help by Individual Psychiatric Disorders and Age

Age Group/Disorder (No. of Children)[a]	*% Needing Help*
4 – 11	
Conduct Disorder (16)	31.3
Hyperactivity (30)	23.3
Emotional Disorder (107)	28.0
Multiple Disorders (45)	62.2
None of the above (1090)	2.3
12 – 16	
Conduct Disorder (37)	21.6
Hyperactivity (22)	9.1
Emotional Disorder (44)	21.5
Somatization (42)	4.8
Multiple Disorders (76)	32.9
None of the above (978)	2.5

[a] Reduced sample size from Table 3–1 due to missing responses on perceived need of professional help.

The overall prevalence of perceived need of professional help was 6.6%—much less than the 18.1% identified with one or more disorders. The low prevalence of the former explains why so few children with disorder were associated with the need for help. This discrepancy arises from the fact that there are a variety of ways to define need, and that different ways will lead to different estimates (Bradshaw, 1972; Lind and Wiseman, 1978; Clayton, 1983).

The gap between prevalence of disorder and perceived need for help in the OCHS could be narrowed by using more stringent criteria to define disturbance. For example, one might decide that disturbance exists when criteria for two different disorders are met. If these criteria were in place, then the prevalence of disorder would be 4.9% (from [45 + 76]/2,487 in Table 3–2) and 43.8% of these children would be perceived to need professional help. Alternately, one might decide that disturbance exists for children that meet criteria for disorder from both respondents. Based on these criteria, prevalence would be very low indeed: 1.6% in the 4–11 age group and 3.7% in the 12–16 age group (Table 3–1); among those meeting the criteria, 75.0% in the young age group and 45.2% in the older age group would be perceived to need professional help.

If we are to develop mental health programs for children in the general population then attention must focus on constructing definitions of need to serve particular objectives. For example, in pursuing primary prevention among groups of children, the definition of need might broadly encompass characteristics such as economic disadvantage associated with higher prevalence of emotional, behavioural and academic problems (Offord, Boyle and Jones, 1987). In expanding the use of effective treatments, the definition of need might focus on the types of mental health problems that the treatments are known to address.

The definition and measurement of need poses many of the same problems posed by the definition and measurement of mental disorder. To begin, need is an elastic concept. Very broad definitions will include large numbers of people while narrow definitions that focus on severe illness will identify relatively few (Goldsmith, Lin, Jackson, Manderscheid and Bell, 1988a). Second, the concept of need encompasses many separable elements. Although psychiatrists are prone to equate need with diagnostic criteria (Tischler, Leaf and Holzer, 1988), this definition is far too limited, particularly in the general population. Other features such as symptom severity, personal distress, co-existing health problems, impairment, willingness to use help and the existence of effective interventions all bear on the definition of need. These separable elements of need are ignored at the risk of developing instruments to assess need that are at best incomplete and at worst irrelevant. Third, the issue of perspective in defining need deserves careful examination. In the child mental health area, there are many perspectives to consider—children, parents, teachers and clinicians. Ironically, children's perspective of need has never been investigated thoroughly. This is a grave omission. It seems unlikely that relevant child mental health interventions can be developed in the general population without directly assessing the priorities of children.

Use of Mental Health/Social Services

All available evidence suggests that only a small fraction of children identified with mental disorder in the OCHS could have used mental health or social services. Examination of government documents for 1983 indicates that about 0.5% of children aged 0–17 years used services provided by CMHC's in the province (Boyle and Offord, 1988); use of Child Welfare Services in the same age group was more frequent but still under 2.0%—far below the overall prevalence of disorder estimated by the OCHS.

Information on the use of mental health/social services was collected in the OCHS. This variable was based on a parental report that the child (4–16 years of age) was the focal point of a consultation in the preceding six months with staff from a mental health service (i.e. a mental health clinic or private practitioner such as a psychiatrist, psychologist, or social worker), a social service (i.e. the Children's Aid Society or the courts or after-care officer), or some other mental health/social/correctional service not specified. At the outset, it should be known that the most frequently reported category of use was "other not specified," and that only two children were reported to have used CMHC's. Thus, the results apply to a broad conception of child mental health services and not necessarily to CMHC's in particular.

About 6.5% of children were reported to have used mental health/social services in the six months prior to the study (Offord et al., 1987). Among children with mental disorder, about one in six (16.1%) used services; among children without disorder, 4.3% used services. These results are alarming for two reasons: First, about five of six children with disorder did not use mental health/social services. Second, large numbers of children using these services did not meet criteria for mental disorder. If one begins with the 6.5% of children who used mental health/social services, about 53.9% did not meet the criteria for disorder.

One might argue from the discussion in the previous section that it is unfair to evaluate the use of mental health/social services by focusing on children with one or more disorders. As noted earlier, the division between normal and abnormal rests on clinical judgments about symptom levels perceived to be in the disturbed range. Also, the concept of need for services and disorder are not interchangeable. There are many other elements of need that must be considered to assure adequate assessment.

Although it is not possible to consider all the features that might be used to define need, data are available in the OCHS to alter the definition of a case so that some of the features relevant to needs assessment are taken into account. These altered definitions include the following: (1) a child with pervasive mental health problems who exhibits one or more disorders on the basis of both respondents—from Table 3–1; (2) a child with multiple disorders regardless of respondent—from Table 3–2; (3) a child with one or more disorders who is also perceived to need professional help—from Table 3–1; and (4) a child with one or more disorders who also shows signs of impairment in social function and/or school performance. A child was classified with impaired social function if he/she was rated by one or both respondents (i.e. parent and teacher in the 4–11 age group, parent and youth in the 12–16 age group) as having problems getting along with the family, teachers or peers. A child was classified with impaired school performance if he/she was reported by the parent or teacher to have failed a grade ever.

Table 3–3 shows the percent of children using mental health/social services in the OCHS when the criteria for a case are altered to identify subsets of children more likely to need help. The results are striking. First, more children meeting the criteria for a case are reported to have used mental health/social services, but the increases above 16.1% are not that large, going from 20.6 to 37.0% (Table 3–3). In contrast, the reduction in prevalence of disorder associated with the altered criteria (shown in brackets in Table 3–3) is large, going from 5.2 to 2.6% from the original estimate of 18.1%. Second, only 23.1% of children with pervasive disorder (criteria for disorder met on ratings from both respondents) used services. The primary reason for this low percent is that use of mental health/social services is tied mostly to parental evaluations. For example, if the identification of children with one or more disorders is subdivided by respondent to specify parent only, teacher or youth only and both respondents, the respective percent of children using services are 20.1, 10.7 and 23.1. Teachers and adolescents may identify disturbance more frequently than parents but their assessments are less likely to result in help seeking. Finally, when criteria for a case are

Table 3–3: Percent Using Mental Health/Social Services When Altering the Criteria for a Case

Criteria for a Case (Prevalence)	% Using Mental Health/Social Services		% of Mental Health/Social Service Users Who are Noncases
	Case	Noncase	
(1) > 1 Disorder: both informants (2.6/100)	23.1	5.9	90.6
(2) > 2 Disorders: regardless of informant (5.2/100)	20.6	5.4	82.6
(3) > 1 Disorder + needs help (5.0/100)	37.0	4.8	71.1
(4) > 1 Disorder (18.1/100)	16.1	4.3	53.9

made more stringent, higher percentages of children using specialized services are classified as non-cases. This would be acceptable if the revised criteria yielded prevalences that were considerably lower than the prevalence of service use. However, this is not true as only 6.5% of children in the OCHS were reported to have used mental health/social services (Offord, et al., 1987).

These data raise important questions about the use of child mental health services in the community. Other studies (Rutter, Tizard and Whitmore, 1970; Langner et al., 1974) have confirmed the findings here that only a minority of children with mental disorder gain access to professional services. Admittedly, childhood mental disorder is a limited indicator of need. It is likely that earlier studies and the OCHS, by using mental disorder as the basis for establishing community need, have overstated the problem of unmet need. Unfortunately, the use of more severe criteria to assess need in the OCHS did little to improve the match between need and service use.

There are a wide range of factors that influence help-seeking behaviour and some useful models have been developed to explain this phenomenon (e.g. Goldsmith, Jackson and Hough, 1988b). However, research on help-seeking behaviour in the child mental health area is virtually non-existent. Clearly, this research should be a priority if we wish to develop programs and services that will attract the intended recipients.

The problem of unmet community need has a counterpart: use of child mental health services by those who do not meet need criteria. As noted earlier, many children in the OCHS who were reported to have used mental health/social services did not meet the criteria for mental disorder. Not surprisingly, as the criteria for defining need become more stringent, increasing numbers of children using mental health/social services failed to meet them.

Studies of adults using mental health services have also shown that a sizeable proportion of users do not meet the criteria for a psychiatric diagnosis (Regier, Shapero, Kessler and Taube, 1984; Shapero, Skinner, Kramer, Steinwachs and Regier, 1985). One might argue, of course, that other dimensions of need related to mental health could justify the use of services by these individuals. Unfortunately, there is a fundamental problem that has to be considered. When the criteria for defining need are relaxed (e.g. to include psychiatric disorder or distress or disability etc.) to justify the use of services by those who seek help, then proportionally more of the general population will meet the need criteria. At the outer boundary, everyone will be deemed to need help. When the criteria for defining need are tightened, the prevalence of unmet need in the general population will go down, but the proportion of those using services who do not meet the criteria will go up. The central issue, of course, is the apparent mismatch between need and service use, and the question is whether criteria should be developed to set priorities for allocating services to individuals requesting help. Clearly, when demand exceeds supply, some rationing mechanism must be put in place given that additional resources are unavailable and that increased efficiency is not possible. The more ticklish question focuses on the division of resources between those who seek help and those who do not. Directing resources to those who meet criteria for need but do not seek help may yield more benefits to the population than continuing to respond to those who seek help in the absence of clearly defined need.

Summary

Analysis of the provision of child mental health/social services in Ontario discloses some potentially thorny issues. In the first place, there appears to be a dramatic mismatch between the use of mental health/social services and community need. Most children meeting the criteria for mental disorder and perceived to need professional help are not receiving any. In contrast, the majority of children using mental health/social services do not meet case criteria. This finding is not an indictment of CMHC's because only two children in the OCHS were identified clearly as using these particular services. However, the finding does raise concerns about the child mental health system in its broadest sense.

Second, the concept of mental disorder, on its own, has limited usefulness as a surrogate measure of need. If we wish to understand need in the community and to evaluate intelligently the provision and use of child mental health services then we must direct our attention to conceptualizing need and developing standardized measurements.

IV. EFFECTIVENESS OF MENTAL HEALTH
INTERVENTIONS FOR CHILDREN

Mental health interventions for children are divided here into two fundamental groups: (1) those for children (and families) exhibiting problems of mental health; and (2) those for children (and families) who are apparently healthy. Interventions for group (1) can be further subdivided into treatment services intended to restore health and rehabilitation services intended to minimize the adverse consequences of a chronic problem. Interventions for group (2) fall under the headings of health promotion, which seeks to improve health generally in the population, and of primary prevention, which seeks to prevent the occurrence of mental disorder among those free of disorder.

Each of the two broad groupings of mental health interventions for children can be subdivided by their general orientation: (1) child-focused; and (2) family- and community-based. Child-focused interventions attempt to reduce symptoms directly and would include a variety of therapies: individual, group, cognitive, behavioural, drug and residential. Family- and community-based interventions include activities such as family therapy, parent management training, family support programs, community-based interventions, and health education.

Properly conducted experimental studies of mental health interventions for children and adolescents are not extensive. For example, two current reviews identified less than 150 controlled treatment trials on interventions for children and adolescents (Casey and Berman, 1985; Weisz, Weiss, Alicke and Klotz, 1987). The authors of these reviews concluded that disturbed children and adolescents who received psychotherapy benefited more than those who received no treatment. However, it has been noted that the interventions assessed by most existing studies have been administered under carefully structured conditions, usually limited in scope and duration. The concern is that the potential effects of promising interventions will not be realized under the conditions of usual clinical practice in applied settings (Institute of Medicine, 1989, pp. 119-58).

In general, the outlook of those reviewing child treatment research is gloomy. Comments such as "the meagre state of child psychotherapy research" (Tuma and Sobotka, 1983, p. 417) and "disappointing and insubstantial" (Kovacs and Paulauskas, 1986, p. 497) recur too often. In the primary prevention literature, the volume of opinion in support of prevention initiatives far outweighs the demonstrable evidence that such endeavours are useful (Offord, 1987).

Treatment Studies

The bulk of treatment outcome studies has focused on disruptive behaviour disorders in children, particularly conduct disorder and attention-deficit hyperactivity disorder. In his concluding remarks about the effectiveness of treating antisocial behaviour in children, Kazdin (1987, p. 195) writes:

> To date, little in the way of effective and empirically established treatments is available. Several promising techniques were discussed, including parent man-

agement training, functional family therapy, problem solving skills training and community based treatment. Even with the most promising treatments, there are too few controlled trials with clinical populations. For a large number of other techniques that are applied clinically, the bulk of information is anecdotal.

Treatment studies of children with attention-deficit hyperactivity disorder have a long history (Dulcan, 1986; Cantwell, 1986). Medication using ritalin, parental training and classroom behaviour therapy have been shown to be effective over the short-term (about 3–6 months) but long-term beneficial effects have not been documented. It is notable that poor compliance with treatment regimens is a limiting factor with these interventions and that benefits arising during treatment appear to fall-off after completion.

Studies evaluating treatment for emotional problems are extremely rare. A recent review by Fleming and Offord (1989) concluded that there is a paucity of firm evidence for the efficacy of any treatment modality in childhood depression. Among hospitalized 6–12 year olds, modest evidence existed in one study for the effectiveness of imipramine over placebo as long as the drug achieved certain plasma levels (Preskorn, Weller, Hughes, Weller and Bolt, 1987). Studies of the effectiveness of psychosocial treatments for depressed children are inconclusive. Among depressed adolescents, there are two randomized controlled trials in which the results are promising for the effectiveness of group cognitive-behaviour treatments (Reynolds and Coats, 1986; Lewinsohn, Hops, Williams, Clarke and Andrews, 1987).

Primary Prevention Studies

Methodologically sound evaluations of primary prevention initiatives are also very scarce. The tone of reviewers is optimistic for the future, although the current evidence is weak. Rutter (1982, p. 833) notes:

critical appraisal of primary prevention of children's psychosocial disorders indicates that our knowledge on this topic is limited and that there are a few interventions of proven value. Nevertheless, there are possibilities for effective prevention.

A more current review by Offord (1987, p. 16) concludes similarly:

It is evident from this review that there is an increasing number of promising leads in the prevention of emotional and behavioural disorders of childhood, but the number of established facts are few. Why is there such a paradox between the large quantity of work and the relatively meagre amount of sound knowledge?

Summary

In reviewing the literature on the effectiveness of mental health interventions for children, it is all too apparent that the scientific basis for practice is thin. This is true for all types of mental health interventions—promotion, prevention, treatment and rehabilitation. The fundamental issue concerns the extent to which one's activities should be guided by scientific evidence. Against the back drop of exponential growth in scientific advances and their effect on our lives, it is difficult to understand the slowness in which scientific methods are applied to the study of child mental health problems. Unfortunately, signs of progress in this area are hard to discern (Kazdin, 1987).

V. ORGANIZATION OF MENTAL HEALTH SERVICES TO CHILDREN—DEMAND, COST, FISCAL RESTRAINT AND SERVICE IMPERATIVES

Although empirical evidence is rarely cited, concern has been expressed repeatedly about structural deficiencies in the provision of child mental health services. For example, in Ontario a recent consultation paper developed by Sullivan (1988) for MCSS identified seven directions for program development in child treatment and intervention. Four of these directions focused on structural aspects of service provision: responsiveness of service, continuity of service, coordinated and responsive services for the seriously and chronically disturbed and structuring a spectrum of services (Sullivan, 1988, pp. 63–79). Analyses done within local planning areas have also pointed to structural problems in the organization of mental health services to children. Special attention has focused on lack of coordination among the Ministries of Community and Social Services, Health, and Education in their responses to child mental health problems (Waterloo Region Social Services Council, 1987; Niagara Children's Services Committee, 1988). Evidence also exists for geographic disparities in funding child mental health services (Boyle and Offord, 1988), suggesting that area differences exist in the accessibility to care. Perhaps not surprisingly, the structural problems identified in Ontario bear remarkable similarity in kind to those in the United States (e.g. Saxe, Cross and Silverman, 1988).

Structural Problems—Historical Perspective

Originally, the initiative to provide social services to children in Ontario came from charitable organizations and voluntary groups in the mid-1800s (Ontario Ministry of Community and Social Services, 1979). With passage of the Act to Provide Gaols for Young Offenders (1857), the principle of using government funds to pay for social services provided by private organizations was introduced. These funds were allocated to service deliverers through provincial grants-in-aid and compulsory municipal taxation.

Attempts to distinguish between neglected, disturbed and delinquent children began seriously in the 1930s and 1940s. In 1946, the Department of Reform Institutions was created which drew distinctions between child welfare services and correction services. The Children's Institutions Act in 1963 and the Children's Mental Health Centres Act in 1971 officially introduced a separate children's mental health system to complement the traditional correctional and welfare services systems.

Structural Problems—Today

Today, we speak of a child mental health system as though it were a structural reality under the stewardship of MCSS. This image is somewhat illusory. To begin, enormous variation exists in the size, mandate and capability of CMHC's. These agencies function more or less autonomously, although government policy is nudging them toward increased community responsibility (Ontario Ministry of Community and Social Services, 1987b). Second, services to children with mental health problems are provided by a variety of other agencies funded by MCSS, including Children's and Youth Institutions, Children's Aid Societies and Children's Residential Services. Although the mandates of these agencies vary, evidence exists that the mental health characteristics of children served by them are not well distinguished (Thompson, 1988). Also, it is important to note that the Ministries of Health and Education, as well as voluntary and self-help groups sponsor services and agencies directly concerned with child mental health problems. However, with the exception of CMHC's, it is virtually impossible to estimate the portion of resources expended by other agencies that are directly attributable to child mental health problems. For example, we do not know how much money is being spent by the Ministry of Education on services to behaviourally disturbed children or how much the Ministry of Health is spending on services billed by child psychiatrists in private practice. The inability to account for resources used to address child mental health problems is symptomatic of the fragmentation that exists in the field.

Structural Problems—Sustaining Forces

Although the structural problems behind the organization of child mental health services have historical roots, it would appear that these problems are being sustained by powerful institutional forces. First, government ministries have evolved with mandates to regulate and/or provide services for particular aspects of the individual's life—health, education, employment, etc. But this separation of functions ignores the interrelatedness of problems and issues experienced by individuals, particularly those at the extreme end of the continuum. For example, children with a serious mental disturbance such as autism will experience deficits in almost all areas of living—physical health, cognitive ability, role performance, social relationships etc. Government structure does not permit vision of the whole person, but rather functional segments that are treated as independent parts.

Second, government ministries responsible for health and social services are placed in the unenviable position of having to reconcile the tension between cost containment and demand without recourse to economic barriers. Government response to this tension seems to have unwittingly laid the foundation for a succession of organizational problems that pervade child mental health services—at least those provided by CMHC's. History again provides the perspective.

Child mental health services sponsored by MCSS have passed through two trends (Sullivan, 1988) and appear to be starting a third. The first trend, which began in 1950 and peaked in 1975, was toward specialized care and residential treatment of "disturbed" children. The second trend was toward the proliferation of government funded agencies with a new focus on community-based and non-residential services. This trend began with the provision of 100% provincial funding for CMHC's legislated under the Children's Mental Health Centres Act, 1971 and is currently in its final phase. The third trend is toward the consolidation of services and identification of community responsibility for care. This trend began with the Child and Family Services Act, 1984 and has been given official endorsement at the ministerial level (Ontario Ministry of Community and Social Services, 1987b).

One can argue that these trends have evolved, not from an analysis of child mental health problems, but from attempts to reduce the conflict between limited resources, escalating costs and increasing demands for service. For example, residential treatment is both expensive and inaccessible. Under conditions of fiscal restraint and growing demand, it is inevitable that a service structure founded on a residential treatment model will collapse. The proliferation of less expensive community-based outpatient services is a logical "service" response to the cost and accessibility problems generated by residential treatment. This is not to deny that genuine concern for individuals has contributed to past service trends. Justification for these trends exists, for example, in the adverse effects of institutionalization (end of the residential era); and the unresponsiveness and inflexibility of a disparate service system (end of proliferation of services). Nevertheless, it does appear that political and administrative realities exert far more influence in the provision of human services (including child mental health) than the analysis of human problems or effectiveness of interventions to address them. Given the scientific vacuum within which we operate, the dominance of political and administrative perspectives can hardly be censured.

The tension between fiscal restraint and increased demand has created an unfortunate obsession with services. For example, MCSS funding for a wide range of children's services, including mental health, is now tied wholly to service activity (Ontario Ministry of Community and Social Services, 1987a). Agencies will now be funded by service category (e.g. behaviour management), analogous to physician fees claimed for specific medical procedures. Among the agency data now required by MCSS for service funding, there is virtually no reference to individuals, including the nature of the problems they are experiencing. The focus on service categories is dangerous for three reasons: (1) it draws attention away from a cogent analysis of human problems to a preoccupation with solutions (i.e. services) that may be irrelevant; (2) it reinforces arbitrary divisions among agencies concerned with human problems by defining their interventions and mandate as unique and separable; and (3) it distorts our view of the individual by defining him or her as a service response and not as a person requesting help with problems.

Omitting the person and his or her problems from the funding equation stirs one to ask how it is possible to set objectives for child mental health. Based on the information now sought by MCSS, it would seem that child mental health objectives will arise from a decision about the cost and distribution of services. As in the past, the objective will focus on accommodating demand as efficiently as possible. One way to achieve this objective is to identify less expensive service alternatives. Is it time for a fourth trend in child mental health? This could take us full circle back to reliance on self-help and voluntary community efforts which are, potentially at least, a very efficient way to accommodate demand.

Summary

Analysis of the organization of mental health services to children reveal several important issues. First, a consensus exists that there are structural deficiencies in the provision of mental health services to children. These deficiencies include problems of funding, coordination and responsiveness. Other than expenditures by CMHS's, it is virtually impossible to estimate how much money is directed towards child mental health. In some instances (e.g. services billed by child psychiatrists) there are no ways to account for expenditures.

Second, the structural problems that exist today have historical roots and appear to be sustained by powerful institutional forces. The compartmentalized structure of government is one such force. A second force is the powerful conflict between increasing demand, rising costs and limited resources. This seems to have created an unfortunate obsession with services which is in danger of eclipsing our view of the individual and his or her difficulties.

DISCUSSION

Child mental health issues are points of controversy whose resolution should improve the life quality of our children. These issues can be subdivided into two broad categories: scientific and administrative. Scientific issues focus on the cumulation of knowledge and information whereas administrative issues attend to choices and decisions in the pursuit of objectives. The two categories are frequently interdependent. For example, knowledge and information can tell us about the extent of a problem, its seriousness, origin, likely course and the cost and usefulness of different approaches to resolving it. Decisions aided by such knowledge and information are more likely to be "rational". On the other side, administrative priorities and funding can set the agenda for science by identifying and supporting lines of inquiry. Research stimulated by those making hard choices about policy and program development is more likely to be "useful and relevant." In practice, though, the scientific and administrative spheres often fail to intersect. Factors distinct from scientific evidence such as values, ideology, political expediency, vested interests and tradition, to name a few, inform the development of policy and influence administrative decisions around courses of action to address social problems. In a similar way, the scientific community pursues lines of inquiry that arise from personal interest and training, academic imperatives (e.g. opportunities for publishing), study area issues, to name a few, which are quite distinct from the day-to-day issues faced by administrators and policy analysts.

This chapter has focused primarily on scientific issues associated with child mental health that might be addressed to improve the life quality of children. This focus arises from a perception that little scientific basis exists for what is done in the area of child mental health. Important questions persist regarding the classification and measurement of childhood mental disorder and the data required to assess community need for child mental health services. Information on the problems experienced by those using child mental health or related services is scant, but there appears to be a mismatch between use and need. We are placed in the awkward position of trusting that our interventions are effective because evidence from clinical settings is not available. To make matters worse, there is little evidence that these fundamental issues and questions have attracted serious government attention. Rather, the traditional preoccupation with services has become embedded in funding formula. The opportunity to audit agency activity will be a hollow victory; it cannot be expected to improve our understanding and effective response to individuals experiencing distress and impairment.

What can be done to address these issues? Some suggestions follow, grouped under the following headings:

1. Measurement priorities
2. Research priorities
3. Policy priorities
4. New initiatives

Measurement Priorities

This chapter focused initially on the classification and measurement of childhood mental disorder. It did so to draw attention to our central concepts and some of the difficulties we face in attempting to define and to measure them. At this time, expending more energy on further delineating childhood mental disorder seems ill advised. Already, there are too many categories. Our efforts to evaluate the usefulness of classifying and measuring childhood mental disorder should consolidate around a limited number of categories which, by broad agreement, seem meaningful at a descriptive level.

Although issues pertaining to the classification and measurement of childhood mental disorder are cause for concern, there is room for optimism. Advances have taken place in the definition and measurement of childhood mental disorder as witnessed by the development of standardized instruments to measure DSM-III-R categories (e.g. Diagnostic Interview Schedule for Children: Shaffer, Schwab-Stone, Fisher, Davies, Piacentini, and Gioia, 1988; and Diagnostic Interview Schedule for Children and Adolescents: Welner, Reich, Herjanic, Jung, and

Amado, 1987). Also, there are cadres of clinical investigators strongly interested in validating measures of childhood psychopathology.

Allowing that the measurement of childhood psychopathology will continue to attract clinical and research attention, are there other measurement priorities that need to be considered? The answer to this question is definitely yes and two of the priorities supported here are: a broadened conceptual focus on mental health and associated features; and the measurement of need for mental health services.

Broadened Conceptual Focus

Recent attempts to define mental health as distinct from mental disorder (e.g. Epp, 1988) remind us that opportunity exists for broadening our conceptual focus. In a sense, our preoccupation with classifying mental disorder has caused us to overlook important attributes of the child that contribute to or reflect directly or indirectly on mental health. The following examples are used for illustration and are by no means exhaustive.

First, the experience of psychological well-being is a concept that reflects directly on mental health. At a theoretical level, it is distinguishable from mental disorder and should be included as part of child mental health assessments. At a practical measurement level, psychological well-being allows for a full continuum from positive to negative and may be particularly suitable for discriminating levels of mental health in essentially well populations.

Second, interpersonal functioning indexed by the quality of social relationships is, strictly speaking, in the domain of social health, but clearly reflects indirectly on mental health. In children, especially, the distinctions between social health and mental health are blurry.

Third, family functioning, indexed by the quality of nurturance, communication and affection bonds in the family is, conceptually, quite distinct from mental health, but logically an important determinant of mental health, especially in children.

The point of these examples is to show that there are other concepts, in addition to mental disorder, that reflect on mental health and deserve measurement development efforts. The conceptual framework suggested here identifies mental health as the superordinate concept. Mental disorder and psychological well-being (among other concepts) would provide the basis for subdividing mental health. Other concepts such as interpersonal and family functioning, role performance and achievement would be identified as important and relevant to mental health, though not direct representations of this concept. It should be noted that the conceptual framework suggested here differs from the one developed by Health and Welfare Canada (Epp, 1988). In this author's view, the schema proposed by Epp is so broad and encompassing that it offers little or no measurement potential.

Extending our focus beyond mental disorder has three potential advantages. First, concepts such as psychological well-being permit more sensitive discriminations among individuals. This feature is important in the assessment of well populations and the evaluation of interventions. Our concepts of mental disorder permit only crude discrimination among individuals and may be too insensitive for the purposes of mental health planning and program evaluation.

Second, the notion that mental disorder is a property of individuals has practical measurement advantages but overlooks the fact that mental disorder is a social construct. The social forces (e.g. family, school, neighbourhood) that influence the inner experiences and behavioural expression of children are, quite rightly, important foci for measurement. It is conceivable that our limited success in validating measures of mental disorder have arisen, in part, because of our reluctance to include contextual data in our assessments.

Third, broadening our focus on mental health and associated features may help identify novel interventions that improve the life quality of children without necessarily altering their diagnostic status.

Measurement of Need

A second area that has been neglected in the study of childhood mental disorder is the measurement of need for mental health services. The concept of need is central to program planning and evaluation and should be a priority for measurement development work. The following examples are used to illustrate how adequate measures of need could be used to improve the distribution and use of child mental health services. First, measures of need could be used to set clinical and research priorities among children classified with mental disorder. At present, instruments for classifying mental disorder focus almost exclusively on symptom groupings. These symptom groupings provide little or no information on important aspects of need, including subjective distress, impairment, willingness to use help and the existence of effective treatment. Second, at a clinical level, measures of need could be used to assess the relevance and urgency of individual referrals. This is especially important when demand for services exceed supply.

Third, at a program level, measures of need could be used to evaluate the appropriate use of services. This is particularly important now that concern exists about a mismatch between need for and use of child mental health services.

Finally, at a planning level, measures of need could be used to identify target groups for intervention initiatives.

Measurement development and evaluation has never been a high priority in government funded research. Such work does not address social problems, although it provides the means for doing so. The benefits of measurement work are "downstream" and not immediate. Nevertheless, standardized measurement is a fundamental requirement for science. It is inconceivable that any scientific basis will emerge for setting program priorities and for developing effective child mental health interventions without upgrading our measurements of core concepts.

Research Priorities

Scientific upgrading of our child mental health interventions is the second priority identified in this chapter. There are, of course, certain prerequisites that must be met before such upgrading can occur. First, the will to experiment needs to be in place. This assumes the following: (1) acknowledgement that current interventions may be ineffective or even harmful; (2) fiscal commitment to support research in clinical settings; and (3) adoption of standardized procedures for classifying mental health problems and carrying out interventions. The research capability available to most agencies providing children's mental health services is generally low, if existent. This could be upgraded in a number of ways—by sponsoring research positions within specific agencies, by pooling resources of member agencies in different geographic areas to hire research personnel or by establishing formal linkages with universities.

Second, existent interventions need to be clearly delineated to facilitate replication in a standardized way. This means a clear specification of the problems addressed, of the mechanisms by which the interventions are suppose to work and of the procedures that make up the interventions. For purposes of clarity, it would be preferable to develop intervention modules specified in manual form. These modules would be developed with specific preventive or therapeutic objectives in mind and could address a variety of pertinent issues including client engagement and compliance.

Third, new intervention models need to be developed that better reflect existing perspectives on childhood mental disorder (Kazdin, 1987). It is well known for example, that the more debilitating childhood disorders, such as autism, mental retardation, childhood schizophrenia and conduct disorder are severe, chronic in nature and, for the most part, intractable. Children with more extreme mental health problems will experience multiple deficits in their own functioning and be at increased risk for living in problem laden families. This would suggest a need for broadly based interventions capable of addressing multiple child and family problems over an extended period. This lesson applies equally to programs with therapeutic, rehabilitative or preventive orientations. It is sometimes thought that primary prevention activities will provide an inexpensive alternative to treatment but in all likelihood this will not be the case (Rutter, 1982).

Fourth, research priorities need to be established for evaluating mental health interventions. Some promising interventions have been identified (Kazdin, 1987; Dulcan; 1986; Rutter, 1982, Offord, 1987) and these should provide the point of departure for future work. Clearly, the first step is to identify interventions that can work under ideal circumstances. For interventions that can work, the next step is to find out if they are effective in usual clinical circumstances.

Policy Priorities

Consensus has emerged that structural difficulties plague child mental health services (Sullivan, 1988; Waterloo Region Social Services Council, 1987; Niagara Children's Services Committee, 1988). It was argued in this paper that these problems have historical roots and are being sustained by powerful institutional forces—the somewhat artificial division of government ministries and programs and the fundamental tension that exists between the desire to accommodate service demand and the need to exercise fiscal restraint.

The optimal organizational structure for delivering child mental health services is not clear. The reason for this stems, in large part, from the absence of child mental health objectives, operationally defined and potentially attainable. Although the Child and Family Services Act, 1984 (Government of Ontario, 1987) consolidates and advances previous legislation, it does not provide direction to the field; it is primarily a code of conduct to be observed by agencies serving children.

In the absence of child mental health objectives that could serve to integrate activity in the field, the irresistible temptation is for individual service settings to concentrate on the problems of accommodating demand for their "products." One might expect that this pressure would narrow rather than broaden our perspective of the child and his or her difficulties. Our inattention to the whole child and our reluctance to define community mental health objectives have led us to substitute means for ends. The means are service categories and functions whose provision, in light of requests for help, has become our primary objective. Added to this problem are the personal allegiances that government departments and agencies develop for their services and functions. These allegiances are primarily divisive and sustain the fragmentation of activity in the field.

It is beyond the scope of this chapter to look in depth at the issues associated with setting objectives. Suffice it to say, a statement of community mental health objectives for children must include two basic elements: (1) a reference population; and (2) a desirable outcome. The reference population might focus on children in the general population or a subset thought to be at excess risk for mental health problems. The desirable outcome might focus on mental disorder or some other indicant of mental health (e.g. psychological well-being). The idea would be to reduce the incidence of childhood mental disorder and to increase psychological well-being in selected communities.

Although it might be possible for MCSS to articulate community mental health objectives for children, the means for attaining such objectives clearly extend across interministerial boundaries. Data presented earlier suggest that teachers (Ministry of Education) are quite able to identify children with mental health problems. Being poor is strongly related to childhood disorder (Offord, Boyle and Jones, 1987) and many children living in poor families reside in public housing (Ministry of Housing). Over a six-month period, about 50% of children with mental disorder will use ambulatory medical care services (Ministry of Health) (Offord et al., 1987). The very process of trying to set community mental health objectives for children should make clear the need for coordinated responses to child mental health problems.

New Initiatives

The measurement, research and policy priorities identified in the previous sections encompass broad issues to be addressed in the long-term. One might ask, are there specific, immediate initiatives that might facilitate the pursuit of these priorities? Some ideas for initiatives are sketched below.

Standardized Assessments in Clinical Settings

The informational vacuum that exists in our knowledge about the mental health, and characteristics related to the mental health, of children using clinical services needs to be overcome. Although CMHC's and other agencies providing child mental health services invariably do assessments of some kind, the emphasis here is on highly structured instruments that are self-completed or interviewer administered. To be potentially useful, the same information must be collected across agencies using standardized procedures. A common pool of information is needed to facilitate geographic and service sector comparisons of those requesting help.

There are four reasons for recommending that standardized assessments be required in clinical settings. First, it would pressure mental health professionals to agree on the definition and measurement of core concepts. Second, it would provide some basis for evaluating the targeting and use of mental health services. Third, it would provide the opportunity for longitudinal follow-up studies which are needed in the field. Fourth, it would refocus attention on the child and his or her difficulties, reminding us that services are means to ends, not ends in themselves.

Research Funding

Commitment to research in clinical settings will only be realized when additional funds are dedicated to research purposes. It is proposed here that research funds be generated in two ways. First, the onus should be on clinical settings to set aside funds for research even if it means taking away money for services. Second, government ministries, particularly MCSS and Health, should provide matching funds to acknowledge and support the commitment of agencies to research.

Centres of Excellence

The research capability of most agencies serving child mental health is likely to be low. Without access to experienced investigators, it is not clear how useful research projects will arise—financial commitment to research activity cannot assure the development of good studies. However, the creation of centres of excellence in clinical settings, focused on particular areas (e.g. measurement, treatment effectiveness, primary prevention etc.) and adequately funded, would provide a strong inducement to researchers interested in child mental health questions. The idea here is to draw clinical and research expertise from academic settings. It would be important that the funding be managed by community agencies and its use evaluated independently.

Final Comment

The most pressing issue in child mental health is the lack of a scientific base for practice. This issue extends back to difficulties we have in defining and measuring core concepts and forward to problems we have understanding the usefulness of activities to promote mental health and to prevent or treat mental disorder. Research focused on improving our understanding of child mental health problems will lead to improved life quality for our children. These improvements will be neither immediate nor dramatic. However, they should be perceptible over time and cumulative. This would be an important advancement in the field.

APPENDIX 1

The target population for the OCHS included all children aged 4 to 16 on January 1, 1983 whose usual place of residence was a household dwelling. Children living on Indian reserves, in collective dwellings such as institutions and in dwellings constructed since June 1, 1981 (Census Day) were systematically excluded from the survey but accounted for only 3.3% of the target population. The sampling frame (source of subjects) was the 1981 Canada Census with the sampling unit, household dwellings. The sample was obtained by stratified, random and cluster sampling from the census file. Interviewers collected information from the female head of household (parents) and youth aged 12 to 16 during a home visit. With parental consent, teachers of children in school were mailed a problem checklist to be completed and returned in a stamped self-addressed envelope. The field work was done in January and February, 1983 by Statistics Canada—responsible at the federal level for the census, labour force survey and other data collection for government. Among eligible households, 91.1% participated and only 3.9% refused.

The OCHS investigated four childhood psychiatric disorders: conduct disorder, hyperactivity, emotional disorder and somatization (the last for 12–16 year olds only). As discussed elsewhere (Boyle et al., 1987), measurements of these disorders relied on problem checklist assessments completed by multiple informants (i.e. parents and teachers in the 4–11 age group; parents and youth in the 12–16 age group). Ratings of problem behaviours for each disorder were summed to obtain scale scores. The thresholds for identifying disorders as present or absent were the scale scores that discriminated best, diagnoses made by child psychiatrists in a separate study.

4

CHILD AND FAMILY POLICIES FOR THE 1990s
Justice Issues

Nicholas Bala

The last three decades have seen dramatic changes in patterns of family behaviour and attitudes towards familial relationships in Canada. During the past fifteen years there have also been enormous changes in the role of law and the courts in Canadian society. There has been a veritable revolution in the laws governing families and children. Those concerned with the future of families and children are increasingly aware of the importance of the justice system.

Since 1960 the divorce rate has increased more than six-fold, though it may now be stabilizing with about one marriage in three ending in divorce. There is now a much wider social acceptance of unmarried cohabitation and same sex couples are starting to demand recognition. There is also much greater acceptance of children born out-of-wedlock. Family size has fallen, and the role of women in the family and the labour force has been irreversibly altered. Perceptibly, but more slowly, the role of men in the family has also been changing.

The 1960s witnessed the "discovery" of physical abuse and neglect of children as a major social problem, while the 1970s and 1980s saw parallel developments in regard to sexual abuse. Although the abuse and neglect of children have always been very serious problems, their dimensions have only become apparent in recent years. The 1970s and 1980s also saw challenges to the traditional approaches to dealing with the problems of children who were in need of protection or who had violated the criminal law.

The last decades have been an era of rapid legal change and have seen a fundamental change in attitudes towards the role of law in society. Some of the new emphasis on the law can be traced to the American civil rights movement, but it is now evident in Canada in the efforts of feminists, Native groups, consumers, tenant advocates and environmentalists. These developments have been reflected in and reinforced by the introduction of the *Canadian Charter of Rights and Freedoms* in 1982. We now live in a rights-based society, one which increasingly looks to the courts to resolve social problems and controversies. Fundamental political and social values support the protection of legal rights. The courts are regarded as an appropriate forum for dealing with society's most contentious and difficult issues.

The last decades have seen the rise of the rights of children and parents. The laws governing families and children changed little in the first half of this century. However, reflecting the enormous social change, though inevitably lagging behind it, the last few years have been ones of revolutionary change in the laws governing these matters. The "modern era" of Family Law in Canada can be traced to the enactment of the federal *Divorce Act* in 1968. Then Justice Minister Pierre Trudeau liberalized the grounds for divorce, reduced the importance of fault for support and custody, and made support laws theoretically gender neutral.

Matrimonial property law was not reformed until later. In 1975, and again in 1978 and 1986, Ontario enacted new property laws, gradually increasing the rights of married women. Subject to some exceptions, all property acquired during a marriage is now divided equally on termination of a marriage. Encouraged by the new *Divorce Act 1985*, the courts are now placing increased emphasis on spousal self-sufficiency after separation. The laws governing custody, access and other matters related to children in the context of separation have also been changed, most notably with the enactment of the *Children's Law Reform Act* in 1978, and its amendment in 1982. These statutes abolish old rules and emphasize the "best interests" of children. Legislation recently proclaimed in force attempts to improve the enforcement of child support and custody orders.

Court decisions and legislative changes have given new rights to common law spouses and the concept of illegitimacy was legally abolished in 1978.

Child protection and adoption laws were significantly amended in 1979, and a new legislative scheme was put into place with Ontario's *Child and Family Services Act* of 1984. These new laws placed increased emphasis on the legal rights of children and parents. The federal government also introduced sweeping reforms to deal with youth in conflict with the law, bringing in the *Young Offenders Act* in 1984 to replace the *Juvenile Delinquents Act* of 1908. The new law replaced treatment oriented legislation with a law emphasizing responsibility and due process, though trying to balance these concepts with a recognition of the special needs of youth and their limited accountability in comparison with adults.

Increasingly rapid developments in medical technology are also facing society with new problems associated with families and children; inevitably we are now looking to the law for solutions. As we move into the 1990s, it is an appropriate time to reflect on the interaction between social and legal change. Have all the reforms been improvements? Do we now have an adequate legal framework to deal with the problems which families and children will face in the next decade?

I. CHILDREN AND PARENTAL SEPARATION

About one marriage in three ends in divorce, and in almost one half these cases there are dependent children. In a large majority of cases mothers retain custody of the children, though increasingly use is made of some form of joint custody or shared parenting.[1] There are a number of important issues concerning the adequacy of present laws governing the care and support of children whose parents separate.[2] These issues relate both to the substantive law and to the manner in which the law is applied and disputes are resolved. Parental separation is inevitably distressing for children, and sometimes has long-term traumatic effects. The question which must always be asked is whether the law and the court system are minimizing the damage or exacerbating it.

Custody Rules: Best Interests or Primary Parent?

While the question of which parent will receive custody is usually resolved by the parents without the need for a trial,[3] the laws governing this matter are very important since they provide the context in which informal arrangements, formal separation agreements and mediated settlements occur.

In the nineteenth century fathers had a near proprietary right to their children, and in the then rare event of separation, inevitably received custody. This rule was replaced by one strongly favouring mothers, at least if they had not proven themselves "morally unfit" by committing adultery. In the last decade federal and provincial legislation[4] has specified that custody disputes are to be decided on the basis of the "best interests" of the child, a theoretically gender neutral rule which requires the court to assess all the circumstances of a case and decide what is best for a child.

---

[1] D.C. Mckie et al., *Divorce: Law and the Family in Canada* (Statistics Canada, 1983), at 207 report that in the 1969–79 period in Ontario the woman received custody in 85.6% of divorces and the man in 14.4% of the cases; there was no appreciable change in this figure over the decade. There are no more recent Ontario statistics available.
C.J. Richardson, *Evaluation of the Divorce Act, 1985—Phase I: Collection of Baseline Data*, (Department of Justice, 1987) reported on a 1985 study of divorce cases in four Canadian cities, including Ottawa. Women received sole custody in 76.9% of the cases and men in 9.5%; 13.2% resulted in some form of joint parenting and in 0.4% custody was awarded to a non-parent. Only 14.9% of the cases were resolved by a court hearing; in these cases the woman received custody 68.9% of the time, the man 26.2% and joint custody was ordered in 4.9% of the cases. It should be noted that the sample of cases was deliberately selected to include a high proportion of contested cases.

[2] Almost all the available literature deals with children whose parents were married, though all of the same issues arise if parents have had a common law relationship.

[3] Richardson, supra n. 1, 52 & 89 reports that custody was initially in dispute in less than one third of cases: 14.9% were resolved by a court hearing, 44.4% by parties negotiating, 16.0% by lawyers negotiating, 6.6% by mediation, 4.4% by custody investigation and 13.8% by other. As noted earlier, contested cases were over-represented in this study.

[4] *Children's Law Reform Act*, R.S.O. 1980, c.68, s.24; and *Divorce Act, 1985*, S.C. 1986, c.4, s.16; subs. 16(9) specifies that marital misconduct, like adultery, is not to be taken into account "unless the conduct is relevant to the ability of that person to act as a parent". [Hereafter *C.L.R.A.* and *Divorce Act.*]

A major criticism of this rule is that it gives judges a too broad discretion to decide cases on the basis of their personal views about appropriate parental roles. It may also lead judges to rely too heavily on "experts" to tell them what will be in the child's best interests; in making their assessments and predictions, these experts are also influenced by their personal and professional biases. It is argued that the indeterminacy of this rule promotes uncertainty and thus encourages litigation.[5]

A number of commentators and judges in the United States have advocated the adoption of the "primary parent" test in place of the potentially vague and arbitrary "best interests" custody rule.[6] Under the primary parent approach, for young children[7] custody is awarded to the parent who took greater care of the children during the marriage. The presumption may be rebutted if it can be shown that the primary caretaker is likely to harm the child. The non-custodial parent continues to have access rights. Under the primary parent approach, courts would not attempt to assess which parent *will* provide better care for a child in the future, but rather would engage in a retrospective inquiry as to which parent actually *has* provided more care. A child's continuity of care would be assured. It has been also been argued that this is a simpler, less speculative approach than one based on the "best interests" of the child. Further it would reward those who have actually provided care, and might serve as an incentive to parental involvement in intact families.

In practice, Canadian courts already place significant weight on parenting roles assumed during marriage when determining a child's "best interests" and resolving a custody dispute.[8] It is true that in most cases the woman would obtain custody under the primary parent rule, but as noted earlier, women also win most contested cases under the present best interests approach. Both at present and under the proposed rule, the fact that men relatively rarely obtain custody is not a result of judicial bias, but a reflection of the reality of the division of responsibility for child care in most families.

---

[5] See e.g. R.H. Mnookin, "Child-Custody Adjudication: Judicial Functions in the Face of Indeterminacy" (1975), 39 *Law and Contemporary Problems* 226.

[6] See *Pikula* v. *Pikula*, 374 N.W. 2d 705 (Minn. 1985); Chambers, "Rethinking the Substantive Rules for Custody Disputes in Divorce" (1984) 83 *Michigan Law Rev.* 477; Elster, "Solomonic Judgments: Against the Best Interest of the Child" (1987) 54 *University of Chicago Law Rev.* 1; and Singer & Reynolds, "A Dissent on Joint Custody" (1988) 47 *Maryland Law Rev.* 497.

[7] For "older" children, the child's wishes may affect or determine the outcome, at least if such wishes are not the product of improper coercion or bribery, and not clearly contrary to the child's best interests. The concept of the "older" child varies from 7 to 13 in different formulations of the primary parent rule.

[8] See *Harden* v. *Harden* (1987), 6 R.F.L.(3d) 147 (Sask. C.A.).

The primary parent approach would not resolve all disputes. Increasingly couples are equally sharing all parental responsibilities; in these cases courts will still have to use the best interests test. It may be argued that the abandonment of the "best interests" test would be a negative symbolic act. However, the adoption of a new legal approach has the potential to facilitate negotiations and lessen the complexity and expense of litigation. It may also serve as important symbolic recognition of the value placed on the assumption of parental responsibilities during marriage. Certainly this is an issue which merits further study.

Joint Custody

One of the most important developments in recent years been the increased use of "joint custody". The term "joint custody" is ambiguous, and is used to describe a number of distinct but related arrangements. In some cases the child may spend roughly equal amounts of time with each parent, regularly alternating residences. In others, one parent has "primary care and control", but the other has frequent access and there is joint responsibility for making decisions about the child.

While Ontario and federal legislation permit parents to have joint custody arrangements, there is no real statutory guidance as to when it might be appropriate to order it.[9] In a number of American states, custody statutes specify that there is to be a preference or presumption in favour of joint custody.

In Canada joint custody is usually the product of a parental agreement, whether negotiated directly by the parents or arranged with the aid of lawyers or a mediator. Canadian courts have demonstrated a reluctance to order joint custody without the consent of both parents, though recently courts have shown a greater willingness to order joint custody despite the objections of one or both parents.[10]

---

[9] *Divorce Act, 1985*, s.16(4); *C.L.R.A.* s.21. See V.J. Mackinnon & J.R. Groves, "Some Proposals to Reform Custody Litigation" (1988), 3 Can.F.L.Q. 287–312 for an argument in favour of a presumption in favour of joint custody. The authors make a number of other proposals, including a recommendation that "parental motivation" in seeking custody should be taken into account by a court seeking to resolve a custody case.

[10] See e.g. *Kruger* v. *Kruger* (1979), 25 O.R. (2d) 673 (C.A.); but for a more liberal approach see *Abbott* v. *Taylor* (1986) 2 R.F.L.163 (Man. C.A.); and *Nurmi* v. *Nurmi*(1988), 16 R.F.L.(3d) 201 (Ont. U.F.C.).

Joint custody remains controversial. Proponents argue that it can serve to continue patterns of care assumed during marriage, to encourage the involvement of both parents in the life of their child, and to share the responsibilities involved in child care after separation. There are studies that support the view that joint custody is usually beneficial to children and likely to lead to greater parental satisfaction. However, much of the empirical work is based on somewhat biased samples.[11] Recent studies from California indicate that joint custody is not a panacea. In situations in which parents have a distrustful or disturbed relationship, the judicial imposition of joint custody may be harmful for children. Joint custody is especially likely to be problematic if one spouse has been abusive towards the other.[12] In the summer of 1988 California enacted legislation eliminating its statutory preference for joint custody, though courts in that state may still order joint custody.[13]

In the spring of 1988 a private member's bill was introduced into the Ontario legislature by Jim Henderson, an M.P.P. and psychiatrist, which would have created a presumption that in the absence of evidence to the contrary, there should be joint custody.[14] This legislation would allow a court to impose joint custody without the agreement of both parties. If enacted, it would not only affect the relatively small number of cases resolved in the courts, but also the large number dealt with by negotiation. At present, advocates of joint custody point out that a parent with a strong claim to sole custody has a virtual veto power over joint custody, since it will rarely be imposed without the consent of both parents. On the other hand, opponents of such a law point out that it might make it more difficult to resist demands for joint custody, even with an abusive or manipulative partner.

The controversy over a presumption of joint custody will doubtless continue. While better knowledge about the effects of different types of custody arrangements will help deal with the question, the law-makers cannot wait for more definite answers; cases have to be resolved today, regardless of the state of knowledge. In the political arena, many of the strongest opponents of such a presumption are feminists, and some of the proponents are members of men's rights groups, keeping the debate lively.

---

[11] For a review of much of the law and literature on joint custody, see Ryan, "Joint Custody in Canada: Time for a Second Look" (1986) 49 R.F.L. (2d) 149. The author describes the deficiencies of much of the empirical work on the subject.

[12] California, *Final Report of the Senate Task Force on Family Equity* (Sacramento: Joint Publications, 1987); Center for the Family in Transition, "Child Outcomes in Joint and Physical Custody Families", by M. Kline et. al. As yet unpublished paper to Annual Meeting of the American Orthopsychiatric Association, Chicago, March 30, 1988.

[13] S.B. 1306, 1988 c. 1442, amending s.4600(1)(d) of the California Civil Code.

[14] Bill 95, 1st Sess., 34th Leg. 1988, s.1. The Bill also stipulates that where practicable the child shall reside with each parent for an equal period of time.

If joint custody is to be used extensively a number of related issues must also be resolved, such as the effect of such an arrangement on the right of parents to change residence and the appropriate amount of child support in situations where a child is spending significant periods of time with each parent. If parents have such an arrangement, what should be the role of the courts in resolving disagreements about such matters as schooling or religious training? To what extent and in what manner should the views of the child be considered in resolving a dispute over the terms of joint custody? All too often the reports of disputes over such matters as education or religion seem to focus on parental positions, while ignoring the children's views.[15]

Enforcement of Custody Rights

In a relatively small number of cases very serious problems have arisen with respect to the enforcement of custody rights. A parent who is not prepared to use the legal system or who is unsuccessful in using the courts may resort to "parental abduction". This promotes disrespect for the law and understandably causes great anguish to parents whose custody rights have been frustrated. It has the potential to cause great harm to children. They live with the parent who is often not the best caretaker. They often lead a "life on the run;" they are moved around, sometimes without proper schooling and medical care. Further, they are denied access to the other parent, often after being falsely told that parent is dead or does not want to see them.

Until relatively recently the courts and police were reluctant to deal with parental abduction, but in the last few years steps have been taken by the federal and provincial governments to deal with the problem. Parental abduction has been made a criminal offence, encouraging police involvement in the location and apprehension of children. An Ontario government agency can provide assistance with civil enforcement of custody rights and new legislation provides access to government data banks to assist in the location of abducting parents. Canada is a signatory to the Hague International Convention on Child Abduction.[16]

The great majority of young children who disappear or are abducted are not taken by strangers, but by parents without custody rights. If the recently introduced measures do not prove effective in dealing with this problem, further measures may be necessary.

---

[15] See e.g. *Chauvin* v. *Chauvin* (1987), 7 R.F.L.(3d) 403 (Ont.Dist.Ct.); and *Young* v. *Young* (1988), 16 R.F.L.(3d) 306 (B.C.S.C.).

[16] On new criminal provisions and federal legislation, see Johnstone, "Parental Abduction Under the Criminal Code" (1987) 6 *Canadian Jour. Fam. Law* 271. The Ontario Director of Support and Custody Enforcement is authorized to act pursuant to the *Support and Custody Orders Enforcement* Act, S.O.1985, c.6 [hereafter *S.C.O.E.A.*] The provisions of the Hague Convention are found in the *C.L.R.A.* s.47.

Access Issues

Continuing post-separation contact between the non-custodial parent and child is usually important and beneficial to both. It is only in the most extreme situations that a court will deny a parent the right of access. In a very significant number of cases the most contentious issues concern the manner in which access is exercised.[17] Post-separation visitation will be a continuing basis for interaction between the parents long after other matters have been resolved.

One source of friction is non-custodial parents who fail to exercise their access rights at the specified times. This can be disappointing to the children, as well as inconvenient or expensive to the custodial parent who may have been relying on the non-custodial parent to care for the children. Equally frustrating are situations in which the custodial parent makes it difficult or impossible for the other parent to exercise access rights. Perhaps the most insidious problems arise when the custodial parent, consciously or otherwise, convinces the children that they do not want to visit.

In some cases children may have valid reasons for not wanting access to occur, either at the specified time or at all. Problems may range from abusive conduct by the access parent to upsetting a child's recreational plans.

It often seems easiest for courts or lawyers dealing with access close to the time of separation simply to specify that there is to be "reasonable access", with the details of access to be arranged and varied by the parents. This can give the parents sufficient flexibility to deal with changes in their lives and those of their children. It may also be a continuing source of disagreement between the parents, and makes it difficult to enforce access rights. Problems with access may be exacerbated if one or both parents move, a not uncommon event in our mobile society, especially following marital breakdown.

The *Divorce Act*, 1985 recognizes the importance of contact with both parents:

16(10)...the court shall give effect to the principle that a child...should have as much contact with each spouse as is consistent with the best interests of the child and, for that purpose, shall take into consideration the willingness of the person for whom contact is sought to facilitate such contact.

---

[17] Richardson, supra. n. 1, at 95 reports: "As we learned over the course of this study, while custody may not be quite the burning issue as it is often portrayed, lawyers, mediators, judges and, sometimes clients themselves, are in agreement that access is almost invariably contentious and tends to remain so long after the final settlement."

This so-called "friendly parent" provision is sometimes cited by the courts in awarding custody to the parent who is more likely to encourage access by the other, or even to make an order for joint custody.[18]

There are, however, substantial difficulties in using the legal system to resolve access problems. In theory the courts may enforce an access order by finding a custodial parent who refuses to comply in contempt of court, or even by altering the custody arrangements. It is even possible for a court to order that the police assist in the enforcement of access rights. Inevitably such remedies are cumbersome and expensive, and the courts find them too draconian to employ.[19] Further, there is no effective remedy which can be used to sanction the non-custodial parent who fails to exercise access rights.

The government of Ontario has introduced a controversial bill to deal with problems related to access.[20] The bill provides for expeditious judicial hearings to resolve access disputes and for new remedies, most notably "compensatory access", to make up for wrongfully denied visits. The courts would also have been able to make financial awards to reimburse for expenses incurred as a result of a denial of access or a failure to exercise access.

The continuing nature of access problems makes them very difficult for courts to resolve and concern has been expressed that the new law may encourage unnecessary and ultimately unresolvable litigation. While the law allows for mediation to assist parents in resolving access disputes, it does not provide for the funding of mediation or access supervision services. As much as possible parents must be aided and encouraged to settle access disputes without resort to

---

[18] See e.g. *Mooney* v. *Mooney* (1988), 15 R.F.L.(3d) 347 (P.E.I.S.C.); and *Kaminura* v. *Squibb*(1988), 13 R.F.L.(3d)31 (B.C.S.C.).

[19] See *C.L.R.A.* s.37; *Rutherford v. Rutherford* (1986), 4 R.F.L.(3d) 457 (B.C.S.C.); *Genua v. Genua* (1979) 12 R.F.L.(2d) 85 (Ont. Prov. Ct.—Fam. Div.). For a case where custody was varied because of access difficulties, see *Tremblay* v. *Tremblay*(1987), 10 R.F.L.(3d) 166 (Alta. Q.B.).

[20] *Children's Law Reform Amendment Act, 1989*. S.O. 1989, c.22 (Bill 124), to come into force on date to be set by proclamation. See "Parents, lawyers split over bill to enforce access", Globe & Mail, Feb. 14, 1989, p.1; and "Ont family law practitioners vexed by access enforcement amendments", Lawyers Weekly, Feb. 17, 1989, p.2.

In *Frame* v. *Smith*(1987), 9 R.F.L.(3d) 225 (S.C.C.) the Supreme Court of Canada held that one parent could not sue the other parent for monetary damages as a result of a wrongful denial of access; for a critical comment, see J. Leon (1988), 3 C.F.L.Q. 397.

the courts. It would, however, seem that the threat of effective judicial sanction is also needed and may encourage the parents to settle disagreements on their own.

Dispute Resolution—Mediation, Experts and Courts

Recently, increasing emphasis has been placed on encouraging parents to resolve disputes concerning their children without resort to the courts, and in particular through the use of mediation. While this trend may on the whole be desirable, it has problematic aspects. Mediation is a new and unregulated profession; individuals without any training or experience can declare themselves mediators and begin to intervene in disputes. Mediation may lack some of the protections of the legal system. This is a particular concern of some feminists who argue that women may be in a weak bargaining position and subject to exploitation in the mediation process.[21] Government commissioned studies have recognized some of the benefits and limitations of the mediation process, but have largely endorsed at least some use of mediation.[22] Some proponents are arguing in favour of mandatory attempts at mediation in custody and access disputes. If governments accept that some form of mediation is a desirable method of dispute resolution, then regulation is needed. Further, there should be fairer access to this type of service; government paid mediators are affiliated with the courts in some Ontario localities but not others.

While non-adversarial methods of dispute resolution may be desirable, inevitably some cases will have to be resolved in the courts. The traditional adversarial system has been modified to deal with disputes concerning custody and access. Ordinary rules of evidence and procedure are relaxed; judges may take a more active role in encouraging settlements at the pre-trial stage. If there is a trial, judges may be more involved in questioning witnesses, in order to ensure that they have all the available evidence. However, there remain serious difficulties with the methods for resolving these cases, which are among the most important and difficult our justice system faces.

---

[21] See A. Bottemley, "What Is Happening in Family Law? A Feminist Critique of Conciliation", in Brophy et al. eds. *Women-in-Law* (London: Routedge & Kegan Paul, 1985) 162. C.J. Richardson, *Court-based Divorce Mediation in Four Canadian Cities; An Overview of Research Results* (1988, Department of Justice, Ottawa) concluded that women were not exploited in mediation. Indeed, in the sites studied, on average larger amounts of support were arranged through mediation than through litigation or lawyer negotiation.

[22] Richardson, supra n. 21; Zuber, *Report of the Ontario Courts Inquiry* (1987, Ontario Ministry of the Attorney General); *Report of the Attorney General's Advisory Committee on Mediation in Family Law* (1989, Ontario Ministry of the Attorney General), all of whom recommended the increased use of mediation to resolve family disputes in Ontario, though recognizing that in many cases mediation may not be appropriate.

The 1987 Zuber Report[23] made many recommendations for the fundamental restructuring of the Ontario court system. Included is a proposal to have all family law cases dealt with by a single court. This would prevent the possibility of different proceedings occurring simultaneously in different levels of court in regard to the same family. While the Zuber Report itself does not recommend specialization of judges, the establishment of a single court to deal with all family cases would provide an opportunity for specialization; specialization should help ensure that judges who decide cases involving children have appropriate expertise and interest. The establishment of a Unified Family Court should be a priority, though this will require federal-provincial cooperation and a number of issues are to be resolved.[24]

In addition to unifying the family court, certain basic issues of court management must be resolved. Our entire court system is characterized by delays in having trials. This is a particularly serious problem in cases involving the future of children. Their growing up cannot wait. Time is never neutral in a case involving the future of a child; delay inevitably affects the position of the parties and the children.

Courts dealing with the future of children require the assistance of a number of different professionals. In contested cases, the independent opinions of such experts as psychologists, psychiatrists and social workers may be vitally important. Ontario courts do not always have ready access to experts; the establishment of a Unified Family Court may facilitate the establishment of assessment services, mediation and other services associated with the justice system.

There must also be appropriate mechanisms for ensuring that a child's views about a mediated, negotiated, or court-imposed custody or access arrangement are brought forward. Caution must be exercised in ascertaining a child's views, since most children in the context of a divorce are understandably reluctant to appear disloyal to either parent and are ambivalent about their feelings.

At present the Office of the Official Guardian has a discretion to appoint a lawyer for the child in a custody or access dispute. A lawyer for the child will normally take instructions from the child, if the child has a clearly stated preference, but some lawyers apparently feel that they may have the discretion not to follow the child's instructions. An expert conducting an assessment will usually interview a child, and the child's views may be conveyed to the court through the expert. While lawyers for children and expert assessments evidently have value, their efficacy merits careful study. It should also be noted that there do not seem to be effective mechanisms for presenting a child's views in the mediation process.

---

[23] Zuber, supra n. 22.

[24] Perhaps the most contentious issue relates to the level of such a court; should it be a lower court, i.e. a Provincial Court, or a higher court? A number of matters are related to the level of court, including the nature of the court procedures and the level of government which makes the appointments.

Child Support Issues

One of the salient features of childhood poverty is that it is much more prevalent among single parent families, particularly those headed by a female, whether these families are a result of separation or of birth out of wedlock. While there are many complex issues associated with the support of children in single parent families, it is apparent payments from non-custodial parents are inadequate to prevent many children from living in poverty.

Though accurate Canadian data on child support payments are not available, it is clear that child support orders are generally quite low.[25] The legislation governing child support rather vaguely provides that it should meet the child's "needs" and be apportioned between the parents in accordance with their ability to pay.[26] Ambiguities and assumptions embedded into the judicial application of this standard have tended to produce low orders.

One important implicit assumption that is regularly made is that child support is intended to benefit only the child, and not the custodial parent. Since the custodial parent and child will inevitably share the same standard of living, the poverty of the custodial parent will result in the poverty of the child.

One of the realities of child support is that the majority of payors and potential payors enter new relationships with new support obligations. There is a considerable ambiguity as to how support obligations to the two family units relate to one another, though some judges give priority to the second family, which clearly reduces the amount of support payable to the first.[27] Similarly many recipients of child support enter new relationships; how should this affect support obligations?

The 1988 *Report of the Social Assistance Review Committee*[28] noted the inconsistencies between private support obligations and social assistance law and recommended that this problem should be studied by the government. There may be situations in which a low support order is made because the applicant is on public assistance; this is particularly problematic when social assistance ends.

Some of the most fundamental issues in regard to child support concern the process under which it is obtained. At present the onus is on the custodial parent to pursue the other parent, typically with the assistance of a lawyer. If an agreement cannot be achieved in regard to child support, the matter can be brought to

---

[25] For available data, see M.L. McCall et al., *The Process and Economic Consequences of Marriage Breakdown*, (Calgary, Canadian Research Institute for Law and the Family, 57, 1988.

[26] *Divorce Act,1985*, s.15(8); *Family Law Act*, S.O.1986, c.4.,s. 33(7).

[27] See e.g. *Sawchyn v. Sawchyn* (1985), 46 R.F.L.(2d) 169 (Sask. Q.B.), and accompanying annotation by McLeod; also Weisman, "The Second Family in the Law of Support" (1984), 37 R.F.L.(2d) 245.

[28] *Transitions: Report of the Social Assistance Review Committee* (Ontario Ministry of Community and Social Services, 1988), p.491.

court, where the judge has considerable discretion in determining the amount of support.

A number of jurisdictions have substantially altered this traditional approach. Several American states now have guidelines which are used to help establish the amount of support payable, based on respective parental incomes. These guidelines produce much more consistent outcomes than individualized judicial determinations, and generally result in higher child support payments. Further, they reduce the amount of litigation over child support issues, thereby saving expense and reducing parental hostility.

An important recent development in Ontario has been the establishment of a government agency which will enforce child and spousal support obligations without charge to the beneficiary.[29] This agency can get access to government records to locate defaulters and appears to be aggressively dealing with the very high rates of default. In a number of European countries the state has a role in establishing the initial support obligation. If there is a default, the state will not only assist in enforcement, but actually may pay an assured minimum benefit for each child.[30]

The process and law governing child and spousal support in Ontario are clearly in need of careful study. While recent measures to improve enforcement are a step in the right direction, further changes appear necessary to ensure that children who are the victims of divorce are not forced to live in poverty.

II. CHILD WELFARE

Child Protection

Parents in our society have primary responsibility for the care and upbringing of their children, though the state establishes certain standards for parental conduct, for example through compulsory school attendance and child immunization legislation. Perhaps the most dramatic form of state intervention in the family is through the child protection system. The state will become directly involved in supervising parents or caring for children if parents are unwilling, or are deemed unable, to care for their children.

In Ontario, child protection services are provided by 54 Children's Aid Societies (C.A.S.'s). The C.A.S.'s receive the bulk of their funding from the province and the balance from the municipalities. These agencies are largely geographically based; a few are religiously restricted (3 Catholic and 1 Jewish) and in 1987 the provincial government authorized the establishment of C.A.S.'s specif-

---

[29] *S.C.O.E.A.*; and *Family Orders and Agreements Enforcement Act*, S.C. 1986, c. 6. The effectiveness of the Ontario program has not yet been studied, but concerns have been expressed about the system; see "437,000 in federal payouts seized from men flouting family-support orders" *Globe & Mail*, Dec. 8, 1988, 1. It would be useful to compare the effectiveness of different Canadian and foreign government enforcement agencies.

[30] See *Transitions*, supra n. 28, 493 for a description of some of these programs. The Report endorses evaluation of these programs and study of their implementation in Ontario.

ically to serve Native children in northern Ontario. While there is significant local autonomy, with each agency having a board of directors, the agencies exercise a state function and are regulated by legislation. In most Canadian provinces child protection services are provided directly by civil servants.

In Ontario, the provision of child protection services is governed by the *Child and Family Services Act* (C.F.S.A.). This legislation came into effect in 1984, and largely adopts a "due process" model for the provision of services. While services can be voluntarily provided,[31] if the state becomes involuntarily involved in the family then parents, and in some cases children, are granted significant legal rights. The process of involuntary involvement is controlled by the courts.

The C.A.S. deals with physical, sexual and emotional abuse, neglect, and children suffering from a emotional, developmental or mental condition whose parents are unwilling or unable to care for them. Less than one quarter of the children in the care of C.A.S.'s are there because of physical or sexual abuse.

Native children and children from certain ethnic minorities are over-represented in the child welfare system, as are children from lower socio-economic groups. Some of this over-representation may be attributable to cultural and other biases or to inappropriate expectations of social workers and courts. Certain provisions of the C.F.S.A. attempt to take account of cultural differences, in particular for Ontario's Native population.[32] However, fundamental questions remain about systemic and other biases in the child protection system and it is apparent that further efforts are needed to ensure that the system is responsive to the culture and needs of an increasingly diverse population, and to ensure that aboriginal peoples have adequate control over services received by their children and families.

Agencies may provide services to families and children in their homes, voluntarily or involuntarily. Children may be removed from their homes and placed in the care of a C.A.S., either temporarily or permanently. If removed from their homes, children may be placed with relatives or neighbours, in foster homes, group homes or some other treatment facility. The number of children in the care of Ontario C.A.S.'s are shown in Table 4–1.[33]

---

[31] It may be that some parents and children who agree to "voluntary" services and placement may feel coerced. While some provisions of the C.F.S.A. are intended to ensure voluntariness, there is a concern about the effectiveness of these provisions. This may be an appropriate issue for further study.

[32] See e.g. C.F.S.A. s.1(e) & (f), Principles; s. 53(4) & (5), Placement of children in their communities; Part X, Native C.A.S.'s.

[33] Ontario Association of Children's Aid Societies, *Info—88*. One day count, June 30, 1988. There were a total of 8,845 children in care on that date; 4 agencies (813 children) did not provide an age breakdown.

Table 4–1: Number of Children in the Care of Children's Aid Societies, by age, Ontario, 1988

	0-5 years	6-12 years	13-16 years	over 16
Care by arrangement and special needs agreement (voluntary)	26%	17%	20%	6%
Interim care (pending court resolution)	23%	12%	6%	1%
Society wardship (temporary)	22%	20%	23%	8%
Crown wardship (permanent)	27%	51%	50%	55%
Extended care				30%
Total numbers	**1688**	**2364**	**3315**	**1478**

The child protection system has changed considerably in recent years. Increasingly efforts have been made to support children in their homes, and this is reflected in the C.F.S.A., which places an onus on the C.A.S. to prove that its plans for involuntary intervention are the "least restrictive alternative" consistent with a child's welfare. Making a greater effort to help children in their families has had real benefits, but it may also have costs. Some critics suggest that some of the older children who are coming into care have serious behaviourial and emotional problems which might have been alleviated if they had been taken into care earlier.[34]

There are many complex and interrelated issues in the child protection field which require careful attention. One problem which has recently received considerable publicity relates to facilities to care for children who have been removed from their homes. Historically, the bulk of children were placed in foster homes, which simulate normal family life and are relatively inexpensive. It has become increasingly difficult to find foster homes. Fewer families have a person at home willing to serve as a foster parent, and many of the older children who are coming into care are disturbed, making it difficult to find suitable foster homes. Foster parents have begun to demand more adequate financial compensation for their often very demanding responsibilities.

---

[34] Clearly the entire question of the costs and benefits of providing more services in the home merits careful study. See D.A. Wolfe & P. Jaffe, "Children in Care of the State: Policy Issues for the 1990s", in this volume.

There have also been cases in which foster parents have wanted to claim custody or adopt a child, against the wishes of the C.A.S.[35] This has raised very difficult questions, as foster parents have very limited legal rights but sometimes have a much closer relationship with the child than anyone else. Serious consideration should be given to the creation of the legal status "foster guardianship", a status between foster parent and adoptive parent. A foster guardian might have a significant set of "parent-like" rights, without the necessity of severing all links to the C.A.S. or the natural family.[36]

At the same time as foster parents are demanding better compensation and more rights, there are increasing concerns about the adequacy of some foster homes and group homes. Because of the urgent need for placements and heavy caseloads, some placements are not adequately screened and supervised. While efforts have been made to ensure that the rights and needs of children in care are met, this remains a serious concern.[37] Clearly there are issues concerning children in care and the child care system which must be addressed.

The legal framework for child protection also requires scrutiny. A number of issues have arisen since the enactment of the Child and Family Services Act in 1984. For example, if a child is apprehended by a C.A.S. on the grounds of suspected abuse or neglect, a court must return the child to parental care pending a full hearing unless the court is satisfied that "there are reasonable and probable grounds to believe that there is a *substantial* risk to the child's health or safety" which requires the child's immediate removal from the home.[38] Does this make it too difficult to protect children and promote their best interests? Or is this necessary to prevent unnecessary disruption in children's lives and protect parental rights?

---

[35] See e.g. *B.* v. *A.* (1988), 13 R.F.L.(3d) 209 (Ont. H.C.). For a very interesting American decision recognizing the rights of foster parents, see *Smith* v. *Organization of Foster Families*, 97 S.Ct. 2094 (1977).

[36] See Ontario Ministry of Community and Social Services, *The Children's Act: A Consultation Paper*, 1982, 152, which proposed "foster guardianship".
For a recent case where a court allowed the foster parents to adopt, but expressed regret at not being able to preserve links to the natural parents, see *C.A.S of Renfrew Cty.* v. *J.M. and E.W.* (1988), 15 R.F.L.(3d) 329 (Ont. Prov. Ct.—Fam. Div.).

[37] R. Dawson, *The Abuse of Children in Fostercare*, Ontario Association of Children's Aid Societies. Part V of the C.F.S.A. provides for the "Rights of Children in Care", including the right of free access to the Office of Child Advocacy.

[38] In *C.C.A.S. of Metro Toronto* v. *P.L.*, [1986] W.D.F.L. 1254 Felstiner Prov. J. referred to s.47(3) of the C.F.S.A. as a "very dangerous statute".

This type of issue is symptomatic of a broad range of fundamental issues about the child protection system. In comparison to the prior legal regime, the C.F.S.A. has increased the level of external scrutiny of decisions in the child protection system, both in terms of initial C.A.S. involvement and in regard to the placement of children in different facilities.[39] The C.F.S.A. attempts to structure the discretion of child protection staff and the courts.

The extension of legal and procedural rights was partially motivated by a desire to promote notions of fairness and due process. A failure to recognize legal rights of parents and children may violate the *Charter of Rights*, and the enactment of such legislation may be viewed as having forestalled judicial action to grant rights.[40] The recognition of parental rights also reflects fundamental beliefs about the appropriate role of the state in family life. Further, there was a belief that due process is necessary to ensure that the best possible decisions are made for children; reviews and hearings tend to ensure that information is brought forward and opinions of professionals carefully scrutinized.

There was also a recognition that state intervention is not always beneficial. Though invariably well intended, state intervention is sometimes inappropriate and damaging to a child's long-term best interests.

Some of the original proponents of the C.F.S.A. may feel that the legislation did not do enough to protect rights and respect due process.[41] There is, for example, a concern that some of the evidentiary provisions of the Act are too broad and make it very difficult for parents to challenge evidence.[42] On the other hand critics of the C.F.S.A. argue that the system has placed too much emphasis on due process. They point out that the enhancement of legal rights has been expensive, and that some of the resources devoted to due process might be better directed towards the provision of services to children and families.

When child protection cases are dealt with in the court system, there are often considerable delays in resolving them. This is frustrating for all concerned, and may be damaging for children who may be left in limbo for months or even years pending completion of judicial proceedings. While there are steps which can be

---

[39] The C.F.S.A. ss. 34–36 create Residential Placement Advisory Committees which control placements in a range of facilities. Sections 105–107 create a complaints procedure for children in care.

[40] See e.g. *Re C.P.L.* (1988), 70 Nfld. & P.E.I.R. 287 (Nfld. U.F.C.); *S.S.* v. *Director of Child and Family Services* (1987), 8 R.F.L. (3d) 430 (Man. Q.B.); and *H.M.* v. *Director of Child Welfare* (1989), 22 R.F.L. (3d) 399 (P.E.I.S.C.). However, contra in Ontario *Catholic C.A.S. Metro Toronto* v. *T.S.* (1989), 20 R.F.L. (3d) 337 (Ont. C.A.).

[41] See e.g. Ontario Ministry of Community and Social Services, *The Children's Act: A Consultation Paper*, 1982.

[42] C.F.S.A. s.46; see e.g. *T.T.* v. *C.C.A.S. Metro Toronto* (1984), 42 R.F.L.(2d) 48 (Ont. Prov. Ct.—Fam. Div.).

taken to improve the efficiency and speed of the court system, due process inevitably entails a certain degree of expense and delay.

One aspect of the granting of legal rights has been the provision of counsel for children through the Office of the Official Guardian, either by staff lawyers or by a member of a panel of lawyers in private practice. Representation of children may be ordered by the court under the C.F.S.A., and occurs frequently in child protection cases. In cases where a child is unwilling or too young to instruct a lawyer, questions have been raised about the role of a child's lawyer and even about the value of having a lawyer to "represent" a child.[43] While there clearly are cases in which a lawyer for the child has an important function in terms of effecting a settlement or bringing evidence before the courts, the overall value and effectiveness of this program in Ontario has not been adequately assessed.

We have now had several years of experience with the child protection provisions of the C.F.S.A. and it is an appropriate time to assess whether the province has struck an appropriate balance between the protection of children and due process. To what extent was the legislation successful in achieving its original objectives? Does the increased emphasis on due process result in better decisions being made? Are the courts and other review bodies getting the appropriate information to allow them to make the best possible decisions? Are children's interests being sacrificed for the sake of due process, or to the contrary do C.A.S.'s still have too much unfettered discretion? To what extent do children have the inherent human right to be free from unwanted state intervention which is perceived to be in their best interests? What level of consistency is there between key decision-makers—e.g. are judges interpreting legislative provisions in the same fashion?

Criminal Prosecutions and Child Abuse Prevention

While the focus of the child protection system is on helping children and parents, increasingly efforts are also being directed towards prevention and reducing the incidence of child abuse.

The criminal justice system has a role to play in combatting child abuse. It is believed that the prosecution of those who have sexually or physically abused children may serve as a deterrent and as an important social symbol. It can also cause abusers who have been denying their behaviour to confront their problems and obtain treatment. In 1988 new federal legislation came into effect to facilitate the prosecution of child abusers, for example by making it easier for young children to be permitted to testify, by permitting videotapes of an interview with a child to be received in evidence, and by allowing a child who may be intimidated by the presence of the accused to testify from behind a screen or via closed

---

[43] See e.g. *Bonenfant* v. *Bonenfant* (1981), 21 R.F.L.(2d) 173 (Ont. H.C.); *Re J. and C.; C.C.A.S. Metro Toronto* (1985), 48 R.F.L.(2d) 371, 381 (Ont. Prov. Ct.—Fam. Div.).

circuit television. Innovative programs have been established to prepare children for testifying in court and provide assistance with "court induced trauma".

Ontario has been relatively slow to implement the new legislation.[44] Video-taping of interviews with children is not done extensively in this province. Closed circuit television has very rarely been used for child abuse prosecutions in Ontario. Perhaps most seriously, training and human resources are not adequate. Crown Attorneys often lack the training and time to deal sensitively with child witnesses, and other services to assist these children are lacking. Criminal prosecutions involving child victims are not receiving priority in the courts, and cases can drag on for very long time periods.

Parliament is required to review its child sexual abuse legislation in 1992–93.[45] At that time advocates for children may be seeking further reforms, for example to allow expert witnesses to give evidence about whether a child has been abused and to permit witnesses to testify about what a child may have told them out of court. It is also apparent that some defence lawyers will be seeking to have many of the recent amendments rescinded, to the extent that they have not succeeded in having them struck down as being in violation of the *Charter of Rights*.

The justice system can only respond to abuse which has already occurred. As a society we must be taking long-term steps to reduce the incidence of child abuse. There is clearly a need for research into the most effective measures and programs to achieve this objective, though some broad areas for action are apparent.

New federal legislation to deal with child pornography might be a welcome first step. Improvements in the screening and training of those who work with children are needed.[46] There must be changes the education system; already greater emphasis is being placed on teaching children to respect and protect themselves, but more must be done to prepare adolescents to act as parents and ensure that they do not become abusers. Support programs are needed for parents, especially those who are at high-risk of being abusers, such as teenage parents and victims of abuse.

Intergenerational cycles of abuse and domestic violence must be broken. Perhaps most fundamentally there must be changes in societal attitudes to children and sexuality. There is clearly a need for research into effective long-term strategies to reduce the incidence of child abuse, including study of the role of the justice system.

---

[44] For a description of the new legislation and Ontario's implementation efforts, see C. Stewart and N. Bala, *Understanding Child Sexual Abuse Prosecutions: Bill C–15 and the Criminal Code, Toronto*, Institute for the Prevention of Child Abuse, 1989.

[45] Bill C–15, 2nd Sess. 33rd Parliament, 1987, s.19.

[46] On the issue of screening, see N. Bala et al. *Review of the Ontario Child Abuse Register* (Queen's Social Program Evaluation Group, Kingston, 1988).

Adoption

Adoption was introduced in Ontario in 1921 to establish permanent family relationships for children whose biological parents were unwilling or unable to care for them. Originally most adoptions involved the newborn infants of unwed mothers; almost all adoptions were arranged by Children's Aid Societies. The nature of adoption and attitudes towards this type of familial relationship have changed dramatically in the last couple of decades. Some of the laws which govern this relationship may be out-dated and require reconsideration.

Originally it was felt that children who were adopted should have no contact with or knowledge about their biological parents. It was not uncommon for adoptees never to be told that they were adopted. Recently, attitudes have changed; it has been recognized that adoptees often have an interest in their background and that contact with biological parents need not undermine the relationship to adoptive parents. In 1987 a new adoption disclosure system came into effect in Ontario, which allows adult adoptees to request a search for a biological parent or relative. Unfortunately, due to inadequate staffing, it can take as long as eight years for a search to occur.[47] It may be that the disclosure provisions should be extended to allow biological parents to initiate a search. Any disclosure program should have sufficient resources to be implemented.

The question of post-adoption access is being increasingly raised. Although not appropriate when a newborn infant is placed for adoption, there may be circumstances involving the adoption of older children where visitation with biological parents may be in the child's best interests. In particular, in situations of step-parent adoption, which is now the most common type of adoption in Ontario, legislation allowing for post-adoption access may be desirable; such legislation now exists in Manitoba.[48]

While at one time there were more newborn infants available for adoption than adoptive homes, there has been a dramatic change. With improved birth control, easy access to abortion, and increased social and financial support for single mothers, there has been a steady decline in the number of unwed mothers

---

[47] The new legislative scheme is found in ss.155–158j (enacted as S.O. 1987, c.4, s.7). For a description of some of the problems of implementation, see "Finding birth parents could take 8 years", *Globe and Mail*, Sept. 16, 1988, 1.

[48] See e.g. *C.C.A.S. Metro Toronto* v. *T.S.* (1987), 10 R.F.L.(3d) 343 (Ont. Dist. Ct.), revg. (1985), 48 R.F.L.(2d) 371 (Ont. Prov. Ct.—Fam. Div.). Manitoba legislation specifically allows post-adoption access in stepparent situations, *Child and Family Services Act*, S.M. 1985, c.8, s.67. Some advocates propose that there should be more support for "open adoption", with possibilities for relatively extensive contacts between natural parents and children, even when the adoption involves a newborn infant being adopted by strangers. The merits of "open adoption" deserve careful study. See L. Caplan, "A Reporter At Large: Open Adoption", *New Yorker*, May 21, 1990.

wishing to have their children adopted. The C.A.S.'s have very long waiting lists and infertile couples are increasingly turning to private adoption agencies. The field of private adoption may require closer regulation. There is evidence that the wealthy and well-connected may have a priority and that birth mothers may be subject to pressure to place their children through the private process.[49]

There are other issues in the adoption area worthy of close study. For example, are adequate programs in place to assist in adoption from underdeveloped countries where abandoned or orphaned children may face a very bleak future? Are there adequate legal protections for biological fathers whose children may be placed for adoption without them even being aware of their birth? [50]

III. YOUNG OFFENDERS

When the *Young Offenders Act* [Y.O.A.] came into effect in 1984, it marked a fundamental change in the Canadian approach to dealing with young persons who have violated the criminal law. The *Juvenile Delinquents Act* [J.D.A.], first enacted in 1908, placed an emphasis on treating delinquents as "misguided children". The J.D.A. was criticized for giving judges and correctional officials too much discretion to do whatever they considered in the "best interests" of a youth. There were also concerns about the effectiveness of the J.D.A. in dealing with the problem of youthful criminality and adequately protecting society. The Y.O.A. places emphasis on the responsibility and legal rights of young persons. The implementation of the Y.O.A. has been controversial, especially in Ontario where the provincial government has been accused of taking a "minimal compliance" approach to the new federal regime.

One of the broad concerns expressed about the Y.O.A. is that it is too legalistic and places too much emphasis on due process, making it difficult for troubled youths to receive needed assistance. One aspect of this concern has been the increased presence of lawyers in youth court; under the Y.O.A. every youth who is unable to afford a lawyer is entitled to have one paid by the government. There have been complaints that the process of obtaining counsel has been cumbersome and resulted in delays and adjournments. More fundamentally questions have been raised about the value of the participation of some lawyers, especially in the crucial dispositional stage.[51]

As long as the legislation places an emphasis on the accountability of young persons and their corresponding rights to due process, it seems that extensive

---

[49] See e.g. "Heavy demand for adoption forces closing of waiting lists" *Globe and Mail*, Sept. 16, 1988, A11.

[50] *A.G. Ontario* v. *Nevins Prov. J.*(1988), 13 R.F.L.(3d) 113 (Ont. Div. Ct.), revg. [1988] W.D.F.L. 215 (Ont. Prov. Ct.—Fam. Div.).

[51] See e.g. Felstiner, "Some Observations on Practice and Procedure under the Young Offenders Act" (1985), *Ontario Association of Professional Social Workers Metro News* (Spring), 19–23; and D. Hanscom, "The Dynamics of Disposition in Youth Court" March 1988, as yet unpublished paper for LL.M. at University of Toronto [available at Law Library, Queen's University].

involvement of lawyers in the process is inevitable. However, steps can be taken to facilitate and expedite access to counsel, to ensure that all lawyers appearing in youth court have appropriate training and familiarity with resources and that they have access to the support services which will enable them to provide effective representation.

Alone among Canadian provinces, Ontario was unwilling to implement the provisions of the Y.O.A. which permit young persons who are charged with relatively minor offences to be diverted from the court system and dealt with by "alternative measures". The government has offered several rationales for this decision. There is some questioning of the efficacy of this process in terms of reducing recidivism, and there is the possibility that the rights of youths may be violated if they are dealt with informally. Further, there is the potential for "widening of the net," if police charge more youths with the expectation that some may be diverted. However, Ontario's failure to implement the alternative measures provisions of the Y.O.A. was widely criticized in the province. Critics argued that alternative measures have the potential for increasing community and victim involvement, destigmatizing youths, and dealing relatively expeditiously and inexpensively with minor offenders.

The failure of Ontario to provide for alternative measures was successfully challenged in 1988 in the Ontario Court of Appeal as discrimination on the basis of geography, in violation of s.15 of the *Charter of Rights*.[52] The case is under appeal to the Supreme Court of Canada. As an interim measure, the Ontario government has established a program that some observers consider cumbersome and inadequately resourced. Regardless of the outcome of the case in the Supreme Court, the issue of alternative measures in Ontario seems likely to remain controversial until the government establishes a sound and clear policy.

One of the most significant effects of the Y.O.A. has been the change in the age jurisdiction of the juvenile justice system. The minimum age of criminal responsibility has been raised from 7 to 12. Children under 12 who violate the criminal law are to be dealt with by their parents or pursuant to provincial child welfare legislation. Certain groups in Ontario, most notably the police, have been highly critical of the raised age jurisdiction. Others, however, have pointed out that Ontario has been less responsive than some other provinces in terms of enacting appropriate legislation and establishing suitable programs for dealing with this age group.[53] The federal government is continuing to study the question of the minimum age jurisdiction for youth court, including consideration of different provincial responses to under twelves. It is apparent that society must take steps to deal with at least some of the offences committed by those under 12; the issue is what response is best for these children and for society.

---

[52] *R. v. Sheldon S.* (1988), 63 C.R.(3d) 64 (Ont. C.A.).

[53] See Metro Children's Advisory Group, *Kids not Cons: A Problem in Search of a Policy, Children Under Twelve in Conflict With the Law*, Toronto, 1985; and Leschied & Jaffe, "Implementing the Young Offenders Act in Ontario", in Hudson et al. eds. *Justice and the Young Offender in Canada*, Toronto, Thompson Educational Publishing, Inc. 1988.

The Y.O.A. sets a uniform maximum age jurisdiction for youth courts running to the 18th birthday, with the date of the alleged offence establishing jurisdiction. While some provinces, such as Quebec and Manitoba, used the 18th birthday under the J.D.A., in Ontario the Y.O.A. raised the maximum age jurisdiction by two years. Ontario's response was to establish a two-tier juvenile justice system. Youths aged 12 to 15 are largely dealt with by Family Court judges and the Ministry of Community and Social Services, while 16 and 17 year olds appear in the adult Provincial Court (Criminal Division), albeit with judges nominally sitting as youth court judges, and receive services from the Ministry of Correctional Services. This scheme perpetuates the divisions of responsibility established under the J.D.A.

The two-tier implementation has been criticized as being inefficient and unfair. There is a need for better research about the differences in treatment for the two age groups, in part to determine whether they are simply a response to the age differences. However, there is already significant evidence that older youths are receiving fewer services while being dealt with in a more punitive fashion by the courts.[54]

Since the Y.O.A. has come into force, Ontario has refused to participate in the surveys of youth court activity carried out by the Canadian Centre for Justice Statistics. This makes it difficult to engage in longitudinal and interjurisdictional analysis of data, though some information has been made available about young offenders in Ontario. In 1987, 20,741 youths 12–15 were charged under the Y.O.A. in Ontario, and 25,495 youths aged 16–17 were charged. Roughly 10% of police apprehensions of young persons involved violent offences and over 60% involved property offences. In the 12–15 age category, almost one third of charges were dismissed or withdrawn before disposition; 20,741 youth court orders were made: 1,031 for secure custody (5.0%); 1,614 open custody (7.8%); 10,906 probation (52.6%); 1,845 restitution or compensation (8.9%); 4,077 community service (19.7%); 3,085 absolute discharge (14.8%); 2,266 fine (10.9%); and 705 other (3.4%). In the 16–17 age category, about 2,280 of the estimated 26,400 youths received a sentence of secure custody (8.6%), while about 31% of charges were disposed of by probation.[55]

---

[54] See e.g. Ontario Social Development Council, *Y.O.A. Dispositions: Challenges and Choices*, Toronto, 1988, 99–109.

[55] These figures come from Ontario Ministry of the Attorney General, Research Services, "An Analysis of Data Relating to Young Offenders", June 6, 1988. The data from this source are presented in a fashion which makes analysis difficult.
It should be noted that many Ontario young offenders are placed in open custody facilities by correctional officials pursuant to a probation order made under s. 23(2)(f) of the Y.O.A., which allows a Youth Court to order that a young person should "reside in such place as the provincial director may specify." This practice makes it impossible to determine accurately the number of youths in custody from dispositional data. The practice is highly controversial and merits study. For conflicting views as to the legality and appropriateness of this practice, see *R.* v. *Joe L.* (1985), Y.O.S. 3497–3 (Ont. Prov. Ct.—Fam. Div.) and *R.* v. *James R.* (1986), Y.O.S. 3497–7 (Ont. Prov. Ct.—Fam. Div.).

While deficiencies in data make accurate comparisons impossible, it is clear that the number of youths placed in custodial facilities in Ontario under the Y.O.A. and the duration of their sentences has increased above levels under the J.D.A. It is, however, very important to note that in some provinces, most notably Quebec, the enactment of the Y.O.A. has not been accompanied by a rise in the use of custody.[56]

There are a number of possible explanations for the increased use of custody in Ontario. It has been suggested that the possibility of committing youths to open custody has inadvertently increased institutionalization, as judges have regarded this as the best option for youth who would otherwise be placed on probation or receive some other form of community placement. The tendency to utilize open custody may be exacerbated by a lack of adequate community resources.

It has also been suggested that some 16 and 17-year-olds are receiving harsher sanctions because they are no longer being treated as youthful adults without prior involvement with the adult justice system, but as older young offenders with extensive youth court records. It may also be that the process of court review of custodial dispositions is not working as effectively as it might; youth court judges seem more reluctant than adult parole officials to permit release from custody.

Much of the responsibility for increased use of custody rests with youth court judges. It has been suggested that some judges may be placing too much emphasis on the principles of responsibility and the protection of society, and failing to appreciate that the Y.O.A. also explicitly recognizes the principles of the limited accountability and special needs of young offenders.[57] Clearly there is a need for research into the causes and consequences of the increased use of custodial dispositions in Ontario.

There are other dispositional issues related to the Y.O.A. In particular it has been claimed that the Act does not meet the special needs of youth with emotional problems. The Act specifies that a youth court may only order that a youth receive "treatment" if the youth consents. There is some ambiguity about the significance of this provision, since young offenders receive rehabilitative services which may be broadly considered "treatment" in custodial facilities. Clearly young offenders cannot be placed in mental health facilities without their

---

[56] Ontario Social Development Council, supra n.54, 25.

[57] The Ontario Court of Appeal has recognized that the protection of society is not paramount to the needs and interests of society [see e.g. *R. v. Joseph F.* (1986), 11 O.A.C. 402], but the extent to which actual sentencing patterns of youth court judges have been affected by this type of appellate decision remains unclear. For a discussion of possible causes of increased use of custodial dispositions in Ontario, see *Y.O.A. Dispositions*, supra n. 54, 76; Leschied & Jaffe, "Impact of the Young Offenders Act on Court Dispositions" (1987) 29 *Can. Jour. Crim.* 421–430; and Bala, "The Young Offenders Act: A Legal Framework", in Hudson et al., supra n. 53, 26.

consent; while some have attacked this requirement as interfering with needed treatment, others have argued that it is essential to protect the rights of youths and questioned the value of involuntary treatment.[58]

There is also a concern that Native youths and members of visible minorities are over-represented among those brought before the youth courts and placed in custodial facilities. Does this reflect systemic or other biases in the justice system, or is it simply a reflection of broader societal issues? Judicial inquiries in Alberta Manitoba and Nova Scotia are exploring related questions, largely in the context of discrimination against Natives in the adult justice system. They clearly merit specific study in the context of the youth justice system, with a view to making the system more responsive to the needs of Native and visible minority youth.[59]

Recently, considerable attention has been focused on the adequacy of the maximum disposition provision of the Y.O.A., three years in secure custody. While virtually no research has been done on the deterrent or rehabilitative effects of different lengths of sentences for young offenders, a three-year maximum seems adequate for the vast majority of offenders. Public attention has centred on the adequacy of a three-year sentence for the small number of youths who commit very serious offences, in particular homicide. Under s. 16 of the Y.O.A. the Crown may apply to a youth court judge to have a serious case transferred into the adult system, where a youth will receive the same sentence as an adult for first degree murder: life imprisonment with no possibility of parole for twenty-five years. In one case in which the Ontario Court of Appeal refused to order transfer to adult court, Mackinnon A.C.J.O. expressed the view that "three years for murder appears totally inadequate to express society's revulsion", and suggested that Parliament consider amending the Y.O.A.[60] A leading juvenile forensic psychiatrist, Dr. Clive Chamberlain, has argued that for a few very disturbed youths, three years is also an insufficient time to permit rehabilitation.[61] Courts dealing with transfer applications have faced the dilemma of choosing between two inadequate alternatives, an insufficient three years in the youth system or totally destructive confinement in an adult facility for at least twenty-five years.

The federal government has responded to these concerns by introducing Bill C-58 to amend the Y.O.A.[62] This new law will extend the maximum sentence that a youth court can impose for murder to five years less a day, and provide

---

[58] Y.O.A. ss.20(1)(i) & 22. See Leschied & Hyatt, "Perspective: Consent to Treatment Under the *Young Offenders Act*" (1986) 28 *Can. Jour. Crim.* 69–78.

[59] See LaPrairie, "The Young Offenders Act and Aboriginal Youth", in Hudson et al. supra n. 53, 159–167.

[60] *R.* v. *M.A.Z.* (1987), 35 C.C.C.(3d) 144, 162(Ont. C.A.).

[61] Quoted in *The Medical Post*, Dec. 8, 1987, 61.

[62] 2nd Session, 38th Parliament, First Reading Dec. 20, 1989. Expected to be enacted by the fall of 1990.

that young persons who are transferred into adult court and convicted there of murder will be eligible for parole in five to ten years instead of the present 25. It also provides that where the "interests of society" and the "needs of the young person" cannot be reconciled under the Y.O.A., the protection of the public shall be "paramount" and the youth shall be transferred.

When assessing the effects of the Y.O.A on young persons, it is extremely important to attempt to distinguish between the effect of the federal statute and its implementation by the provincial governments and the courts. While it may be necessary to consider amending the federal legislation to deal with some concerns, it is apparent that there are more contentious issues in Ontario than in other provinces, and the effect of provincial implementation must be closely studied. Perhaps more fundamentally, if we wish to reduce the incidence of youthful criminality, we should avoid simplistic solutions. We will have to find the underlying causes of juvenile crime and attempt to eliminate these. While the question requires further research, it seems unlikely that taking a get tough approach will in itself reduce the incidence of offences by young persons.[63]

IV. OTHER LAW REFORM ISSUES

Virtually every area of children's and family policy is affected by law and the justice system. Issues like truancy, special education, corporal punishment, consent to treatment and access to mental health facilities all have legal dimensions. Anyone concerned about these issues will have an agenda for law reform.

There is one area which is particularly complex and controversial where there is a clear need for government action. A number of related medico-legal issues have arisen as a result of advances in medical knowledge and technology. The government has failed to act on a 1985 report of the Law Reform Commission of Ontario dealing with reproductive technology and surrogate motherhood. While the Report is controversial[64] and some of the recommendations may have to be reconsidered, there is a need for government action to regulate this field.

Another related issue concerns the extent to which the state should be involved in requiring prenatal medical care. There are cases in which mothers have refused to receive medical care at the time of birth, or refused to have a medically recommended procedure in connection with the birth, such as a caesarian

---

[63] See Leschied et al., *The Changing Profiles of Young Offenders With Special Needs: Trends and Critical Issues*, 1988, London Family Court Clinic; and Leschied, Austin & Jaffe, "Impact of the Young Offenders Act on Recidivism Rates of Special Needs Youth" (1988), 20 Can. J. Beh. Scien. 322.

[64] Ontario Law Reform Commission, *Report on Human Artificial Reproduction and Related Matters, 1985*. For a critique of the report and a discussion of related issues, see Somer Brodrib, *Women and Reproductive Technologies* (Canadian Council on the Status of Women, Ottawa, 1988).

section. Can the C.A.S. obtain a court order so that the mother receives care regarded as medically appropriate? What should be done with mothers who are drug addicts or alcoholics and pose a risk to their unborn children? While cases involving this type of issue have come before Canadian courts, the Ontario legislation is silent on how to deal with these problems.[65]

V. CONCLUSION

We have clearly moved to a rights based model of society. Fundamental political and social values support the granting of legal rights. As society becomes increasingly complex and sophisticated, it seems highly unlikely that we will return to a society which does not place a high value on due process and fundamental freedoms.

It seems inevitable that for the foreseeable future considerable reliance will continue to be placed on the courts to deal with problems of children and families. In each situation we must critically examine the value and efficacy of our laws and justice system. There may be situations involving families and children in which too much faith is placed on laws and courts to resolve very difficult social and human problems.

It also behooves us to have a justice system which operates as humanely and efficiently as possible. This requires lawyers and judges with better training and increased sensitivity. It requires a court system which minimizes delay and ensures that cases in which a child's future is at stake receive priority. It requires a Unified Family Court, with ready access to appropriate support services, like assessment clinics, and to alternatives to the court system, like mediation and alternative measures. Most fundamentally, it requires social commitment and adequate resources.

---

[65] See *Re Baby R.*(1988), 15 R.F.L.(3d) 225 (B.C.S.C.) and *C.A.S. Belleville* v. *L.T.*(1987), 59 O.R.(2d) 204, 7 R.F.L.(3d) 191 (Ont. Prov. Ct.—Fam. Div.). See also the Yukon *Children's Act*, S.Y.T. 1984, c.2, s.134, which expressly allows for prenatal intervention.

ISSUES IN EDUCATION
A Discussion of Policy

Penny Moss and Donald Rutledge

This chapter describes the state of education in Ontario today and outlines proposals for change. In our discussion of critical policy issues now under debate—streaming, equity, drop-outs, teacher education, evaluation of student achievement—we will be leading to an integrated proposal for organizing schools in a new way. While we recognize the importance of many other issues—day care, gender equity, the place of alternative schools, private schools, education for Franco-Ontarians, the relation between schools and society, apprenticeship programs, cooperative education—we do not address these explicitly and at length. Instead we discuss what we believe must be the central focus—an organization of schooling that will serve more students better, particularly during the crucial adolescent years. We hasten to add that our proposal is not completely original with us. Something like it has been considered earlier in Ontario (Hope, 1950) and it resembles the Minnesota Plan (Berman, 1985) in several ways. The problem has been recognized before and is still with us.

There is ample evidence that some such proposal for change is badly needed. Public satisfaction with the situation in Ontario schools has declined over the past ten years. The OISE Survey of Educational Issues indicates that in 1978 68 percent of survey respondents were very satisfied or satisfied with the "current situation in Ontario elementary and high schools with regard to the school system in general". By 1982, that percentage had dropped to 55 percent and by 1986 less that a majority, 42 percent reported being very satisfied or satisfied. This decline continues with only 36 percent reporting satisfaction in the 1988 survey. But the public has no doubt about the importance of education. In a poll conducted for the Canadian Education Association (1984), in answer to the question "In your opinion, how important are schools to one's future success? ", 82.3 percent of Ontario respondents said "extremely important", while another 15.5 percent said "fairly important". When asked in the same survey "What are the biggest problems with which the schools in this community must deal? ", the four most frequently mentioned problems by Ontario respondents were, drugs, smoking, alcohol (20.2 percent), lack of discipline (18.3 percent), pupils' lack of interest, truancy, attitudes (16.0 percent) and curriculum problems (10.4 percent). While these issues are ones that recur in local school board and government policy initiatives, the current political agenda in Ontario education is dominated by concerns about the purpose and outcomes of schooling in an increasingly technological and economically competitive society. This theme is identified by the Premier's Council in its 1988 report *Competing in the New Global Economy*:

> increasing the commitment to educational achievement and completion is the central educational challenge facing Ontario policy makers, educators and students (p. 233).

In his report to the Minister of Education, the *Ontario Study of the Relevance of Education and the Issue of Drop-outs*, (1987), Commissioner George Radwanski, writes:

> In this new economic environment, our young people will not long feel fulfilled, nor will their self-esteem long endure, if they find themselves unemployable or unqualified for other than the most menial, dead-end work because they lack the requisite knowledge or skills. And our collective sense of fulfilment and self-esteem as a society will scarcely be enhanced if our standard of living goes into steady decline because an under-educated population has made us uncompetitive in an increasingly rigorous global economy.

So concerns about both personal development and economic growth call for educational reform.

I. EDUCATION IN ONTARIO TODAY: SOME PROBLEMS

The Present Scene: A Crisis of Confidence

The Adolescent School Attendance Act raised the age of compulsory school attendance from 14 to 16 years beginning in 1921. Prior to that time in Ontario the average pupil left school in Grade 5; [1] today about two-thirds of students persevere until Grade 12.[2] Yet public discontent with the schools seems to have reached an all-time high. Moreover, public opinion concerning the nature of needed reforms is also solidifying into a conservative mass—not very detailed or technically pondered—which calls for more compulsory content, more emphasis on control of behaviour, and a widespread testing program designed, somehow, to produce higher levels of achievement by at least some of our students so that we can compete economically. "Excellence" is in; equity is less important.

Most recent legislation for children is aimed at protecting them and ensuring advocacy for their rights, as in the Young Offenders Act, the Public Health Act, and the Day Nurseries Act. But the public debate about education policy continues to centre on "unsatisfactory standards" and tends to view the child as deficient, lazy, potentially dangerous. Something like an adversarial role for the student lurks in many discussions about education.

---

[1]   Kel Crossley, oral, guest lecturer OISE, 1977.

[2]   Ministry of Education, oral report, See also calculations of drop-out rate.

Not everybody agrees, of course. In the teaching profession there is considerable resistance to these public attitudes, and the split between political rhetoric and informed professional opinion shows up everywhere. For example, in 1984 reforms to secondary education culminated in a new governing document for secondary schools, *Ontario Schools: Intermediate and Senior Division* (O.S.I.S.). It was launched as a conservative reform document, calling for fewer student options, more core content and closer links to employment. But this public political launching is at some variance with the real reforms introduced, which show up in the new guidelines issued for each subject. It is true that these are solid and detailed as to content, and impose content more specifically at a lower grade, but they are more progressive as to methodology than any document previously issued by the Ministry. They require the teacher to modify the domination of classroom conversation and emphasize the social nature of learning. If implemented thoroughly, they will bring about a dramatic change in teaching methods over the next decade, putting much more emphasis on meaning and on the use of language by the student in all subjects.

Analysis of educational policy suffers from a "quick fix" mentality. Although media love to talk about the schools' failings, in Ontario the provincial legislature rarely debates educational policy. Usually improvements to education are invoked politically as a means to a Great Society, or at least a way of competing economically. And the present debate about educational change in Ontario could well lead to merely superficial changes in our schooling arrangement, mere repair and maintenance. Even worse, the reforms may be politically imposed and positively harmful, producing more alienation and less achievement. We wish to argue that our present challenge is to move to a new plateau of learning—one in which more students learn more, learn in depth, learn how to learn. Current reform proposals will not take us to this new plateau.

Recently, George Radwanski's report has been studied by a Select Committee of the Legislature (reported, 1988). Radwanski's recommendations were worrisome in their failure to recognize the reality of the student as a living creature bright with purpose. There is no point in calling for more hours and years of remediation if we cannot coopt learner's purposes. We cannot produce independent thinkers by taking away their own intentions, the source and power of their autonomy. Yet there was no provision in his recommendations for a structuring of the school system which could help preserve human connections for these students and give them a sense of purpose throughout their school careers.

By now our bias should be clear. We do not see the question of "standards" and improved education outcomes as being inimical to the issue of equal opportunity and equal outcomes throughout society. We believe, quite simply, that formal education can be both better and more universally accessible. We endorse the statement made by the late Ronald Edmonds, at one time Senior Assistant for Instruction, New York City Public Schools:

> We can, whenever we choose, successfully educate all children whose schooling is of interest to us. We already know more than we need, in order to do this.

Whether we do it must finally depend on how we feel about the fact that we haven't done it so far... (Edmonds, 1979, p. 23).

The Secondary School Question: Policy Development Since 1960

Although several issues have produced some controversy, questions about how to provide secondary education for most of the population have been the most persistent among the major policy questions for at least thirty years. The dissatisfaction and controversy about secondary education have produced new and improved official policies at a bewildering rate, so that many students enter high school under one set of regulations and graduate under another. Indeed, the Ministry of Education has recently announced a review of O.S.I.S. prior to its full implementation. Much of the debate centres around the question of "tracking" or "streaming" students by achievement (for example see Oakes, 1985, Radwanski, 1988).

Some argue that as long as secondary schools serve as both preparatory to university and college for some students and "finishing" schools for other students, there will be confusion and criticism. Goodlad (1986) reports that some international critics even argue that we cannot have universal secondary education and excellence too. For example, in comparing schooling in various countries, Burton Clark contended that "the dream of universal education in the form of the comprehensive school...is a huge burden on the school system...the perceived failure of the U.S. secondary schools is, to a considerable degree, the result of a shortfall in outcomes when they are measured against the expectation that the comprehensive school...can be helpful to all students from all types of backgrounds". But as John Goodlad (1986) has pointed out, there is a growing consensus that secondary graduation is indispensable to every student. Not only that, but the sharply heightened requirements of the workplace are also making more and more people conclude that there are no significant differences between the kind of formal schooling required to prepare for entry into higher education and the kind required to prepare for entry into the work force.

In Ontario, however, the last thirty years have seen increased diversity in high school offerings. In 1960 the injection of federal money for vocational schools[3] broke the pattern of the old high school general course, with its core subjects in Grades 9 and 10, plus university preparation after that. The province responded eagerly to the chance for federal money, altering its whole system to include "vocational" students—students who had not been promoted from elementary school. In 1961 the Revised (or Robarts) Plan produced a new curriculum for secondary schools in three months, and classes began in September 1962.

The Revised Plan went far beyond the provision of vocational education for students who earlier would have left school. It also introduced another stream or level called the "general level;" students who functioned at this level were sup-

---

[3] *The National Training Act* (1960) federal money was available for the building of vocational and technical schools.

posed to receive a good general education and go to work. They were not qualified to enter university. The effect was to produce three levels of achievement—vocational, general, academic. The traditional technical and commercial courses were mostly at the general level.

Failure rates were high in the early sixties; 42% of students had failed once by Grade 10.[4] The Revised Plan came under pressure almost immediately, and the much more flexible Credit System began to take shape, with six secondary schools given permission to experiment with it in 1967. The Credit System made few demands concerning core subjects. A credit was awarded in a certain subject at a certain level for work done and time spent. The accumulation of a certain number of credits resulted in a graduation diploma, with the student having a large degree of choice. In the interests of handling a wide range of ability, levels of achievement were elaborated further, eventually encompassing six allegedly separate and distinguishable levels. Even the lowest of these could count towards a credit, although the worth of the credit was often debated. In 1967 the province-wide Grade 13 examinations were abolished. Although objective evidence indicated that student performance at the highest credit level did not suffer, the looseness of the Credit System and the lack of an external examination together with the free time and the exotic subjects contributed to public scepticism.

For a few years the Revised Plan and the Credit System ran in double harness, although by 1971 about 80% of secondary schools were on the Credit System. By September 1972, the Credit System was mandatory, and was prescribed in the policy document H.S.I. In less than a decade it was under intense public criticism for being too soft and liberal and for lacking mandatory requirements, and by May of 1981 the *Report of the Secondary Education Review Project* (SERP) was released. It examined almost every aspect of secondary school education, focusing on the Credit System, the content and organization of curriculum, standards, discipline, and the role of the school in preparing students for employment. After encouraging public response to the SERP report, the Ministry, in November of 1982, produced *The Renewal of Secondary Education in Ontario* (ROSE), which introduced *Ontario Schools: Intermediate and Senior* (O.S.I.S.), an attempt to preserve the credit system while satisfying demands for rigor, core content and closer links to employment.

O.S.I.S. organizes courses after Grade 8 at three levels of difficulty, advanced, general and basic. The policy advocates that students' programs be made up of courses taken at one or more levels of difficulty and that the needs of non-university bound students be better met. Preliminary findings indicate that little substantive change has occurred, although Leithwood and James (1988) found that general adherence to the technical and administrative requirements of O.S.I.S. had occurred. Many students remain enroled in courses at a single level of difficulty—advanced, general or basic. The changes to school organization and timetables necessary to produce the flexibility inherent in O.S.I.S. have generally

---

[4]   Kel Crossley, oral, OISE 1987.

proved difficult for some schools to make (Leithwood, James, 1988). Thus, students continue to find themselves in streamed programs. It is therefore unlikely that O.S.I.S. will effect any change to the correlations between streaming, dropping out and post-secondary student options.

Who Stays—Who Succeeds

The measure of high school completion commonly used is that of the earning of a Secondary School Graduation Diploma (SSGD) which requires 16 compulsory credits and 14 electives. Six Ontario Academic Courses (OAC) required for university entrance may be earned in addition to or within the thirty credit total. At present Ontario is without direct measures of rates of completion of high school because we lack a system for tracking the progress of individual students. The Student Information System being implemented by the Ministry of Education will soon provide this capacity.

Current estimates of school outcomes compare the numbers of students awarded the SSGD with the number of students enroled in Grade 9 three years earlier. In 1987 102,980 SSGD's were awarded, while in 1983 149,818 students were enroled in Grade 9, suggesting a high school completion rate of approximately 70%. (This method of calculation ignores the number of students who may take 4.5 or 5 years to complete the diploma requirements. Current information on the levels of difficulty at which diploma requirements are earned is not available from the Ministry of Education.)

Can the rate of completion of secondary education be improved? Can higher levels of achievement be obtained? We can only consider these questions by making a careful analysis of what is happening now. Who is leaving? Why? Could they stay profitably? Do they understand their real options, especially if they are in basic level courses?

A current drop-out rate of around 30% is widely accepted (Radwanski, 1987). This rate compares favourably with rates from a number of other North American jurisdictions, but is a significant concern for Ontario, not only because of the increased recognition of the importance of high school, but also because the drop-out rate is not evenly distributed through the student population. As we shall see dropping out is more likely to be associated with socio-economic status, racial or ethnic backgrounds, and level of difficulty at which courses are studied. The concern must be for enhanced social justice or equity by means of raising student achievement.

The completion of secondary school is crucial, and unfortunately few drop-outs get their diploma later. While it is true that many return to school or other educational settings, the sample of drop-outs studied by Ellen Karp (1988) indicates that their overall success rate remains low. Of the 49% that returned to school or continued their education, 30% graduated, 29% were still enroled and 40% had dropped out again.

The patterns of dropping out are well known. The literature on drop-outs from Canada and all industrialized nations consistently confirms the strong link between family background, school achievement and dropping out. Radwanski (1987) found that 12% of students dropped out from advanced level programs, 62% from the general level stream and 79% from basic level. The lure of the workplace is particularly strong for students who are unsuccessful or alienated from school.

It must be recognized that a significant proportion of young people identified as drop-outs have made a deliberate choice to go to work rather than a choice to leave school. Ontario offers few, if any, satisfactory training or education programs outside of secondary schools for 16 to 19 year-olds.

The link between family socio-economic status and school success was reported by Porter, Blishen and Barrados in an Ontario-wide study in 1977. They found that:

> Higher family socio-economic status and higher levels of fathers' education are found to be associated with higher levels of school performance, higher levels of self-concept or ability, higher levels of educational expectations, a greater tendency to be enroled in a five-year program and staying in school longer.

Detailed studies conducted by the Research Department of the Toronto Board of Education (1983) serve to confirm and extend the identification of the relationship between family characteristics and dropping out and streaming. The distribution of students in Grade 9 by program levels of difficulty, advanced, general, basic, was linked with a number of family background characteristics. The findings over four years remained consistent. Students with parents in the upper occupational categories, professional and managerial, were twice as likely to be studying at the advanced level as students whose parents' occupations were in the lower categories, unskilled or semiskilled. These latter students were more likely to leave school early. This finding was true for both mothers' and fathers' occupations. As well, the studies showed that more males than females were enroled in basic and general level programs. Students who identified themselves as Blacks were less likely to be studying at the advanced level and most likely to be taking basic level courses. Native Canadians were the least likely to be studying at the advanced level and more likely to be in the basic level. The racial group with the largest proportion at the advanced level were those identifying themselves as Asian. These are the unsettling facts behind the gross figures. Although such detailed studies have generally not been conducted by other school boards, it seems likely that similar patterns could be expected across the Province.

The added dimension of race or ethnicity in these studies makes efforts to significantly alter these relationships even more urgent. It would be foolish, if not disastrous, to continue to ignore the relationship between school achievement, class and race or ethnicity.

The Province's espoused philosophy of equal educational opportunity, in reality means little more than an equal opportunity to attend school. The consequences of this limitation to opportunity are profound. Not only must we deal with the moral imperative for social justice, but also with the personal and economic consequences to both the individual and to society of school under-achievement.

Recent studies of Ontario students and drop-outs provide some directions for useful reform. In his study of 44,744 students aged 13–19, Dr. Alan King (1986) identified five key elements that might contribute to student satisfaction in their school experience:

- Effective teachers who are fair, accessible, caring, respectful of student individuality, enthusiastic and have clear, reasonable and have consistently enforced expectations of student behaviour;
- A guidance counselling program which reduces student concerns about confidentiality and a perceived bias in favour of university-bound students;
- Effective school principals who treat students as individuals, administer rules fairly, and are highly visible in the school;
- School programs which are linked to students' post-secondary futures;
- The involvement of the majority of students in extra-curricular activities.

Similar results were obtained by Ellen Karp (1988) in a survey of 843 drop-outs aged 15–25 with an average age of 20 years. Drop-outs, parents and teachers were asked for ideas likely to improve the school system for those students most likely to drop out. The top five responses from drop-outs were for more involved teachers, more interesting subjects, more relevant or job-oriented courses, more responsibility on the part of the student and smaller class sizes. Parents recommended more involved teachers, better availability of extra help, more guidance, more discipline and smaller class sizes. Teachers identified the need for more guidance, more relevant courses, smaller class sizes, improved student self-esteem and career awareness.

Both the large and detailed study of King and the more limited study of Karp indicate that students well understand the importance of school to their present and future life chances. Yet it seems that educators are cavalier about the value of a diploma. When asked to respond (in a survey cited by O.S.S.T.F. (1987)) to the statement "a student who is not benefitting from secondary school should be allowed to leave," 52.5% of students and 57.2% of parents disagreed, whereas 79.1% of teachers, 86.7% of guidance counsellors and 90.4% of principals agreed.

Students have every reason to stay, and they know it. Unfortunately many of them feel unsuccessful, unwanted. They yearn for a closer relationship with teachers, more acceptance, less judging. They seem to understand the relationship between teaching and learning.

Parent Involvement in School Success

The link between family background and school success is clear, although it is not a straightforward one of cause and effect. Yet some writers, for example Coleman (1966) and Jencks (1982) have concluded that schools can do little to alter the relationship between family, socio-economic status and academic achievement, even when compensatory programs are provided. The research literature on the effects of parent involvement on children's school achievement indicates that it is not the home that is the cause of some children's lack of success in school, but rather it is, in substantial part, the lack of connection between home and school. In a recent review of the literature, Dr. Suzanne Ziegler (1987) writes:

> There can be no more powerful argument in favour of parental involvement in their children's schooling than the fact that it is strongly and positively associated with children's achievement in school and attitude toward learning (p. 6).

> The evidence is clear that parental encouragement, activities and interest at home and participation in schools and classrooms affect children's achievements, attitudes and aspirations, even after student ability and family socioeconomic status are taken into account. Students gain in personal and academic development if their families emphasize schools, let the children know they do, and do so continually over the school years. However, not all families currently become involved in school-related activities or show interest in their children's school work. And not all schools actively encourage and direct parent involvement (Epstein, 1986, p. 1–2, cited by Ziegler, 1987).

Research cited by Ziegler (1987, p. 9) using a random sample of American families found that while mothers' educational level is a strong predictor of parental involvement, it is important to school achievement only when parental involvement actually occurs (Stevenson and Baker, 1987). But perhaps more importantly, studies have shown that the differences between families as learning environments and in their likelihood of school involvement are not unalterable. Attitudes of parents who have felt powerless to influence their children's schooling and academic outcomes can be changed by parent involvement which is well-planned by the school and long-lasting (Sattes, 1985, cited by Ziegler, 1987). Outreach by the school must be aggressive and may need to include home visits if it is to benefit the children of all families. It is possible that without sustained efforts more inequity may result from approaches that result in only the more enthusiastic parents becoming involved (Toomey, 1986, cited by Ziegler, 1987). Teachers often express the view that the parents they most need to talk with are often the ones least likely to come to school.

In a recent study of characteristics associated with academically successful inner city children Ziegler, Hardwick and McCreath (1989) found the parents of 75% of the small group of poor students were difficult to contact initially, or proved difficult to maintain contact with from the initial contact to actual interview. However, the researchers did find that while perseverance was necessary the task of reaching these parents was possible in most cases. The findings of this study include that successful students work hard at school, ask teachers for help, do school work at home even if not required to, receive help from family members and have parents that demonstrate their belief in the value of education. The study concludes that effective teaching and effective teacher-parent communication can help more inner city children to be successful in school.

Much of the work on the effects of parent involvement on academic achievement has focused on the preschool or primary years, and has looked at the development of reading or literacy. Longitudinal studies indicate that the effects of positive early parent involvement are sustained. The best known of these has studied the participants of the Perry Preschool Program (U.S.A.) into early adulthood, which found significant positive academic, social and employment outcomes (Stallings and Stipek, 1986, cited by Ziegler, 1987). While it is not possible to know to what extent the involvement of parents made a difference, parent involvement in preschool programs, either at home or at school, has been a feature of most successful preschool programs.

The contribution of parents to student success in secondary schools has also received more attention in recent years. Hargreaves (1984), in his report on improving secondary schools, writes:

There is very little that the school can do towards removing poverty or improving the adverse social conditions in which many parents live. Yet, if we want children to achieve more, especially working class children, then improved home-school liaison and increased parental involvement must be a top priority. Cooperative home-school relations will enhance everything the school does...there are some ways in which most schools could improve their home-school relations. In our view, even the best practice does not go far enough in the light of the importance of parent involvement to any serious attempt to reduce pupil underachievement and disaffection. More substantial changes are needed (p. 14–17).

Ziegler (1987) describes a dramatic example of the effects of focused, personal, at-home contact with secondary parents from the work of Marockie, Jones and Lawrence (1987). A West Virginia secondary school (grades 10–12) set out to reduce its drop-out rate of 29 percent. A guidance counsellor position of "home-school visitor" was added to the school of 1750 students to devote full-time to conducting home interviews with students who wanted to drop out and with others identified as at risk by school personnel. A drop-out re-entry program was developed to provide appropriate support and counselling to returning students. Within 7 years, the school's drop-out rate fluctuated between 5 and 11 percent. That school system has now added a drop-out prevention program to the elementary schools and uses retired professionals to make "care calls" daily to all absent students. These callers are trained by the "home-school visitor" to express concern at the absence of the student and to solicit ways the school could help in the return of the student as soon as possible (Ibid pp.202–205). Similar programs have been initiated by a number of Ontario schools.

It is clear that we can no longer look to the home as the cause of poor students' lack of success in school. But it is equally clear that some parents, particularly those of lower socio-economic backgrounds, are unlikely to initiate contacts with schools. Parents, probably most parents, can be and wish to be supporters of their children's education and the effects of such participation are profound. Schools alone are unlikely to solve the problems of under achievement and dropping out. By aggressively initiating and sustaining the genuine and collaborative involvement of parents in their children's education we can reasonably hope to narrow the gap between the achievement of poor students and that of other students. Parents and teachers who collaborate in children's education are more likely to share similar expectations and to have similar knowledge about the child's progress in school.

Evaluation of Student Achievement

Two recurring themes dominate discussion about the evaluation of student achievement—general standards and specific diagnostic information which could help teachers be more effective. The Bullock Report (1975), *A Language For Life*, is succinct on both issues:

> We are in no doubt of the importance of monitoring standards of achievement in literacy, and of doing so by using the most sophisticated methods possible. There will always be keen interest in the movement of standards, and it is perfectly natural that there should be. Where there is no information there will be speculation, and the absence of facts makes room for prejudice...Information of the right quality will be of value to teachers and researchers and will be a reference point for policy decisions at the level of central and local government (p. 37).

Public opinion polls usually show that at any given time there is a perception that standards of school performance are declining. In view of this widespread Cassandra Complex, it is odd that a comprehensive study of school achievement has never been done. An ideal system would look at all the objectives listed in official guidelines and devise measures for seeing how well they are met. Instead, traditionally, a narrow range of attainments has been isolated and tested, usually those which can be measured by paper and pencil tests, and most frequently in English and Mathematics. Furthermore, these standardized tests have usually been given without regard for subject context of any kind, for the students' social setting, or for creating a testing situation conducive to an accurate understanding of the students' real capability—as distinct from performance on a particular occasion. The results have not been of much use to anyone, as the Ministry's 1979 publication on the *Ontario Assessment Instrument Pool* observed:

> Unfortunately many of the evaluative practices both in the past and in other jurisdictions have served neither to improve educational policy nor to stimulate and extend student learning. There is little evidence, for example, that the mere introduction of large scale assessment programs to allow simple annual comparisons of student or school performance can assist students, teachers or administrators. At best the effects seem neutral; at worst, harmful. Ironically, many of these testing programs have not even succeeded in their initial intention of reassuring the public or reducing the level of public criticism.
>
> The absence of a comprehensive, sensitive evaluation program which could provide real information about achievement is usually put down to expense. Yet

a monitoring program can be valid and reliable even if only a small representative sampling of students is involved.

The question of student evaluation is obviously central to reform of education. In the Fall of 1988 the Ministry of Education announced a program of testing Grade 6 students in reading and mathematics. As always, they were responding to "concern expressed in the press and every place else about the literacy and math skills."[5] It is too soon to know the nature of these tests, but early indications are that they will be much like those in the past, pencil and paper tests designed to measure a narrow band of competencies. Two other approaches merit serious consideration, that launched by the Toronto Board of Education in the Spring of 1988,[6] and that outlined in the Hargreaves' Report, *Improving Secondary Schools* (1988).

In 1988 the Toronto Board of Education began a comprehensive evaluation program in English and Mathematics involving 11 hours of one-on-one testing for each child in the sample. The most unusual features of the program are the wide range of competencies it tests and the care being given to the testing situation. It does not rely on standardized tests imported from elsewhere, but uses assessment methods and materials developed by Toronto teachers, coordinators, consultants, and research staff. It matches Ministry and Toronto Board curriculum goals and guidelines, and therefore is concerned with the quality of learning. It does not rely exclusively on written tests, but involves the use of a variety of concrete materials and real experiences. A full description of the Toronto program would be too lengthy for this article and it is much too soon to know how well it works. Undoubtedly experience will improve it. But the insights it will yield into what students actually can do at various grade levels should be extremely valuable to public and teacher alike. Less comprehensive evaluation may be adequate for monitoring standards, but "snapshots" of this complexity are indispensable to improvements in curriculum, teaching methods and public understanding.

Whereas the Toronto Board's work on evaluation aspires initially only to an understanding of results in relation to stated curriculum objectives, the Hargreaves report to the Inner London Educational Authority in 1984 takes a more fundamental look at school achievement. That report declares that pupil underachievement is directly related to our present view of what achievement actually means. It argues that we have relied too much on the measurement of narrow cognitive, intellectual skills to assess achievement (the skills of memory and written expression, which the Hargreaves Report calls achievement *aspect one*). We know, and our official guidelines say, that the ability to apply knowledge (*aspect two*), the personal and face-to-face skills (*aspect three*), and motivation and self-confidence (*aspect four*), are also important and can be attained. By

---

[5] W. Lipsischuk, Ministry of Education, quoted, *Toronto Star*, Oct. 1988.

[6] *Evaluation, System Standards and Reporting to Parents*, Toronto Board of Education, 1988.

identifying these four aspects of achievement, the report calls attention to our failures. We have not created a general understanding of this wider definition of achievement, and we certainly have not developed effective means of assessing such factors as motivation and commitment. Yet we have known for a long time that they are extremely important.

It is probably crucial to evaluation schemes that they keep monitoring of general standards separate from the teacher's responsibility for professional judgment concerning particular students. But it is also crucial that we evaluate what we profess to be teaching, and that we establish useful standards of performance in relation to society's needs. Again in this area we find a sharp difference between public and professional understanding. All the new O.S.I.S. subject guidelines have substantial sections on evaluation. They stress student involvement in designing evaluation strategies; teacher, peer and self-evaluation; the use of a variety of evaluation techniques including observation and checklists; the need for evaluation to be continuous and non-disruptive; the use of evaluation to determine changes in teaching methods and curriculum objectives. All these approaches can diminish the "student as adversary" feeling, and all of them need to be thoughtfully presented to the general public.

Even so, monitoring of achievement and of general standards should proceed independently, and should be the responsibility of a central authority—probably the province. Such monitoring remains essential if public confidence in education is to increase. Indeed, we have devoted considerable space to the evaluation issue because it seems crucial. The debate about educational issues will remain sterile until we can reconcile the justifiable public call for accountability with our improved understanding of how human beings learn. We are beginning to devise evaluation techniques which honour the complexity of human learning, and support rather than impair student performance. Educators must find ways of being accountable and comprehensible without reverting to obsolete understandings of achievement and testing.

Language and Learning

Far away from the rhetorical battles centred on "back to the basics" and "progressive education," a slow but sure change in teaching emphasis has gradually been entering classrooms. In spite of the legendary resistance of teachers to altering their practices, a powerful synthesis concerning the nature of learning is proving effective. This synthesis is based on work in linguistics and learning theory during the past fifty years, that shifts the focus from the teacher to the learner. According to Nancy Martin, it

> is a realization of the way in which language enters into learning from the very beginning—from the first reciprocal exchanges between mothers and infants to the development of mature writers. The way children learn their mother tongue is a potential model for all learning and is in process of being institutionalized as the interactive model of learning begins to take hold. We now have a concept of

teaching and learning which applies to all learners—the spectrum of abilities (Lightfoot, Martin, 1988 p. IX).

The Bullock Report of 1975 endorsed the new approach to teaching and learning, and also provided a brief general description of it:

> ...the kind of approach which we believe will produce the language development we regard as essential...involves creating situations in which, to satisfy his own purpose, a child encounters the need to use more elaborate forms and is thus motivated to extend the complexity of language available to him. It also involves the teacher in charting the process by careful observation of the developing language skills.

This approach is, of course, very different from the traditional mode by which teachers provide an analysis of rules and then teach them as procedures or models. Because the new language-in-use approach is now so pervasive in teachers' understanding, there is a tendency to over-estimate public understanding of it. A brief description of its origins and general features may be helpful.

In the late fifties and early sixties a group of English teachers working in British grammar schools became interested in language as a general human function. Piaget's work was, of course, already quite well known and the publication of Vygotsky's *Thought and Language* in English was a strong stimulus. Sapir, Cassirer, Luria and others were also part of their reading. As the teachers read and discussed the work of these thinkers, they began to be uncomfortable about the nature of language demands made by schools. The connections between language and thought seemed to be damaged rather than improved by the linguistic codes of many schools. Students were not encouraged to use language to explore ideas and thus assist thinking. Instead they were required to express preformulated concepts in borrowed terms without understanding them. They were confronted with texts inappropriate to their linguistic experience. They were not encouraged to use language tentatively, either orally or in writing. The school's demand for a finished performance was immediate; no practice allowed, all mistakes disdained and penalized.

Slowly, convictions began to emerge among these teachers. Perhaps, they reasoned, language really is the key to school success or failure. Perhaps it is the school system which has been egocentric in its language behaviour, alienating millions of very intelligent children whose experience has made them non-academic or whose dialect is unfamiliar to the school. We recognize but do not honour the fact that the language of such children is often rich, lively and subtle.

The basic arguments of the movement were and are persuasive. They began to be enshrined in official curricula and policy statements. Some practices began to have intellectual respectability—more opportunity for talk in small groups, more use of writing to learn in all subjects, more concern for the language in which presentations are made to children either orally or in textbooks.

Emphasis was also placed on how the student's written work was received. It was not to be constantly evaluated and graded with reference to its comprehensiveness, accuracy and freedom from solecisms. Only on rare pre-arranged occasions was that to happen. It was, instead, to be seen as part of an evolving thought process which would both influence and result from the student's linguistic growth. The cumulative writing folder became important. The teacher's job was to deepen both thinking and language by entering into a discussion concerning what is written; clarifying, enlarging, rejecting, or questioning fallacies or wrong information. Pushing the student to think and write better, and dealing with form only as a means to that end.

This brief description of a complicated process and its psychological bases will have to serve. The point is that all these recommended practices are now very familiar, part of received wisdom. Although they are not universally followed, most people who don't follow them feel at least vaguely guilty. The most recent Ministry publication, *Ontario Schools, Intermediate and Senior Division* (O.S.I.S.), contains admirable sections on The Learning Process and Language Across the Curriculum, as do most Ministry subject guidelines. And it takes only a moment's reflection to see how an externally imposed evaluation scheme could destroy these new and very promising practices, which are based on mutual respect and trust. It would be unspeakably ironic if the public zeal for improvement resulted in backward steps and lower achievement, but the possibility is very real. The central myth, as Frank Smith says, "is that learning can be guaranteed if instruction is delivered systematically, one small piece at a time, with frequent tests to ensure that students and teachers stay on task." Such a myth is at variance with our understanding of human learning, but it appeals strongly to our conservatism, our puritanism and our yearning for industrial efficiency.

Teacher Education

James Britton (1982, p. 214) remarks that "what the teacher can't do in the classroom can't be achieved by other means." This notion, central to educational reform, is embedded in the report *Teacher Education in Ontario: Current Practice and Options for the Future*, 1987; a position paper written for the Ontario Teacher Education Review Committee by Fullan and Conelly. Their proposals for reform rest on the explicit assumption that "teacher education must be seen as a continuum, from pre-service through induction to inservice, that is, through the entire teaching career." They provide a theoretical framework for recommendations that include:

- A preservice program following the completion of a four-year degree;
- An induction period in school with a reduced teaching load so that induction activities would contain both academic and practice components;
- An apprenticeship program during which teachers would have the opportunity to work alongside innovative experienced teachers;
- The restructuring of schools so that they are better workplaces, providing opportunity for teacher growth—including the provision of a Teacher Centre to encourage professionalism;

- Review of current arrangements for Additional Qualifications programs, coordination of inservice programs and shared governance of teacher education.

II. A PLAN FOR ONTARIO: SOME SUGGESTED CHANGES

The debate in education in Ontario is not over whether reform is necessary but what should be done. Many of the current prescriptions focus on specific, relatively inconsequential matters, lacking in coherence or likelihood of better than marginal improvements. Some are likely to raise the current failure and drop-out rates. But before we describe a plan for Ontario's schools we must note some of the most pressing problems; many of them hard to solve because of legislative, financial or social constraints.

- Schools are asked to do too much and are over-regulated. Social and medical problems are handed to the schools, often without the accompanying resources to deal with them.
- As they become adolescents students are separated into streams that prevent most from learning as much as they could.
- Teachers are overburdened and cannot spend enough time with each student.
- Principals have neither the authority nor flexibility to create high quality schools.
- Parents of secondary students have inadequate understanding of their child's progress and little connection to their child's teachers.
- Existing policies lack coherence and patterns of implementation are uneven.

Accordingly, we cannot expect individual schools or even school boards to deal with the problems associated with under-achievement. The problems are systemic and require systemic solutions—including less systemic control. It cannot be derived from further tightening of guidelines, prescription of content, additional rules or exhortations to goodness. Rather, we need a provincial framework which describes the purpose of schooling, the intended outcomes and sensible objectives for change.

Our proposal is based on one central conviction: that adolescence is pivotal. It is the time of life when we struggle towards individuality, towards competence, towards social acceptance and ease. We are vulnerable as adolescents, yet capable of far more than most adults realize. We need to have much expected of us, and we need to be personally involved in our own learning. What happens to us in the early years of adolescence profoundly affects the pattern of our life. It is a crucial period in schooling, and we propose its restructuring together with some changes to student evaluation and teacher education to support this restructuring. What emerges, then, has three components:[7]

- A restructuring of schooling so that students attend a four-year school for the Intermediate Division, Grades 7 through 10, and then move into specialized education for two or three years.

- A new concept of evaluation which employs a much wider concept of achievement and replaces external examinations and standardized tests with diagnostic evaluation day-to-day until students are prepared to meet criteria for promotion.

- A new concept of teacher education which calls for pre-service, induction and apprenticeship programs followed by career-long learning through in-service programs and opportunity for the collaboration of teachers in their local schools.

Restructuring of Schooling

Several plans or suggestions about the restructuring of schooling are under debate in the United States at the present time. Most of them, like the Minnesota Plan, advocate new arrangements which would ensure that the school-learning age is marked by a logical point of change in the student's career. Some of the responses to the *Secondary Education Review Project* back in 1980 made similar recommendations—as indeed did the Porter Plan of 1950. Such a plan seems helpful in providing more personal attention to a student in a fashion usually associated with the elementary years, until school leaving age. The studies of drop-outs uniformly reveal that they feel more attention and more personal interest from teachers were what they needed most to persuade them to stay in school.

It is in the Intermediate Division that the greatest change should be made to provide the best possible learning situation for the student. It is essential that the 12–15 year olds receive as much individual attention as can be provided while, at the same time, being able to experience every option in which one could specialize in the Senior Division.

- All students would be grouped in neighbourhood schools. No credits would be offered in Grades 9 and 10 but, instead, there would be listed the expectations of the Ministry for a student entering Grade 11 and the Board would be responsible for seeing that these were met.

- A team of four teachers would be responsible for the teaching of core subjects to each group of students for the period of four years. With the integration of curriculum possible in such an arrangement, the needs of the gifted as well as the slower learner could be accommodated.

- There would be partial rotary with such a system. The school would also be staffed with art, music, technical and family studies, physical education,

[7] Some of our proposal was contained in a Discussion Paper forwarded to the Ministry by the Toronto Board in 1980. The present authors contributed to that paper, and we wish to acknowledge our indebtedness to colleagues who also contributed at that time.

French, and typing teachers so that all students would be exposed to all
options.

- Classes would be integrated to the greatest extent possible, with the Special Education component usually provided either within the classroom or by withdrawal when necessary.
- At the end of four years the teaching team would be in a unique position to assess the interests and abilities of the individual student. Counselling as to placement in the Senior Division School would be given on the basis of four years' observation and assessment by four people who have watched the student develop during early adolescence.

The advantages of such an arrangement are many:

- It allows the child to remain in a neighbourhood school for a longer period of time without confining him/her to the same school for ten years;
- The development of parent-teacher partnerships to benefit adolescent students would be more likely;
- The fears of many parents concerning thirteen- and fourteen-year olds entering large, seemingly indifferent institutions where they are in contact with so many older students would be allayed;
- Parental involvement in the school is made easier until the end of Grade 10;
- The intimate relationship with teachers until the school leaving age is reached would provide a more meaningful education for many students;
- It facilitates a language-in-use policy since teachers get to know students better;
- It allows integration of curriculum to be provided up to the time that specialization becomes absolutely necessary;
- The decision as to specialization is postponed until the student is more mature and has more experience without any sacrifice in program quality;
- It improves the evaluation of student achievement by setting positive criteria and by ensuring a full knowledge of the student;
- Curriculum is delivered in the divisions in which it comes from the Ministry, permitting greater cooperation and less overlap between the teachers of those divisions;
- It provides for an appreciation by all children of the skills required for the various courses offered in the Senior School and gives them the opportunity to experience all areas so that choices for Senior School are based on reality;
- It prevents the alienation which many students encounter when suddenly facing complete rotary, eight teachers, and different classmates in classes, at too early an age;
- It leaves all doors open to any type of education until Grade 11.

The Senior Division Schools would thus become specialized *schools of excellence* which would emphasize certain aspects of a program while still providing the opportunity for a wide choice at the end of Grade 12. The consolidation of language offerings in certain schools would ensure students that such choices would be available into O.A.C.; emphasis on mathematics could ensure more computer time being available for the senior students; art and/or music could be the emphasis at one school. Such senior programs would allow much closer liaison between business, unions, institutions of higher learning and the schools. Work-education programs and apprentice training would be much more acceptable with students of this age. Alienation in this grouping would be at least partially overcome by the common interests which brought the student to a certain school.

Such a scheme would require considerable education of the public to the advantages of the Intermediate School system, particularly in two areas:

1. The opportunity for students to be challenged at their individual level of ability and thus remain interested and involved in continuing their education;
2. The need for and appreciation of excellent technical and commercial programs extended into Ontario Academic Courses.

The establishment of the physical plants to house the Intermediate Schools adequately is not an overwhelming difficulty, although it would require some provincial assistance for funding, as well as the flexibility necessary to meet specific geographic and demographic features.

Such a model, implemented across the province, would permit students moving from one area to another the opportunity of fitting into another school system much more easily than is now possible.

A New Concept of Evaluation

The Intermediate School should serve less as a screen for students, and more as a conduit, leading them to appropriate school or work placement. An evaluation program needs to be devised, with the following features:

1. An external monitoring of general standards by random sampling of an appropriate percentage of students for evaluation annually.
2. A teacher-developed program for the ongoing evaluation of all students based on a combination of features from the Hargreaves plan [wider achievement], the recent work in Toronto [more variety of tests, fuller coverage of curricular goals, more care for the testing situation], and new concepts from recent Ministry guidelines [peer evaluation, collaborative evaluation, non-disruptive evaluation]. This program should be developed gradually as part of curricular improvement programs related to the professional development of teachers. Human resources from the faculties of education and the Ministry of Education should be involved.
3. Development of suitable summative evaluation for students as they leave the Intermediate School. Such evaluation would provide a comprehensive profile of each student, and would include performance on a battery of proficiency demonstrations as the student reaches the end of the Interme-

diate School. The purpose of such demonstrations would be to assist the students' life choices as he/she reaches school-leaving age.

A New Concept of Teacher Education

Every new Ministry subject guideline calls for a new approach to teacher education—one that stresses initial internship and career-long professional development. It seems likely that the recommendations arising from the report of the Teacher Education Review Steering Committee (1988) are going to provide this approach. New curriculum projects, school based, practical and yet supported by theoretical understanding, should be an inevitable and natural part of the teachers' ongoing professional growth. Dummy-runs are not helpful and waste energy. It would be sensible to prepare experienced teachers to teach in the Intermediate School by assisting them to face the practical problems of transition to a new format, and to develop the new evaluation schemes outlined above.

Conclusion

Implementation of such a plan would have to be ordained by the Ministry of Education if it were to occur at all. New regulations covering credits and diplomas would be needed. Then a five-year plan of gradual implementation would be provided by each Board, with funds approved on the basis of this plan.

All of this seems overwhelming, but nothing less can provide the sense of personal meaning teachers and students need. It seems dubious that the new Guidelines' focus on the student as active learner can be made a reality in existing structures, with existing class sizes, groupings of students and evaluation practices.

Under current arrangements children as young as 13 years old make choices or have choices made for them that can direct their future lives. For some the choice results in a lowering of self-esteem, a lowering of expectations and few real future options.

Our proposal has three parts that are inseparable if all students are to learn more and to learn well. We do not underestimate the challenge of such a restructuring. It needs a provincial policy framework which recognises that the essential synthesis of the three parts—structure, evaluation and teacher professional growth—will take place only in the school itself. Surely these policy issues deserve this combination of provincial legislation and local policy.

6

FAMILY CHANGE AND FAMILY INCOME IN ONTARIO
Some Recent Trends

Kevin McQuillan

Ontario has experienced far-reaching social and economic change in recent decades, change which has had important implications for the income of families. As in most Western societies, the nature of economic activity has been altered by the decline of traditional forms of industry while employment in the service sector has grown substantially. At the same time, the face of the labour force has been altered by the rapid and continuing increase in the participation rates of women. As a result, the proportion of the population employed in the paid labour force has risen to an all-time high while, at the same time, unemployment rates remain at historically high levels. Alongside these economic developments, important changes have been taking place in the organization of family life. Growth in the number of lone-parent families and in the number of multiple-earner households has served to undermine the once-dominant breadwinner model of family life in which the father provided economic support while the mother cared for the home and children (Eichler, 1988). Not surprisingly, these developments, and others, have had important implications for the well-being of Ontario families. This chapter will review some of these developments and examine their effect on family income. We will begin by briefly discussing some of the major explanations of changing income patterns that have been advanced in recent years. Then, we will examine income patterns in Ontario in the period 1970–1985 in the light of these ideas. Finally, in a brief concluding section, we will attempt to point out some of the implications of our findings for the development of social policy in the province.

Explanations of Changing Income Patterns

Although a vast literature on the issue of shifting income patterns exists, three competing approaches tend to dominate discussions of the problem. The first approach, suggested by the American economist Richard Easterlin (1978, 1980, 1987), lays primary emphasis on the role of demographic factors and suggests that many of the changes can be traced to the entry into the labour market of the unusually large cohorts born during the Baby Boom. In Easterlin's view, the sheer size of the Baby Boom generation has produced major strains in the economy. As the members of these cohorts have entered the labour force they have faced high unemployment rates and relatively low wages. At the same time, older workers who belong to the smaller pre-Baby Boom generation have bene-fitted from this situation. The relative shortage of older, experienced workers has forced up their wages while keeping their unemployment rate low. The result has been a shift in the age structure of poverty, with young individuals and families experiencing rising rates of economic deprivation. Easterlin argues, however, that this situation will be temporary. While the Baby Boom cohorts will experi-ence some disadvantage throughout their lives, the tendency for income to rise with age will alleviate the worst aspects of their plight while the smaller cohorts which will follow them into the labour force will benefit from less competition and thus higher wages. In his judgment, the 1990s will be a prosperous decade marked by rising incomes and lower poverty rates, especially for the young.

Other writers are less optimistic about the future. A second group of econo-mists has argued that fundamental shifts in the structure of the modern economy will produce lasting negative effects. Among the most important of these will be increasing income polarization and a decline in the size and significance of the middle class (Bluestone and Harrison, 1982; Kuttner, 1983). In their view, the decline of manufacturing and the rise of the service sector of the economy have led to a steady decline in the number of average-paying jobs. What we see instead is growth in the number of high-paying jobs in new high-technology sectors and a rapid increase in low-paying jobs in the service industries. The result has been slow growth or decline in real wages, increasing income polariza-tion and a shrinking middle class. Young workers, seeking their first position in the labour market, are the most likely to be affected by these trends, though older workers may also find themselves losing jobs through plant shutdowns and being forced to seek lower-paying work in the service sector. From this perspective, such developments reflect profound changes in the international economic order and are not likely to be easily reversed.

The third major approach in the literature, while not denying the effects of demographic and economic change, calls attention to the role of the family.[1] Two types of change are seen as having particular significance for family income patterns. One is the steady increase in the proportion of families with more than one income-earner in the labour force. The phenomenal rise in labour force participation rates for married women has made the multi-earner family the norm among husband-wife families. In a period in which the wages of men have stagnated, the movement of wives into the labour force has served to boost the real money income of many families. However, this option is seldom open to another type of family whose numbers have been growing rapidly, lone-parent families. Rising divorce rates and increasing rates of non-marital fertility have combined to produce a large increase in the number of families headed by a

---

[1] The best available review of this extensive literature is presented in Wilson, 1987. For other perspectives, see Moynihan, 1986, and Murray, 1984.

single adult. In addition to the absence of a second earner, lone-parent families typically face other economic disadvantages as well. Where the children in the family are still young, the parent will likely have difficulty in both handling family duties and working full-time outside the home. As a result, single parents frequently have lower rates of labour force participation. And, in addition, since the great majority of lone parents are women, when they do work outside the home, they are likely to be in jobs which pay low wages. The outcome of all this is that lone-parent families typically have incomes well below the average and high rates of poverty. The continued growth of such families combined with the increase in multi-earner husband-wife families holds out the prospect of a widening income gap between different family types (Treas, 1987).

The three theoretical approaches discussed here are by no means contradictory. All three point to important factors which must be taken into account in any effort to understand changing income patterns. In the analysis which follows, we will not attempt to test these three views nor to determine which is most important. Rather we will use them as a guide to identifying the most significant changes which have been taking place in family income patterns in Ontario.

The Income of Ontario Families, 1970–1985

The focus of our analysis will be on the income of non-elderly Ontario families in the period from 1970 to 1985. We will examine the changes which have occurred in the income levels of all non-elderly families but pay special attention to the situation of low-income families. We are especially interested in seeing how the incomes and characteristics of poor families have changed over time. Throughout the paper, the unit of analysis will be non-elderly census families. We have excluded the elderly from consideration here because their economic situation and sources of income differ markedly from those of non-elderly families. We have decided to focus on census families rather than economic families because we believe that the census family definition more closely matches the type of family setting most Canadians aspire to live in. From this perspective, the decision of some family heads to live with other relatives may, in fact, be seen as an indicator of financial hardship. In empirical terms, of course, the differences between census families and economic families are not great and the results presented here are not out of line with other analyses performed using economic families as the unit of analysis. The data used are drawn from the 1971 and 1981 Census Public Use Sample Tapes and from the 1986 Survey of Consumer Finances. There are some differences between these sources in coverage and in the recording of information on incomes.[2] The differences are not so great, however, as to seriously distort changes in income trends over time. Nevertheless, it should be remembered that the presentation of the data in exact dollar amounts lends a spurious accuracy to the findings. In all three sources, the income data

---

[2] See especially Rashid, 1983, for a comparison of the accuracy of income reporting in the 1981 Census and the Survey of Consumer Finances.

Table 6–1: Total Family Income, Total Family Earnings and Per Capita Income of Non-Elderly Families, 1970–1985, in 1985 Dollars

Income Measure	1970	1980	1985	% Change 1970–1985
Total Income	33,585	41,053	41,209	22.7
Total Earnings	31,313	36,973	36,674	17.1
Per Capita Income	10,275	13,401	13,587	32.2

Source: 1970 • Family File. Public Use Sample Tape. 1971 Census of Canada
1980 • Family File. Public Use Sample Tape. 1981 Census of Canada
1985 • Census Family File. 1986 Survey of Consumer Finances

refer to income received in the year preceding the census or survey. All income data have been adjusted using the Consumer Price Index and are presented in constant 1985 dollars.

The data in Table 6–1 show that Ontario families experienced significant growth in real family income during this fifteen-year period. Total family income increased by just over 22% between 1970 and 1985. Virtually all of this growth occurred, however, during the 1970s. Real income remained virtually unchanged between 1980 and 1985.[3] The early eighties, of course, were marked by a severe economic recession, and year-to-year data show that family income declined during the first years of the decade. Since 1984, incomes have once again started to rise but are only now reaching the levels first seen at the beginning of the decade (Statistics Canada, 1987).[4]

Data on per capita income show a similar pattern though they suggest that income growth measured on a per capita basis has been stronger than is indicated by the figures for total income. The reason for this, of course, is the significant decline which has occurred in the size of families in Ontario. The average size of non-elderly families declined by approximately 13% between 1970 and 1985 and this decline, combined with the significant growth in total income, served to boost per capita income by 32.2%.

These significant increases in total income and per capita income exceeded the growth in the earnings of family members. Total earnings grew by just over 17% in the fifteen-year period, significantly lower than the rate of increase in total income, and actually declined slightly in the period 1980–1985. The slow rate of increase is especially striking given the increase which occurred in the number of workers per family during these years. This is a topic we will look at in greater detail later on.

[3] The 1986 data, drawn from the Survey of Consumer Finances, record information on sources of income which were not recorded in the 1981 Census. Our data thus may mask what was, in effect, a small decline in real family income between 1981 and 1986.

[4] After-tax income remains slightly below the pre-recession peak.

In sum, despite the severe recession of the early 1980s, the real income of Ontario families stood at a level in 1985 that was significantly higher than in 1970. Combined with a continuing decline in family size, these data suggest that the average family enjoyed a significant improvement in their standard of living. Several qualifications should be added, however. First, the data refer only to money income. As Judith Treas (1987) has pointed out in her examination of American income trends, data on money income tend to overstate the change in the quality of family life. Many families have increased their income by putting additional workers in the labour force but this normally entails a loss of services performed in the house by family members, or rising costs as families begin to purchase services in the market. Second, the data presented here refer to all non-elderly families. And, as we shall see, not all family types have followed the same path. The different experiences of Ontario's families raise important questions for social policy in the province and in the country.

Having looked briefly at the general trend of family income, we will now examine trends in income among those at the bottom of the income distribution and compare their fortunes to the rest of Ontario's families. Ideally, we would focus on those who fall below the Statistics Canada low-income cutoff, a measure which takes into account the size of families and region of residence in determining whether a family should be classified as poor (National Council of Welfare, 1988). Unfortunately, however, the 1971 census file which forms the base of the present analysis did not include this measure. As an alternative, we have chosen to compare the economic situation of those families who fall into the bottom 20% of the income distribution to those in the other four-fifths of the distribution.[5] While less than perfect, this strategy should allow us to see whether poorer families in Ontario have experienced the same level of income growth as families in general. It will also allow us to see how the characteristics of families at the bottom of the income distribution have changed over time. As noted above, the analysis is restricted to families in which the husband or lone parent was less than 65 years of age.

The data in Table 6–2 present the same information as in Table 6–1 for families in the lowest quintile and for those in the upper four quintiles. Beginning with the data on total income, we see that income for those at the bottom of the distribution increased at a rate slightly higher than that for higher-income families. Real income of those in the lowest quintile increased by 27.2% over the fifteen-year period compared to an increase of 22.4% for the remainder of the population. Nevertheless, the gap between those at the bottom and the average family remained large. The income of the poorest families was 32.8% of the average in 1970 and rose to only 34.0% of the average in 1985. The data on per capita income show a similar trend. Per capita income among low-income families rose by 42.0% between 1970 and 1985 while the increase among higher-in-

---

[5] Obviously, significant differences exist among families in the upper four quintiles. Given our interest in poor families and the data available, the use of two income groups is appropriate.

Table 6–2: Total Family Income, Total Earnings and Per Capita Family Income, by Income Group, 1970–1985, in 1985 Dollars

Income Group	Total Family Income		% Change
	1970	1985	1970–1985
Top Quintiles	39,230	48,016	22.4
Lowest Quintile	11,004	13,997	27.2
All Families	33,585	41,210	22.7
Lowest Quintile as % of Average	32.8	34.0	
Income Group	Total Earnings		% Change
	1970	1985	1970–1985
Top 4 Quintiles	36,925	43,618	18.1
Lowest Quintile	8,865	8,914	0.6
All Families	31,313	36,674	17.1
Lowest Quintile as % of Average	28.3	24.3	
Income Group	Per Capita Income		% Change
	1970	1985	1970–1985
Top 4 Quintiles	11,910	15,658	31.5
Lowest Quintile	3,738	5,309	42.0
All Families	10,275	13,588	32.2
Lowest Quintile as % of Average	36.4	39.1	

come families was 31.5%. The reason for this was a slightly larger decline in the average size of families in the lowest quintile. The change in average size hides an important change in family composition, however. Families in the upper four quintiles actually experienced a slightly larger decrease in the average number of children. The larger decline in family size among poorer families was a function of both declining fertility and a decline in the average number of adults per family as a result of substantial growth in the number of one-parent families. As we shall see later, this fact has had important implications for the economic situation of poorer families.

The different path followed by families in the bottom quintile during this period shows up clearly in the data on total earnings. For lower-income families, real earnings were almost unchanged while for other families they grew by approximately one percent per year. As a result, the total earnings of poorer families as a proportion of those received by the average family fell from 28.3% in 1970 to 24.3% in 1985. At the same time, the proportion of low-income families for whom transfer payments were the major source of income increased from 16.0% to 27.8%. This trend raises a number of important questions which need to be explored further. First, what are the sources of the disadvantage low-income families experience with respect to what might be called market income and, second, why has their situation in this regard worsened? In the rest of the chapter, we will explore these questions by examining the effects of selected demographic, economic and social trends on the economic situation of Ontario families.

The Changing Age Structure and Income

The Baby Boom which the province and the country experienced in the years from 1946 to 1964 continues to have an important influence on the national economy. The number of new job-seekers swelled through the late 1960s and 1970s as those born during the Baby Boom years began to enter the labour force. Despite a rapid rate of job creation, unemployment rates for young people attained historically high levels and incomes were depressed. To assess the effects of demographic change on the economic situation of Ontario families is more complex, however, since this period has seen other demographic developments which have offset some of the effects of the Baby Boom. Most importantly, age at marriage began to rise in 1972 from its post-War low point and, by the mid-eighties, had returned to the levels characteristic of the immediate post-War period. Thus when we look at the income situation of Ontario families we find that, on the one hand, young families have done poorly in terms of income but, on the other hand, a rising age at marriage has meant that fewer families are headed by young people. These facts come across in Table 6–3 which shows both the average earnings and the distribution of families by the age of the husband or lone parent. The earnings data confirm the fact that the recent period has been a difficult one for young people and their families. Total earnings for families headed by an adult under 25 rose by only 7.6% while the increase for families in which the husband/lone parent was between ages 25 and 34 was 13.5%. For the youngest families in the bottom quintile, real earnings actually declined. By contrast, real earnings rose by more than 20% for families with heads in the prime earning ages. Earnings also increased slowly for older families but this likely reflects, in part, changing work patterns, including early retirement. Data on total income show that these families experienced considerable growth in real income (16.5%) despite slow growth in earnings.

A number of factors have contributed to the slow rate of growth in earnings among young family heads. First, growth in real wages has been slowest for workers under age 35 (Myles et al., 1988). This has been true in virtually all industries and occupations and has continued to be true beyond the recession of the early eighties. Second, the growing proportion of lone parents among young family heads has also acted to depress earnings. The proportion of lone parents among families with a head under 25 almost doubled over the fifteen-year period. Among young husband-wife families, the slow growth of the husband's earnings were offset by the increased labour force participation rates of their wives. For young lone-parent families this was, of course, not an option. As a result, while the total earnings of young husband-wife families increased modestly over the period, the earnings of lone-parent families actually declined in

Table 6–3: Total Family Income by Age of Reference Person, and Family Income Group, 1970 and 1985, in 1985 Dollars

Income Group	Age				
	15–24	*25–34*	*35–44*	*45–54*	*55–64*
1970					
Top 4 Quintiles	29,256 (5.6)	34,108 (25.6)	37,788 (27.9)	40,481 (24.7)	37,108 (16.2)
Lowest Quintile	9,270 (14.7)	9,072 (25.7)	8,711 (21.7)	8,979 (18.7)	8,336 (19.2)
All Families	21,310 (7.4)	29,077 (25.6)	33,075 (26.7)	35,456 (23.5)	30,546 (16.8)
1985					
Top 4 Quintiles	34,992 (3.0)	39,685 (25.8)	46,104 (29.3)	49,165 (24.1)	39,184 (17.7)
Lowest Quintile	8,573 (10.2)	9,584 (29.5)	9,388 (23.4)	10,086 (16.1)	6,693 (20.8)
All Familes	22,923 (4.5)	33,001 (26.6)	39,977 (28.1)	43,581 (22.5)	31,816 (18.3)
% Change in Earnings 1970–1985	7.6	13.5	20.9	22.9	4.2

real terms. The increased proportions of these families in the young age groups thus further reduced the already low rate of earnings growth.

Demographic explanations of income change normally focus not only on the rate of change in the incomes of different age groups but also on the effects of changing age composition. For example, a large increase in the proportion of families in the youngest age category, where incomes are lowest, would act to lower the average income of all families. However, the data in Table 6–3 suggest that changes in age composition have not had an important effect on the earnings of Ontario families in the period under study. Whether we consider all families together or examine the income groups separately, standardizing for age using the 1970 age distribution has little effect on the level of earnings.

Earnings, Work Patterns and Family Income

Labour market factors clearly play a central role in the evolution of family income patterns. Trends in wages, unemployment and labour force participation rates bear heavily on family earnings. Rapid increases in real wages will obviously boost family earnings, but families may act to increase their incomes even

Table 6–4: Earnings of Husbands/Lone Parents Employed Full-Time by Income Level, 1970 and 1985, in 1985 Dollars

Income Group	Total Earnings of Husband/Lone Parent		% Change
	1970	1985	1970–1985
Top 4 Quintiles	29,334	31,444	7.2
Lowest Quintile	9,579	10,064	5.1
Lowest Quintile as % of Average	36.4	35.3	8.2

in the face of stagnant or declining wages by increasing the amount of time spent by family members in paid labour. Thus it is important to look at both components of earnings. In this section of the paper, we will attempt to do this by first focusing on changes in real wages among family heads and then by examining changes in the work patterns of family members.

Our data are not ideally suited to examining changes in wage rates but they do allow us to observe the course of earnings among family heads who were employed full-time. The figures contained in Table 6–4 show that the earnings of family heads in the lowest quintile lagged well behind those in the upper four quintiles. Their total earnings in 1970 amounted to only 36.4% of the average received by all family heads who were employed full-time and, by 1985, this figure had fallen slightly to 35.3%. The markedly lower earnings of family heads in the lowest quintile obviously account for much of the financial disadvantage experienced by these families. However, when we compare the data in Table 6–4 with the figures presented in Table 6–2, several important differences stand out. First, the gap in total family earnings is considerably larger than the gap in head's earnings. While the head's earnings amounted to 35% of the average in 1985, total family earnings were only about 25% of the average. Second, while the increase over time in the wages of heads in the upper four quintiles was slightly larger than that experienced by heads in the bottom quintile, the difference in the rate of growth of total earnings was much larger. For families in the top four quintiles, the earnings of the head increased by 7.2% while family earnings grew by just over 18%. By contrast, in the lowest quintile, the earnings of heads employed full-time rose by 5.2% but total family earnings remained virtually unchanged. Thus while the low wages paid to workers at the bottom of the income distribution explain a large part of the disadvantage they experience, changes in wage rates over time do not appear to explain the much slower growth in total family earnings experienced by low-income families in the years since 1970. To account for this, we must look at the changing employment patterns of family members.

The rapid rise in the labour force participation rates of women, and especially married women, has had far-reaching effects on family and society. In 1961, less than a quarter of husband-wife families had both spouses employed outside the home. Today, more than half of such families have both partners working, and among younger families the rates are even higher. Not surprisingly, these trends have had a significant effect on income levels. In Table 6–5, we present data on the distribution of families by number of employment income-earners for the two income groups. The table also shows average family earnings by number of earners. We find, as expected, that income rises sharply with the number of earners. In 1985, for example, a one-earner family made about half as much as families with three or more earners. In addition, while the total earnings of families with only one earner actually declined between 1970 and 1985, the earnings of multiple-earner families increased significantly. The biggest improvement was enjoyed by two-earner families where real earnings grew by over 19%. Of most concern to us here, however, is the substantial difference between low-income and other families in terms of the number of employed family members. In 1970, 65.1% of families in the upper four quintiles had two or more income-earners while only 29.4% of families in the lowest quintile had at least two earners. Between 1970 and 1985, families in both income groups experienced an increase in the proportion of multiple-earner families with the proportion rising to 35.9% among low-income families and to 80.8% for those in the upper four quintiles. In the low-income group, however, this increase was offset by a rise in the number of families with no earners from 14.4% to 19.5%. As a result, the average number of earners per family remained almost constant for families in this group while among the rest of the province's families the average increased from 1.80 to 2.04. This increase allowed families outside the bottom quintile to increase their family earnings significantly in a period of slow growth in real wages.

The data in Table 6–5 refer to all income earners regardless of whether they worked full-time or part-time. Yet much attention has been paid to the growth of part-time work as a source of slow income growth. Unfortunately, neither the census nor the Survey of Consumer Finances provide full data on the work activity of all family members. They do tell us, however, about the work patterns of husbands, wives and lone parents. Table 6–6 presents these data for lower-income and higher-income families in 1970 and 1985. Turning first to the situation in 1970, we see that in 96.5% of families in the upper four quintiles, the husband or lone parent was employed full-time while only 69% of husbands and lone parents in the lower-income category worked full-time outside the home. Moreover, among these poorer families, 17.7% had neither a husband/lone parent nor a spouse employed outside the home, while among other families 53.4% had both partners working on either a full-time or part-time basis. Even in 1970, then, lower-income families were at a significant disadvantage in terms of labour force activity.

Between 1970 and 1985 the gulf between lower-income and higher-income families with respect to work activity widened. The proportion of lower-income families in which husband and wife worked full-time declined slightly while the proportion of families with neither a husband/lone parent nor a spouse employed rose from 17.7% to 24.6%. For the rest of Ontario's families, the change was in

Table 6–5: Total Family Earnings by Number of Employment Income Earners, and Income Group, 1970 and 1985, in 1985 Dollars

	Number of Earners				Total	Average Number of Earners
	0	*1*	*2*	*3+*		
1970						
Top 4 quintiles	0	32,428	36,987	47,420	36,925	
	(0.3)	(34.6)	(49.6)	(15.5)	(100.0)	1.80
Lowest Quintile	0	9,931	11,190	10,775	8,865	
	(14.4)	(56.2)	(26.8)	(2.6)	(100.0)	1.18
Average Earnings	0	25,935	33,916	45,927	31,313	
	(3.1)	(38.9)	(45.1)	(12.9)	(100.0)	1.68
1985						
Top 4 Quintiles	0	33,405	44,022	52,010	43,618	
	(0.9)	(18.3)	(56.7)	(24.1)	(100.0)	2.04
Lowest Quintile	0	8,986	13,910	12,165	8,918	
	(19.5)	(44.6)	(31.1)	(4.8)	(100.0)	1.21
Average Earnings	0	24,173	40,389	50,132	36,674	
	(4.6)	(23.6)	(51.6)	(20.2)	(100.0)	1.87
Change in Earnings all families	0	-6.8	+19.1	+9.2	+17.1	

the opposite direction. The proportion of these families in which both partners worked full-time rose sharply from 36.9% to 48.7%, and in two-thirds of these cases both partners worked outside the home on either a part-time or full-time basis. A family in which both husband and wife are employed full-time outside the home has rapidly become the norm among Ontario's more prosperous families. Among those near the bottom of the income distribution, on the other hand, families have been unable to match these trends. The consequence has been that these families have fallen further behind in terms of money income earned in the market place. In the next section of this paper we will explore some of the factors that have led to this situation.

The Changing Characteristics of Low-Income Families

In any attempt to assess the effect of changing family structures on the distribution of income, most attention focuses on the growth of lone-parent families. Rising rates of divorce and non-marital fertility have produced a rapid increase in the proportion of families headed by a lone parent. This phenomenon has been occurring in all major industrial societies and Ontario has been no exception. Declining rates of mortality and low levels of divorce and non-marital fertility during the Baby Boom period, sometimes referred to as the "Golden Age of the

Table 6–6: Work Activity of Husbands/Lone Parents by Work Activity of Spouse and Income Group, 1970 and 1985

Work Activity of Husband–Lone Parent	Lowest Quintile				Top 4 Quintiles			
	Work Activity of Spouse				Work Activity of Spouse			
	FT	PT	None/Absent	Total	FT	PT	None/Absent	Total
	1970				*1970*			
Full-Time	14.9	8.7	45.4	69.0	36.9	15.7	43.9	96.5
Part-Time	2.0	1.4	7.2	10.6	0.8	0.3	1.1	2.2
Not in Labour Force	1.9	0.7	17.7	20.3	0.4	0.0	0.9	1.3
Total	18.8	10.8	70.3	99.9	38.1	16.0	45.9	100.0
	1985				*1985*			
Full-Time	14.3	10.0	35.9	60.2	48.7	18.6	27.0	94.3
Part-Time	2.0	1.0	8.0	11.0	0.9	0.5	0.6	2.0
Not in Labour Force	2.4	1.8	24.6	28.8	1.4	0.4	1.8	3.6
Total	18.7	12.8	68.5	100.0	51.0	19.5	29.4	99.9

Family" (Beaujot, 1987), brought the proportion of lone-parent families in Ontario in 1961 to an historic low. Only 6.3% of all census families were headed by a lone female while 1.6% were headed by a lone male parent. Moreover, 59.6% of the women who headed lone-parent families had been widowed. The years which followed saw a steady increase in the proportion of lone-parent families and a change in the way lone-parent families were formed. The 1986 census recorded over 290,000 lone-parent families in Ontario, a figure which amounted to 11.9% of Ontario families. The vast majority of them were headed by a woman. Today, almost one in ten Ontario families is headed by a lone female. At the same time, these women are likely to be younger than was true in the past and are likely to have become lone parents not on the death of a spouse but as a result of divorce or the birth of a child outside of marriage.

These trends in family formation have far-reaching implications for the economic health of families. Lone-parent families are, by their very nature, at a serious disadvantage in a society where the two-career family is rapidly becoming the norm. Census data for Canada as a whole indicate that female lone-parent families headed by a woman age 15–24 had, on average, only .43 employment income earners, while those in the age category 25–34 recorded only .60 earners.[6] While the situation improves as the mother ages, the average number of earners in female lone-parent families in Ontario in 1986 was only 1.19 while husband-wife families with children received income from 2.12 earners and those without children from 1.59 earners. And, of course, when employed, these women share with other women the continuing problem of lower wages and salaries.

Lone-parent families possess few resources or alternative sources of income to compensate for the disadvantage they experience in the labour market. Although income from other non-government sources has grown rapidly among wealthier families, the income lone-parent families receive from other sources remains small. Considerable evidence exists that divorced mothers receive only a small portion of the income they are entitled to from their former husbands (Nett, 1988; Eichler, 1988). And the problem is even more acute for the growing number of lone mothers who have never been married. Evidence from the United States suggests that never-married lone parents experience even greater levels of economic deprivation than do lone mothers who entered the status through divorce or widowhood (Duncan and Rogers, 1987).

Given these disadvantages associated with lone-parent status, it is not surprising to find that female lone-parent families experience great financial hardship. In 1973, over 60% of mother-only families with at least one child under eighteen fell below the Statistics Canada low-income line. And, while this figure has since

---

[6] The number of cases in this category for Ontario in the Survey of Consumer Finances was too small to yield accurate estimates. The data reported here are drawn from a special tabulation from the 1986 Census.

Table 6–7: Total Family Earnings by Family Type and Income Group, 1970 and 1985, in 1985 Dollars

Income Level	Family Type				
	HW- No children	HW- Children	MLP	FLP	Total
			1970		
Top 4 Quintiles	37,328 (22.8)	39,273 (73.1)	33,797 (1.4)	30,029 (2.7)	36,925 (100.0)
Lowest Quintile	10,705 (24.6)	10,505 (50.4)	8,215 (2.4)	5,877 (22.6)	8,865 (100.0)
All Families	31,605 (23.2)	35,040 (68.6)	26,142 (1.6)	13,689 (6.7)	31,313 (100.1)
			1985		
Top 4 Quintiles	43,855 (25.2)	48,164 (68.9)	40,327 (1.4)	34,221 (4.5)	43,618 (100.0)
Lowest Quintile	12,045 (27.3)	11,972 (35.2)	8,659 (1.6)	7,702 (35.9)	8,914 (100.0)
All Families	37,077 (25.7)	44,065 (62.1)	33,228 (1.4)	16,561 (10.8)	36,674 (100.0)

declined, current data continue to show half these families live below what is commonly referred to as the poverty line.[7] Our data indicate that these families are greatly over-represented in the bottom quintile. Although they made up only 6.7% of non-elderly families in 1971, 22.6% of families in the lowest-income category were headed by a lone female. By 1986, 10.8% of non-elderly families and 35.9% of those in the lowest quintile were headed by a woman on her own.

The growing number of lone-parent families among those in the lowest quintile has had a significant effect on the number of earners and on total family earnings. Table 6–7 presents these data for 1970 and 1985. They show clearly the large disadvantage experienced by lone-parent families. For both points in time, the earnings of mother-only families amounted to less than half the Ontario average. Even within income groups, the earnings of lone-parent families were significantly lower than those received by husband-wife families. The lower earnings of lone-parent families was a function of *both* fewer earners and lower earnings per employed person.

It was noted above that the average number of earners per family has increased significantly among families in the upper four quintiles while remaining

---

[7] These data were provided by Professor Martin Dooley.

stable among those at the bottom. Here we see that this occurred despite increases in the average number of earners for most family types. Thus among poorer families, the average number of earners in husband-wife families with children increased from 1.34 in 1970 to 1.57 in 1985, while among female lone-parent families the number rose from 0.79 to 0.91. What caused the overall figure for low-income families to remain constant was the change in the composition of the lowest quintile by family type. Growth in the relative weight of lone-parent families offset the increases in number of workers within family types. Had the distribution of families by family type within the lowest quintile been the same in 1985 as in 1970, the average number of earners would have risen to 1.30 per family.

When we turn to the data on average earnings, we see a similar picture. The total earnings of female lone-parent families increased significantly during the fifteen-year period. But the increase occurred from such a low base that, in 1985, their earnings were still considerably below those of other families in the bottom quintile. At the same time, the greater numbers of lone-parent families in the low-income category helped to limit the growth in total earnings. Had the distribution of families remained unchanged, the total earnings of low-income families would have increased by just over 7%, still well below the increase enjoyed by families in the upper four quintiles but significant nevertheless.

There can be no denying the significance of the growth in lone-parent families for the distribution of family income. While poverty rates for both husband-wife and mother-only families have declined over the last fifteen years, the growing proportion of children living in mother-only families has slowed the decline in child poverty (Dooley, 1988). At the same time, it is evident that a significant number of married couple families suffered from low family income as well. In 1985, 6.7% of non-elderly husband-wife families in Ontario fell below the low-income cutoff and 62.5% of families in the lowest quintile were headed by a married couple. Low income among these couples is not a function of family structure but of the characteristics of the couple and the circumstances in which they live. The data presented in Table 6–7 point to one of the important factors, the smaller number of income earners. Husband-wife families in the lowest quintile in 1985 had only 1.57 earners compared to the 2.19 earners in upper-quintile married-couple families. In addition, the earnings of husbands in the bottom quintile who worked full-time in 1985 were less than one-third the amount earned by such husbands in the upper quintiles, a ratio which changed little over the period. Not surprisingly, there was a significant difference in educational attainment as well. Only 27.6% of husbands in the upper four quintiles in 1985 had not completed high school while 47.0% of husbands in the lowest quintile had not done so. Moreover, the difference between husbands in the bottom quintile and those in the others grew over the period. The proportion of husbands who had not completed high school dropped by 46% for those in the upper quintiles but only by 30% for those at the bottom.

Government Transfer Payments and Family Income

Many government programs enacted by federal, provincial and municipal governments affect the economic situation of the poor and the distribution of family income. The goals which lie behind these programs are as varied as the situations of the groups in the population targeted by the programs.[8] Some transfers such as family allowances are universal in nature though they obviously form a more important component of family income for the poor. Others, such as the unemployment insurance program, though not specifically aimed at low-income families, may play a crucial role in supporting those poorer families with members who have experienced unemployment and who qualify for assistance. Still other programs, such as provincial and municipal assistance programs, are explicitly designed to provide income to poor families.[9] In this section of the paper we will examine the overall effect of these transfer programs on family income in the period 1970–1985. Table 6–8 contains information on government transfer payments by family type and income group for both 1970 and 1985.[10] It also shows the proportion of total family income received in the form of transfer payments. The data reveal that government transfer payments grew both in absolute value and as a proportion of family income for all family types. The real value of payments to the average non-elderly family slightly more than doubled over the fifteen-year period and their contribution to family income rose from 2.7% in 1970 to 5.0% in 1985. Even among families in the upper four quintiles, the role of transfer payments increased significantly. The proportion of income received in the form of transfers increased from 1.9% in 1970 to 3.5% in 1985 for families in this income group. Yet despite this growth, it remains the case that transfers play a rather small role in the income situation of families outside the bottom quintile. Indeed had the real dollar value of transfer payments to families in the top four quintiles remained constant between 1970 and 1985, their incomes still would have increased by 19.8%, a figure only slightly below the actual increase of 22.4%. Among families in the lowest quintile, the situation is evidently quite different. Even in 1970, transfers formed an important part of their total family income, accounting for 14% of the income they received. And, as was the case for other families, both the real value and the share of income accounted for by transfer payments increased significantly over the fifteen-year period. By 1985, just over one-quarter of the income of families in the bottom quintile was derived from government transfer programs. Had the real dollar

---

[8] No review of these policies can be undertaken here. Irving (1987) contains an extensive bibliography on the development of social assistance in Ontario. See also Minister of National Health and Welfare, 1988.

[9] A thorough review of the existing Ontario social assistance programs is available in the full report of the Social Assistance Review Committee (1988). An analysis of the adequacy of benefit levels is presented in Ross, 1987.

[10] Data on transfer payments are generally acknowledged to be less than complete. See, for example, Rashid, 1983.

Table 6–8: Total Government Transfer Payments By Family Type and Income Level, 1970 and 1985, in 1985 Dollars

Income Level	Family Type				
	HW-No children	HW-Children	MLP	FLP	Total
1970					
Top 4 Quintiles	331 (0.9)	839 (2.1)	617 (1.8)	1822 (5.7)	746 (1.9)
Lowest Quintile	712 (6.2)	1367 (11.5)	1177 (12.5)	2908 (33.1)	1549 (14.0)
All Families	412 (1.3)	917 (2.6)	785 (2.9)	2557 (15.7)	907 (2.7)
1985					
Top 4 Quintiles	1053 (2.3)	1850 (3.7)	2031 (4.8)	2373 (6.5)	1675 (3.5)
Lowest Quintile	2753 (18.6)	3525 (22.7)	5481 (38.8)	4208 (35.3)	3590 (25.7)
All Families	1415 (3.7)	2040 (4.4)	2804 (7.8)	3595 (17.8)	2058 (5.0)

Note: Numbers in parentheses indicate the proportion of total income derived from transfer payments.

value of payments to low-income families remained at 1970 levels, their incomes would have increased by only 8.6% during the sample period, rather than by 27.2% as in fact occurred. Moreover, if transfer payments to all families had remained fixed at 1970 levels, the average income of families in the bottom quintile would have fallen from 32.8% of the Ontario average to just 27.5%. Thus the growth of transfer payments appears to have offset the slower growth in earnings experienced by low-income families and to have prevented them from falling even further behind in terms of total income. This finding fits with the conclusions of other authors who have noted that while the growth of the welfare state has not significantly reduced income inequality, it has prevented the growth in inequality which would have come about on the basis of market forces alone (Banting, 1987).

When we turn from the role of transfer payments in the two income groups to their role in different types of families we discover some surprising trends. Our data suggest that transfer payments to mother-only families have grown at a slower rate than was the case for other types of families. As noted above, caution is required when interpreting data on transfer payments since the evidence indicates these payments are under-recorded in our sources. Nevertheless, they would appear to indicate a significant change in the role of transfers among poor families. By 1985, transfer payments had come to be a significant component of family income for all families in the lowest quintile.

Summary and Discussion

The results presented above confirm the findings of many other studies indicating that young families have not fared well in the recent period. The work of Myles et al. (1988) demonstrating a continuing pattern of low wages among young workers even in the period of recovery from the recession of 1981–82 raises particular concern. Analysts disagree over the sources of the problems faced by young workers and their families. Supporters of a demographic view suggest these problems may be temporary and that the entry of the smaller post-Baby Boom cohorts into the labour force may actually lead to a shortage of labour and rising wage rates for young workers. Others are less optimistic, however, and doubt that demographic change alone will significantly improve the circumstances of the young. There is also concern that those at the tail-end of the Baby Boom, who have experienced a tough start to their working careers, may not "age out" of their problems as earlier cohorts have done. The situation of young workers is of particular interest since young workers also tend to be the parents of young children, and low family income at this stage of the family life-cycle may imply relatively high rates of child poverty. The difficult situation of the young has been contrasted in a number of recent analyses with the continuing improvements in the economic situation of the elderly (Preston, 1984), and, for some, has led to the conclusion that governments need to consider shifting resources away from the elderly in order to improve the situation of young families. While such talk may be seen as premature, a continuation of current trends will raise important questions about the best way to distribute scarce resources among different age groups in the population.

A second group of special importance for social policy are lone-parent families, particularly those headed by women. These families are disadvantaged in a number of ways. First, the mothers tend to be younger and less educated than other family heads (McQuillan, 1988). Second, as women, the heads of these families share the same disadvantages other women experience in the labour market. Third, the nature of life in a lone-parent family makes it exceptionally difficult for them to compete in the modern labour market. The mothers themselves encounter substantial problems in attempting to find and hold onto full-time employment while also fulfilling their parental responsibilities. Thus we find that only 42% of non-elderly female lone parents were employed full-time in 1985 and almost 30% were not in the labour force at all. In addition, of course, while the children are still young, there is no possibility of placing additional family members in the labour force.[11] In past, lone-parent families found themselves competing against husband-wife families in which virtually all husbands were in the labour force but where the majority of wives worked in the home. With the dramatic rise in paid employment for married women, the situation has changed to the disadvantage of lone-parent families. In terms of employment-income earners, lone-parent families are now outnumbered almost two to one by husband-wife families. Little wonder, then, that over 40% of mother-only families in Ontario fall below the poverty line.

A smaller number of workers in the labour force is not only typical of lone-parent families but of poor families generally. As we have shown, a key element of the widening gap in earnings between those in the bottom quintile and the rest of Ontario families is the sizeable increase in the average number of workers per family among the non-poor. This development has had a profound effect on the economic status of individuals and families, and it is of great significance for social policy. Indeed, it is ironic that at a time when the family is often seen to be in decline, its salience for economic issues has, in some ways, increased.[12] This fact complicates the job of policymakers. When the traditional breadwinner family was dominant, the economic status of families was largely determined by the status of the husband in the labour market. In such an environment, the consequences for the family of policies affecting the labour market were more predictable. In the current situation, the likelihood that policy initiatives may have unintended consequences is probably greater than ever. What, for example, will be the effects of pay equity legislation on the gap between low-income families and others? On the one hand, since more low-income families have a woman as their principal earner, rising real wages for female workers should improve the situation of these families. But, on the other hand, currently-married women whose husbands are employed are themselves more likely to be in the labour force than lone mothers. Thus the net outcome of the policy for poor families is not easy to predict. If nothing else, these questions emphasize the need for high-quality data and analysis of the effects of social and economic change on the well-being of Ontario families.

The finding that transfer payments have grown in importance as a source of income for poorer families also raises important policy questions. A significant increase in transfers over the last fifteen years helped to prevent what would otherwise have been a decline in the relative income of the poor. Low-income lone-parent families are, of course, particularly dependent on transfer income, though the share of their income derived from this source did not increase significantly during the sample period. Should this trend be a source of concern to policymakers? One view is that this trend is indeed a problem, that increasing

---

[11] This statement holds true for lone-parent families according to the census definition. It is not necessarily true in the case of economic families.

[12] Shaw (1986), for example, has shown unemployment does not necessarily imply financial hardship. The economic status of the family or household to which the individual belongs is more important in understanding the individual's situation.

dependence on non-market sources of income is an indication that the poor are slipping out of the mainstream of society. Moreover, reliance on transfer income leaves the poor increasingly vulnerable to cutbacks in social welfare programs, a not unlikely prospect in a period of fiscal restraint. From this perspective, the prime goal of assistance policies should be to move people "off the welfare rolls and onto the job rolls."

An alternative view of the situation is possible, however—one which does not see recent trends as necessarily problematic. This view rests on an analogy between the situation of the poor, perhaps especially lone mothers, and the elderly. The elderly have also become increasingly dependent on transfer payments yet few would view this situation as constituting a social problem. The elderly are seen as both in need of and deserving of income assistance. The fact that this assistance comes from the community as a whole rather than the families of elderly citizens raises little opposition. In his discussion of the American situation, Samuel Preston has put the point well: "We appear to worry very little about whether increased benefits for [the elderly] would undermine their children's willingness to care for them or lead the able-bodied to withdraw prematurely from the labour force. But we're scandalized by equivalent prospects for those we think of as welfare mothers" (Preston, 1984: 448). From this point of view, greater reliance by poor families on transfer payments is not problematic. Indeed, it can be argued that little is gained by encouraging mothers of young children to move into the labour force and that their time might better be spent insuring quality care for their children.[13]

There is no doubt that the situation of some families makes movement into the labour force well-nigh impossible. In such cases, assistance programs should concentrate on meeting the immediate needs of the family rather than encouraging a move to paid employment. In general, however, there are good reasons, I believe, why the general thrust of social policy should be directed toward helping those on assistance, and young family heads in particular, to participate in the labour force. First, there is considerable evidence that lengthy work interruptions disadvantage workers later in their working lives. Second, the very different social situation of young family heads and the elderly undermines the analogy presented above. The vast majority of the elderly do not participate in the labour force and they view retirement as a reward for a life of work. However, there is a strong expectation that young adults will be active in the labour force. With participation rates of over 90% for males 25–44 and over 70% for women in these age groups, those who are outside the labour force are likely to see themselves as being on the margin of society. Finally, the non-monetary benefits of work outside the home, especially for lone parents, should not be ignored. For most people in our society, work is not only a source of income and, perhaps, of intrinsic satisfaction, it is also an opportunity to meet and interact with other adults. The sociability that work can offer may be of particular benefit to lone

---

[13] I owe this formulation of the issue to Professor Martin Dooley.

parents who might otherwise be isolated within the home. For these reasons, it seems reasonable that social policies should assist those who are able to participate in the work force.

While improvements in existing programs to help low-income families are clearly essential, it also needs to be recognized that the paths followed by many families carry with them a high risk of serious economic disadvantage. Among married-couple families in which the husband has completed high school less than 5% fall below the low-income cut-off, while two-thirds of lone-parent families headed by a never-married female live in poverty. Moreover, the life of the lone-parent family is likely to be marked not only by financial hardship but by many other difficulties related to the health and emotional well-being of the family members (Avison, 1988). Discussions of social policy have tended to avoid the issue of the sources of family change, however, viewing the problem as exogenous to the social assistance system and thus beyond the reach of social policy. This no doubt reflects a desire on the part of both researchers and policy-makers to avoid issues which dredge up many sensitive and controversial questions. But the strong links which exist between family characteristics and the probability of living in poverty makes research on the sources of family change essential. Initiatives which encourage young people to avoid patterns of behaviour which carry with them a high probability of economic hardship should form part of a comprehensive family policy.

FROM SCHOOL TO WORK
The Transition Period

Pamela J. Sloan

The transition from school to work has only recently emerged as a separate and distinct issue of public policy. Historically, preparing youth for the labour market was viewed as an element of broader education and training policies. In times of economic growth and labour scarcity, the transition from school to work was one which took place naturally and easily. The exceptionally high rates of youth unemployment in the late 1970s and early 1980s challenged the assumption that education alone would assure young people access to the labour markets. Policies and programs aimed at alleviating high rates of youth unemployment were put in place by governments and, as a result, the transition from school to work emerged as a distinct issue of public policy. As youth unemployment rates dropped in the mid–1980s, school to work transition policies and programs became increasingly focused on helping youth who had particular disadvantages or difficulties in gaining access to the labour markets. With the very rapid and pervasive changes in technology and employment that are now occurring in Ontario's economy, ensuring an effective transition from school to work for all youth is taking on renewed importance.

The Historical Context

The nature of the public policy issues relating to the transition from school to work have changed in step with the changing profile of the youth population and evolving economic trends.

The Demographic Profile of Youth

The demographic profile of the youth population in Ontario has undergone dramatic change in the past six decades, as shown in Figure 7–1. The most significant feature of this chart is the very rapid growth in the youth population from the late 1950s to the late 1970s, when the number of people between the ages of 15 and 24 doubled. During this period, the rate of growth of the youth population far outstripped the rate of growth of any other age group in the province.

Today, there are about 1.4 million people in Ontario between the ages of 15 and 24 (see Figure 7–2). The youth population is almost evenly split between

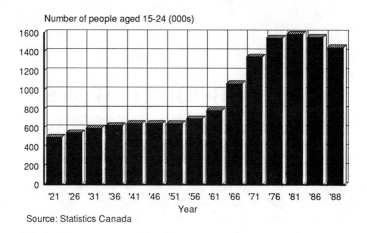

Number of people aged 15-24 (000s)

Source: Statistics Canada

FIGURE 7–1: *Youth in Ontario, 1921–88*

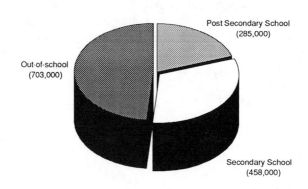

Source: Ministry of Skills Development

FIGURE 7–2: *Activities of Ontario Youth—Attachment to the Educational System, October, 1988*

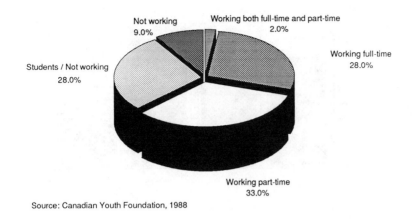

Not working
9.0%

Working both full-time and part-time
2.0%

Working full-time
28.0%

Students / Not working
28.0%

Working part-time
33.0%

Source: Canadian Youth Foundation, 1988

FIGURE: 7–3: *Employment of Ontario Youth, 1987*

those young people "in-school," (that is attending school full-time) and those who are "out- of-school."

Youth and Employment

A very high proportion of young people work either full-time of part-time. A recent survey by the Canadian Youth Foundation which found that only about 37% of young people in Ontario had no involvement in the labour force, while 28% were working full-time and 33% were working part-time (Figure 7–3).

The dominant source of jobs for young people has been in the service sector. Between 1961 and 1981, youth employment in the services sector grew faster than any other sector of the economy (Figure 7–4).

In 1983, youth represented over one-half of the total labour force employed in the accommodation, food and beverages industry and almost one-half of the all employees in the retail industry (Figure 7–5). While many of these jobs accommodate part-time workers, it is also important to note that these occupations are among the lowest skilled and the lowest paying anywhere in the economy.

Youth Unemployment

Although a very high proportion of youth show some attachment to the labour market, the patterns of employment and unemployment differ significantly from those of adults. In particular, youth unemployment rates tend to be significantly higher than those of adults. A comparison of the rates of youth and adult unemployment between 1975 and 1986, shows that the youth unemployment rate has generally been double that of adults (Figure 7–6). There are many reasons for

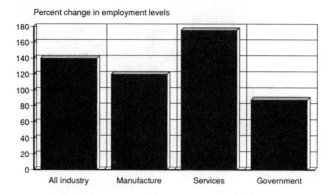

Source: Ontario Study of the Service Sector

FIGURE 7–4: *Changes in Youth Employment, 1961–81*

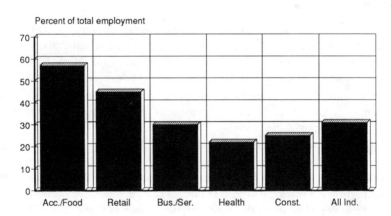

Source: Ontario Study of the Service Sector

FIGURE 7–5: *Youth Employment—Employment Shares in Selected Sectors, 1983*

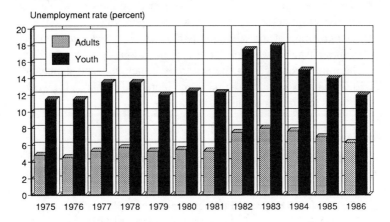

Source: Ministry of Skills Development

FIGURE 7–6: *Ontario Unemployment—Comparison of Youth and Adult Rates, 1975–86*

this. In part it is a reflection of the rapid increase of the youth population, and its entry into the labour force. The relatively higher rates of youth unemployment can also be attributed to the fact that the youth labour market is somewhat more dynamic than the labour market as a whole, which in turn leads to higher rates of frictional unemployment. Finally, many youth, who are students, also seek part-time or temporary employment and are also measured as part of the labour force.

Historically, the youth labour market has also tended to be more susceptible to the influence of economic cycles than is the labour market as a whole. In times of strong economic performance, youth are attracted by the number of job opportunities and their participation rates have tended to increase.

The Experience of the 1970s

While higher than average unemployment rates and greater vulnerability to economic cycles could be generally anticipated for the youth component of the labour market, conditions in the young labour market worsened significantly in the late 1970s.

The rise in the proportion of young people registered as unemployed that took place in most OECD countries in the late 1970s was dramatic. In Canada, the youth unemployment rate more than doubled between 1965 and 1976, as it did in Germany, the United Kingdom and even Japan. The reasons for this deterioration in employment prospects for young people reflected a number of factors, including:

• The entry into the labour force of very large numbers of youths as the baby boom generation reached working age;

- Slowing economic growth in many industrial countries with the accompanying reduction in the growth of new job opportunities;
- The lengthening of the schooling period which raised aspirations and possibly unrealistic career expectations among young people; and
- Technological changes in the economy which reduced demands for unskilled and inexperienced workers and increased demands for workers with new types and higher levels of skills.

The Policy Response

The experience of the late 1970s marked the emergence of the school to work transition as a distinct issue of public policy and challenged the conventional assumption that education alone would assure young people access to labour markets. Governments responded to the problem of high youth unemployment in two ways. First, a number of short-term measures to help youth were put in place. Second, longer term reforms to vocational preparation and training were introduced.

Educational expansion was a standard response in most OECD countries to increases in youth unemployment. In large part, this was a voluntary response by young people to stay in school longer and improve their educational qualifications. However, educational and training solutions were not sufficient to deal with the youth unemployment of the late 1970s and early 1980s. Because the youth unemployment problem was primarily the result of weakness in demand for young people, governments responded with transition programs that were aimed at stimulating demand, including:

- Introducing improvements in job placement services and vocational guidance for school leavers;
- Creating special programs for unemployed school leavers including the provision of work experience, work induction courses and remedial education for low achievers; and
- Increasing the number of cooperative education programs which could give young people both skills and job experience.

In Canada the federal government introduced the short-lived Job Experience Training Program to "provide new entrants to the labour market with job experience as a basis for their successful entry into the labour force." Under this program, employers received a subsidy for employing unemployed school leavers with a view to considering them for permanent employment at the end of the period. The underlying assumption was that work experience in itself would increase the employability of young people.

Since the early 1980s, youth and the problems of youth unemployment have continued to receive policy and program support by government. Both the federal government and the Ontario government provide program support for young people who face difficulties in making the transition from school to work. In 1985, the federal government created a Minister of State for Youth to provide government-wide coordination on all matters related to youth, ranging from summer employment programs to venture capital funding for youth entrepreneurs.

The primary federal vehicle for providing specific support to youth who have had difficulty in making the transition to the labour force is administered through the Job Entry program of the Canadian Job Strategy. This program provides unemployed youth with a combination of on- and off-site training and experience for up to 52 weeks. Eligibility is restricted to employed youth who have attained the legal school leaving age, have been out of the regular school system for at least three months, and who do not hold a post-secondary degree or diploma.

In Ontario, the FUTURES program is the major initiative addressing the issue of youth unemployment and school to work transition. FUTURES was launched in 1985 by the Ministry of Skills Development and has offered pre-employment preparation for severely disadvantaged youth; work experience placements; assistance in obtaining educational upgrading; and a program which enables youth to work part-time and to attend school part-time. Fewer than 50,000 youth have participated in the FUTURES program annually.

The coincidence of strong economic growth and decreases in the size of the youth population make it difficult to attribute the decline in the youth unemployment rates to specific government programs. In addition, critics of the programs, such as the Social Planning Council of Metropolitan Toronto, have argued that the programs are not sufficiently targeted to those youth who face serious difficulty in gaining access to the labour market and long-term opportunity in it.

Youth and the Future Labour Markets

Since the beginning of the 1980s, the economic and demographic environment within which the school to work transition is taking place is changing markedly. With the aging of the baby boom generation, the number of youth in the population has been declining and youth unemployment as a mass phenomenon is disappearing.

At the same time, economic restructuring and technological change will significantly alter the types of skills young people will require to gain access to employment in the future.

A Declining Youth Population

One of the most critical factors that will reshape the nature of the transition from school to work will be demographic trends. Since the late 1970s, the youth component of the labour force has moved from being the most rapidly growing segment of the labour force to the slowest growing component. Since the late 1970s, the rate of growth of the youth population has declined in absolute terms and, only because youth participation rates have continued to rise has there been any positive contribution to the rate of growth of the youth labour force (Figure 7–7).

The youth component of the labour force will continue to decline over the next decade. The high overall rates of population growth of the 1960s and 1970s

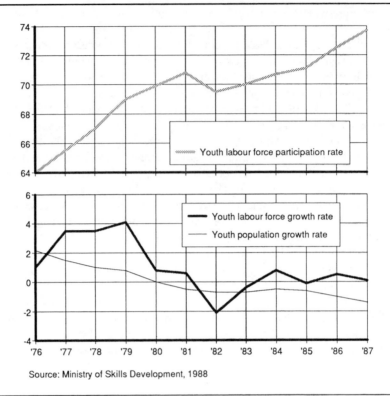

Source: Ministry of Skills Development, 1988

FIGURE 7–7: *Youth in the Labour Force, Ontario, 1975–87*

have diminished and the demographic projections of the Government of Ontario suggest that the population will grow at an annual average rate of only 1.6% between 1986 and 1996, less than one-half the rate of the 1960s and slightly over one-third the rate of the 1970s. The youth component of the labour force is forecast to decline further. By the end of the century, the youth population is forecast to shrink to under 1.4 million, a decline of 25% from its peak level in 1980 (Figure 7–8).

These demographic factors will have the effect of turning youth into a segment of the labour force that has been in relative over-supply to one which, before the end of the decade, will be relatively scarce component of the labour force. Everything being equal, this should eliminate a major part of the problem of youth unemployment and facilitate the transition from school to work. However, the effect of technological change and restructuring of the Ontario economy will mean that even a youth labour force which is in relatively short supply will face new challenges in gaining access to the labour force and to the types of jobs which will have long-term potential for growth and opportunity.

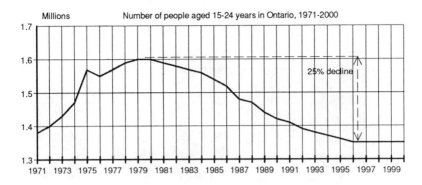

FIGURE 7–8: *Youth Population—Demographic Projections, Ontario,*
1971–2000

A Changing Economy

The restructuring of Ontario's economy, and the rapid introduction of new technologies in the workplace are significantly changing the employment opportunities for youth. A great deal of industrial restructuring has already taken place in Ontario. This industrial restructuring has been characterized by a decline in share of employment in the primary and goods producing sectors and an increased share of employment in the services sector. Between 1975 and 1984, the average rate of growth in employment in the services sector was 2.8%, compared to 1.4% for the good-producing sector. As a result, the share of employment in the services sector grew to 67% of total employment in the province in 1987.

The relative decline in employment in the goods-producing sectors has not been a reflection of the decline in importance of these industries in Ontario's economy; rather it has been a reflection of the productivity increases caused by investments in new capital, new technologies and new skills. Even in the services sector, the most rapid rate of growth of new jobs is in the knowledge-intensive highly skilled business services sector.

Industrial restructuring will continue to reshape the labour markets of the future. International competition is causing a decline in the low wage sector of the economy and the move to more knowledge intensive activities, with the resulting loss of low skill jobs and increasing demand for higher level skills.

The Impact of New Technologies

The introduction of new technologies is another major factor that is redefining jobs and the skills required to do them. There is already evidence that skill

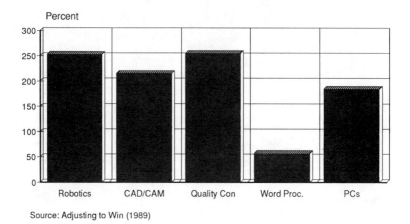

Source: Adjusting to Win (1989)

FIGURE 7–9: *Adoption of New Technologies—Estimated Rate of Increase, 1985–90*

requirements will be different and generally higher than has been the case in the past. A 1986 survey by the Economic Council of Canada of 1,000 employers found that between 1980 and 1985, 75% of employers had introduced new technologies in the workplace and of these, 75% reported the need for new or substantially altered skills.

The rate of adoption of new technologies is forecast to accelerate in the future and affect a very wide range of jobs. The use of robotics and automated inspection and quality control systems are forecast almost to triple between 1985 and 1990, while the use of personal computers will double (Figure 7–9). Adopting these new technologies, such as the more sophisticated machinery and equipment to automate office work (word-processors, computerized payroll, management information systems) or goods production technologies (computer assisted design and manufacturing) will significantly alter the skill requirements of the future.

The recent report of the federal Advisory Council on Adjustment, *Adjusting to Win,* predicted that while 44% of jobs in 1986 required a higher level of education than high school, 64.3% of the jobs to be created between 1986 and the year 2000 will require a higher level of education (Figure 7–10).

Not only will skill requirements change, but technology will also affect the types of jobs available in the future. A 1985 survey by Ontario's Taskforce on Employment and New Technology concluded that technological change is likely to cause changes in the relative importance of occupations within the economy.

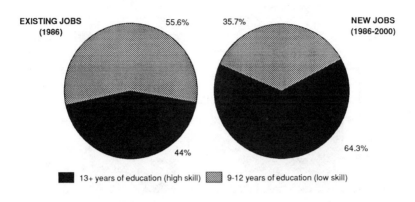

Source: Adjusting to Win, 1986

FIGURE 7–10: *Changing Skill Requirements, Canada, 1986–2000*

In broad terms, the Ontario Task Force identified the following trends for the occupational mix:

- The shift from blue-collar to white-collar occupations will continue, in part because a high proportion of new jobs will come from service-related industries;
- There will be relatively more demand for managerial and administrative occupations and for occupations in natural sciences, engineering and mathematics;
- Professional and technical personnel who will be particularly in demand include production and financial managers, engineers, engineering technologists and technicians, systems analysts and computer programmers;
- High-skilled trades personnel who will be in demand include machinists, industrial machinery mechanics, tool and die makers and equipment installers and repairers;
- There will be relatively less demand for semi-skilled and unskilled production-related occupations.

The Task Force concluded that not only are good basic skills in literacy and numeracy essential, but skills in higher level mathematics, applied science, communication and interpersonal skills, analytical and problem-solving skills and computer literacy will be increasingly important in dealing with the change and uncertainty brought on by technological change.

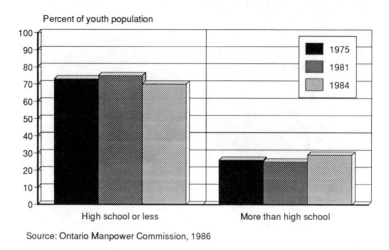

Source: Ontario Manpower Commission, 1986

FIGURE 7–11: *Education Ontario Youth—Level of Attainments, 1975–84*

The Opportunities for Youth

The Ontario economy will shift steadily to knowledge-intensive, higher skilled activities. Growing competitiveness in international markets will mean that Ontario businesses will be required to compete with more sophisticated and higher value-added products, technologies and services. As a result, the employment opportunities for youth are likely to be quite different in the future than they have been in the past.

While in the past, the dominant source of jobs for young people has been in the relatively lower skilled occupations within the services sector, future employment opportunities are likely to require youth to have different and generally higher level skills. There is a growing consensus that the core skills required for successful entry to the work force and performance in it are changing. This reflects a number of considerations:

- First, a number of traditional entry level jobs may decline or disappear;
- Second, the occupations in high demand are likely to have higher skill requirements than has been the case for entry level jobs in the past;
- Third, access to these jobs may require more than formal education and training alone: direct work experience may become an increasing prerequisite.

These developments have important implications for the transition from school to work.

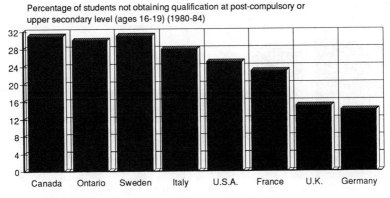

Percentage of students not obtaining qualification at post-compulsory or upper secondary level (ages 16-19) (1980-84)

Source: Premier's Council, 1988

FIGURE 7–12: *Educational Completion Rates—International Comparisons*

Matching Skills to the Emerging Economic Priorities

The degree to which skill requirements are changing and the rate at which the changes are taking place is causing a refocusing of policy in the issue of school to work transition. A rapidly emerging policy issue is to ensure that the education and skills that young people receive match emerging economic priorities.

There are a number of indicators that suggest that youth in Ontario are not developing the skills that they will need to gain access to or sustained success in the labour market of the future.

Educational Attainments

Levels of educational attainment are an important indicator as to whether Ontario's youth will be equipped with the skills that will be sought by employers in the future. Labour force surveys show that the level of educational attainment in Canada tends to be low both in absolute terms and by international standards. The relatively low commitment by Ontario's youth to higher education is emphasized by the fact that only about 30% of the population in Ontario between the ages of 15 and 24 have any post-secondary education at all and that this level has remained relatively constant over time (Figure 7–11).

Not only do Ontario youth not pursue higher education, there is a very serious problem of educational completion even at the high school level. About 30% of Ontario students drop out of the formal education system without a secondary school graduation diploma or certificate of training from a publicly or privately funded school (Figure 7–12). Ontario lags behind other countries in terms of both lower rates of education completion at the secondary level and lower rates

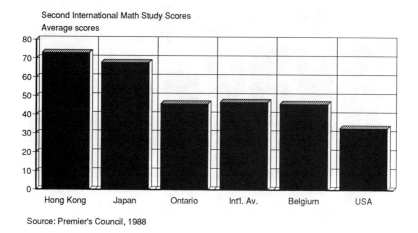

Second International Math Study Scores
Average scores

Source: Premier's Council, 1988

FIGURE 7–13: *Performance in Mathematics—Results of 1984 SIMS Tests*

of participation in education past the post-compulsory age. The Ontario rates are lower than those in many other industrialized jurisdictions, including the United States, Japan and West Germany.

Skills and Competencies

Levels of educational attainment are one measure of how well youth are equipped to enter the work force and to enjoy long-term sustained success in it. However, educational attainment alone is not sufficient to ensure youth access to or success in the labour market. Youth must also have the types and levels of skills that will be in demand, as well as the capacity to acquire new skills over time.

Projections of future skill requirements indicate that youth will require not only a solid foundation in basic skills (basic literacy and numeracy skills), but that new and higher level skills in science and technology will be in growing demand. Although the provision of skills as a means of ensuring employability has been one of the long-term goals of the education and training system in Ontario, a growing body of evidence suggests that there are major deficiencies not only in the area of scientific and technical skills, but also in the competence of Ontario's youth in the most basic core skills.

Basic Skills in Ontario

Concerns about competencies in basic literacy have recently emerged as a key policy priority in preparing youth for the workplace. In its 1988 report, *Competing in the New Global Economy*, the Premier's Council in Ontario found that

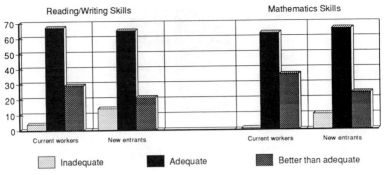

Ranking of Basic Skills of Ontario Auto Parts Workers

FIGURE 7–14: *Perceptions of Basic Skills—Auto Parts Industry, Ontario, 1985*

almost 20% of the population in Ontario aged 15 and over could be classified as illiterate or functionally illiterate. Within the 20–24 year-old age group, almost 4% had reading skills below ninth grade level.

The problem of illiteracy among youth exists even among college and university students. The Premier's Council also reported that the failure rate on literacy tests administered to first year post-secondary students in Ontario ranged from 20% to over 40%, while the average failure rate in Ontario's 22 Colleges of Applied Arts and Technology was 25%. Not only is there evidence that youth is ill-equipped with basic literacy skills, there is also evidence that Ontario's performance in mathematics at best only achieves the international averages.

The results of the Second International Mathematics Study (SIMS) which compared secondary school student achievement in about 20 countries, placed Canadian and American students well behind their international competitors in applied mathematics skills. Ontario's performance was only average in comparison with the superior performance of students from Hong Kong and Japan (Figure 7–13). Employers have been expressing dissatisfaction with the level of basic skills in Ontario's youth for some time.

A 1985 survey of managers in the automotive parts industry revealed that 29% found their current workers literacy skills inadequate, while 36% perceived their workers' mathematical skills to be insufficient. The skills of new entrants to the industry may be perceived as better than those of current workers, but there is still a very high proportion of new entrants with less than adequate skills (Figure 7–14).

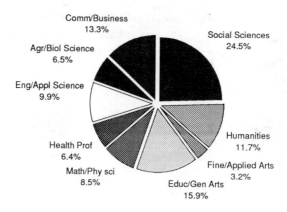

Source: Ontario Survey of University Graduates, 1987

FIGURE 7–15: *Ontario University Graduates—Percent of Graduates by Field of Study, 1985*

A 1988 survey of the members of the Canadian Federation of Independent Business also found dissatisfaction with the skill levels of new employees: in Ontario fully 64% of the small and medium-sized businesses surveyed expressed dissatisfaction with how high school had prepared workers for employment in their firms.

Higher Level Skills in Ontario

The implications of ongoing low levels of education attainment and deficiencies in basic skills are of major concern when considering the labour market of the future. The basic skills are not only important in their own rights, but they are also the building blocks for all higher level skills and training.

Youth in the past have had access to jobs which required relatively low level skills. These entry level jobs are disappearing, replaced by those with higher education and skill requirements. Increasingly, youth will need a variety of higher level skills, particularly in the scientific, technical and technological areas, in order to compete in the labour markets of the future. As a result, the ease with which young people will make the transition to the work force and the long-term opportunities that they will enjoy will increasingly be determined by their ability to perform technical and technologically-oriented jobs.

Canada has a poor track record in equipping young people with scientific and technical skills. A study by the Science Council of Canada, *Science for Every Student; Educating Canadians for Tomorrow's World*, showed that science is rarely taught, if at all, in elementary schools across the country. The Science

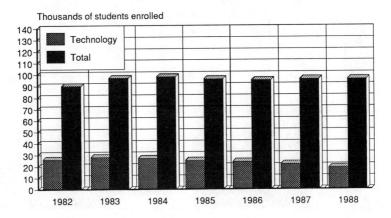

Source: Ministry of Colleges and Universities

FIGURE 7–16: *Enrolment in CAAT's—Total Enrolment and Technology Enrolment, 1982–88*

Council, attributed this failing to teachers' reluctance or inability to deal with the subject: most of the teachers surveyed had not taken a college or university-level course in a subject other than education in the last ten years; over 50% of elementary school teachers had no university level mathematics; and almost 75% did not have university level science.

The poor foundation in science is reflected in how students make their choices for future education. The vast majority of students who pursue secondary education do so in the social sciences or humanities. A 1985 survey of university graduates by field of study found that almost 35% of university graduates in Ontario received degrees in either humanities or social sciences; by comparison less than 10% received degrees in engineering and applied science (Figure 7–15).

Even in Ontario's Colleges of Applied Arts and Technology (CAAT's), the proportion of students enroled in the technology streams is both low and declining. Both the absolute number and the proportion of technology students has declined since the mid-1980s (Figure 7–16). Apprenticeship training programs should be another important means of training young people in technical skills. While enrolment in apprenticeship programs has increased in the past decade, the growth has been primarily in the construction trades and to a much lesser extent in the industrial trades (Figure 7–17).

While the low rates of participation in scientific and technical training is a problem for all youth, it is a much more serious problem for females. Women have historically been under-represented in scientific and technical education

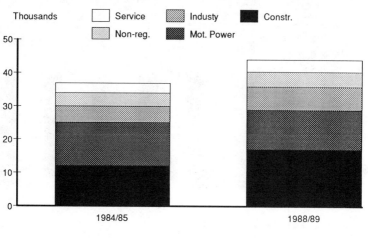

Source: Ministry of Skills Development

FIGURE 7–17: *Apprenticeship in Ontario—Active Apprentices by Trade, 1984–89*

and training. A 1988 report released by the Council of Ontario Universities on attracting and retaining women students in science and engineering found that, while women constituted 53% of students graduating with first degrees from Ontario universities, their representation in engineering and applied sciences (12.3%) and mathematics and physical sciences (29.1%) was conspicuously low.

Participation in apprenticeship has also been traditionally dominated by males. Of the over 45,000 apprentices in Ontario, only about 5% are women, and these are concentrated in the so-called "pink collar" trades such as hairdressing.

Implications for Public Policy

The low levels of educational attainment, deficiencies in basic skills and low level of commitment to the development of technical and scientific skills should become areas of major concern for educators and policy makers in Ontario. The assumptions of the past that the educational system will adequately prepare youth for the workplace are being challenged. Deficiencies in even the basic skills of young people reflect on the quality of education that they have received; the handicaps that these kinds of deficiencies place on young people will only grow as the workplace of the future becomes more demanding and complex.

The current low level of attainment in science and mathematics, and the fact that very few youth pursue any formal education in the technical and technological disciplines, is a matter of serious concern for public policy. Increasingly the educational system must orient itself toward providing education which ensures

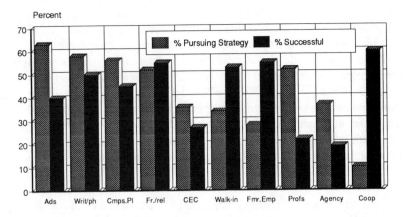

Source: Survey of 1985 University Graduates, 1987

FIGURE 7–18: *Job Search Strategies Pursued by Ontario University*

that young people have the skills and competencies that they will need in the workplace of the future.

Facilitating Entry to the Work Force

Given the degree to which skill requirements are changing and the rate at which the changes are taking place, a second policy requirement that is emerging is the need to improve the ease with which young people enter the work force.

The youth labour market of the future will be significantly more complex than has been the case in the past. Some traditional sources of youth employment will decline and may disappear; new types of jobs will be created, requiring new and higher level skills; and direct or relevant work experience will take on increased importance in securing employment in the future.

Better Information and Counselling

Providing effective counselling and information about job career choices, educational choices and job opportunities will be an essential requirement to facilitate entry into the work force for young people.

There is growing concern that Ontario's students may not be receiving adequate guidance about future educational and occupational opportunities. Within the school system, guidance counsellors must deal with a very wide range of issues that include not only career and educational counselling, but also social and personal counselling. Not only are guidance counsellors faced with a widening responsibility but it is increasingly difficult for them to keep up-to-date with new and changing educational options and labour market demands.

The perception of the value of guidance counsellors within the high school system is reflected in a recent survey by the Canadian Youth Foundation. Approximately two-thirds of Canadian students surveyed indicated that they had met with school guidance counsellors. Of these, over 70% had found the sessions helpful in terms of selecting courses, but less than 60% found them helpful in terms of career or educational plans. There are also few if any effective counselling mechanisms for youth who have left the formal educational system. Counselling is available to youth from the Canada Employment Centre of the Federal Department of Employment and Immigration but much of this is intended to deal with youth who have had difficulty in gaining or sustaining employment rather than in preparing youth for new employment opportunities.

Better Placement Services

Youth rely on a wide variety of strategies to gain employment (Figure 7–18). For example, university graduates rely heavily on newspaper ads or writing or telephoning potential employers as means of obtaining jobs. On-campus placement or career counselling services are also used by more than half of Ontario's university graduates.

Despite the popularity of these strategies, they by no means assure young people of finding a job: while over 60% of university graduates seek jobs by responding to advertisements, only about 40% of those who pursue this strategy are successful.

The success rates of the more formal and structured placement services cause the effectiveness of these services to be questioned. Less than one-half the students who seek employment through on-campus career counselling or placement services are successful; only one-third of those who use private employment agencies are successful; and less than one-quarter of university graduates who seek employment through the services of a Canada Employment Centre find jobs using that strategy.

The means by which university graduates find jobs and the relative rates of success in pursuing different kinds of search strategies raise a number of questions for public policy. First, the majority of youth have not tended to rely on formal and structured means of entering the labour force, instead seeking employment through the more random means of responding to advertisements or by writing or telephoning employers. As employment opportunities for youth undergo significant change in the future the need for more structured means of determining those choices will grow. Second, the relatively low success rates of the more formal placement services cause their relevance and effectiveness to be questioned. Ensuring that placement and counselling services can effectively match young people to employment opportunities will be increasingly important for youth and for employers.

More Opportunities for Work Experience

The relative success rates of job search strategies of Ontario university graduates also emphasize the value of direct work experience in making the transition from school to work. The most successful job search strategies were those that involved seeking employment from former employers and cooperative education employers. In particular, cooperative education has proven to be an extremely effective mechanism for bridging the gap between education and the workplace. Students involved in cooperative education programs not only have the opportunity to develop job-related skills as a result of direct work experience, but as reported in a recent Science Council study, *Postsecondary Cooperative Education in Canada*, students also develop useful personal and interpersonal skills— greater self-confidence, the ability to work independently, and the ability to work well with others. Cooperative education is also important to employers. The study also found that cooperative education was perceived as beneficial to employers in selecting and recruiting employees.

There has been a marked increase in cooperative education programs in place in Canada. The first Canadian co-op program was established at the University of Waterloo in 1957 with 75 students. Today over 26,000 students and over 4,000 employers participate in over 50 colleges and universities. While there has been a very rapid growth in the availability of cooperative education programs, there are still relatively few students enroled in them with only 6.5% of undergraduate enrolment in Ontario's universities and only 9.8% of total college enrolment. Cooperative education is also beginning to occur in the secondary school system. In 1987, about 35,000 high school students—over 5% of all secondary school students—participated in coop courses in almost 600 schools. Pilot programs, such as the School to Work Apprenticeship program being developed by Ontario's Ministry of Education are also helping to facilitate the transition from school to work.

The importance and value of cooperative education programs at both the secondary and post-secondary levels will only grow in the future. As the skills required for entry into the work force become higher level and more complex, it will become increasingly important for young people to have opportunities which allow them to combine their formal education with on-the-job experience.

Ensuring Equal Opportunities

While there has been a decline in the aggregate rates of youth unemployment and while this decline can be expected to continue in the future as a result of demographic trends, there will likely continue to be certain segments of the youth labour market who will continue to face high levels of unemployment and difficulties in gaining access to stable, long-term employment. For this reason, there will continue to be the need for public policy measures ensure support for those who face difficulties or disadvantages in making the transition from school to work.

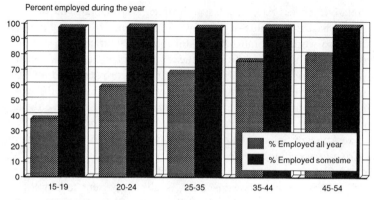

Source: Ministry of Skills Development, 1987

FIGURE 7–19: *Employment of Out-of-School Youth—Comparison to Adult Employment, 1985*

FIGURE 7–20: *Education Level & Unemployment—Out-of-School Youth, 15–19, 20–24, Ontario 1985 (000's)*

Age and Educational Level of Out-of-School Youth	Average Number of Weeks of Labour Force Activity	Percent of Labour Force Who Expect Unemployment
15–19		
Elem. Education or less	41.42	-
Some or Complete High School	43.32	37.13
20–24		
Elem. Education or less	46.08	-
Some or Complete High School	47.09	29.99
Post High School Education	49.08	19.7

Source: Ministry of Skills Development, 1987

A Dual Labour Market for Youth

The youth labour market is not homogeneous. Certain categories of youth have relatively greater difficulty in getting jobs and face higher rates of unemployment and longer durations of unemployment than does the youth population as a whole. While changing demographic trends have diminished and will continue to reduce the problem of overall youth unemployment, there will remain a

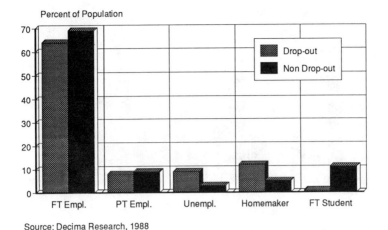

Source: Decima Research, 1988

FIGURE 7–21: *Employment Status of Drop-Outs—Comparison to Non Drop-Outs*

core of young people for whom the transition from school to work will be neither easy nor effective.

A 1987 study by the Ontario Ministry of Skills Development reviewed the experience of out-of-school youth, a sub-group of the youth population who experienced particular problems in the labour force. Out-of-school youth are defined as those young people who had no attachment to an educational institution and had completed the transition from school to the labour force. Out-of-school youth comprise almost one-half of the total youth and are primarily in the 20–24 year age group. The study found that in 1985, although the proportion of out-of-school youth who had jobs was high and comparable to that of the adult labour force, the proportion who were employed all year was significant lower. This is illustrated by the fact that while fully 98% of 20–24 year-olds experienced some employment during the year, only about 60% were steadily employed (Figure 7–19).

Education and Youth Unemployment

While lower rates of stability of employment can be expected for youth than for adults, there is evidence of a direct relationship between levels of educational attainment and a successful transition to the labour force. The study of out-of-school youth also found a strong inverse relationship between the level of education and the incidence of unemployment. Among 20–24 year-olds, the probability of being unemployed during the year for those with complete or

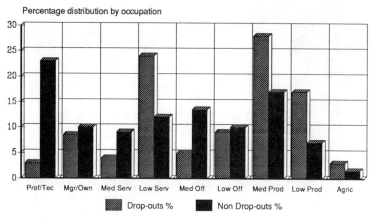

Source: Decima Research, 1988

FIGURE 7–22: *Education and Occupations, Ontario, 1988*

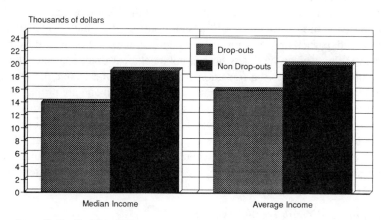

Source: Decima Research, 1988

FIGURE 7–23: *Incomes of Drop-Outs—Comparison to Non Drop-Outs*

partial high school education was 30%, while for those with some form of post-secondary education, it was 20% (Figure 7–20).

The relationship between educational attainment and a successful entry into the labour force is further emphasized in a recent survey by Decima Research on behalf of Ontario's Ministry of Education. The rate of unemployment of drop-outs (who are defined as those people who have left secondary school, for whatever reason, prior to graduating) is three times the rate of unemployment of non-drop-outs (Figure 7–21). Not only is the unemployment rate higher among drop-outs than non-drop-outs, but the likelihood and duration of unemployment is significantly higher among drop-outs than for non-drop-outs: the Decima survey found that the likelihood of unemployment for drop-outs was double that of non-drop-outs, as was the average duration of unemployment.

Other Consequences of Low Educational Attainment

The consequences of low educational attainment go beyond an increased likelihood of unemployment and unstable employment. There is also a major effect on the type of jobs that are available to youth with low levels of educational attainment, which in turn affects income levels and opportunities for advancement. The Decima survey found that the most likely occupations for drop-outs tended to be concentrated in low level service jobs and medium and low level production jobs, with almost negligible access to professional and technical jobs (Figure 7–22).

The types of jobs that drop-outs have is reflected in their income levels. The average incomes of drop-outs is only about 8% that of non-drop-outs and their median income is only three-quarters as high (Figure 7–23). Access to jobs with prospects for advancement is also limited by perceptions of the skills and commitment of drop-outs. A survey by Goldfarb Consultants, also on behalf of Ontario's Ministry of Education, found that the generic skills of drop-outs, including skills at problem solving and the ability to make decisions, were often perceived by employers to be worse than those of non-drop-outs (Figure 7–24).

The Attitudes of Youth

The attitudes of youth will play a vital role in their commitment to educational attainment and their prospects for future success in the labour markets. The recent survey by the Canadian Youth Foundation found that more than three-quarters of high school students did not like going to school nor did they find their courses interesting. At the same time, the survey found that the perceptions of the value of education of youth who were still in school increase with the level of their education, with 56% of vocational students and 48% of university students believing that their education would help them later in life (Figure 7–25). Even out-of-school youth recognize both the inadequacy of their current levels of education and the growing importance of education to their future. The Canadian Youth Foundation survey also found that, of those young people who

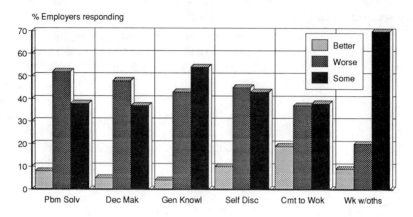

% Employers responding

Source: Goldfarb Consultants, 1988

FIGURE 7–24: *Employment Perception of Drop-Outs—Comparison with Graduates*

FIGURE 7–25: *Attitudes of Students to School, Canada, 1987 (%)*

	All Students	High School	Vocational	University
Do you like going to school?	29	23	36	43
Are your courses interesting?	29	23	39	43
Is your school work meaningful and important?	41	32	59	54
Is your learning going to help you later in life?	45	41	56	48

Source: Canadian Youth Foundation, 1988

were no longer in school, 4 out of 10 felt that they had enough education while 6 out of 10 said that they did not think that their education was adequate.

Many out-of-school youth also have aspirations for further education. Seven in 10 would like to pursue post-secondary studies, particularly in the technical and vocational areas (Figure 7–26).

Policies to Ensure Equal Opportunity

The correlation between educational attainment and success in the labour markets points to the need to ensure educational completion as a fundamental

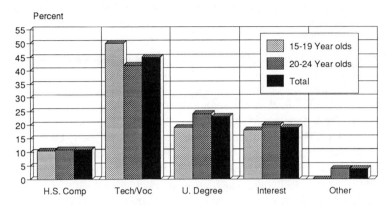

Source: Canadian Youth Foundation, 1988

FIGURE 7–26: *Aspirations for Further Education—Canadian Youth Population, 1987*

objective in promoting equal opportunity for all youth. This goal may not be easy to attain. Youth have expressed considerable dissatisfaction with their interest in high school, and their perceptions of its relevance. Changing these attitudes and increasing educational completion rates set an enormous challenge for Ontario's educators. For those youth who fail to complete their education, there will continue to be a need for specific programs which help them either to gain access to the labour force, or to upgrade their education as a means of promoting equality of opportunity. The current programs offered by both the federal and Ontario governments which aim to reduce the barriers to entry for young people who have experienced long periods of unemployment by offering a combination of training and work experience will continue to be important in the future. However, giving the rising skills requirements generally, policies to ensure equitable access to jobs with long-term opportunities may have to address more youth than only those who have failed to complete their basic education. Youth recognize that their skills and education may not be adequate for the future, and express aspirations for additional education and training. Policies and programs which place a new emphasis on allowing young people to return for educational upgrading are likely to become increasingly important.

An Agenda for Public Policy

The next decade poses many challenges for public policy makers. Facilitating the transition from school to work will become an increasingly complex task.

Changing occupational trends and skill requirements have significant implications for how youth will make the transition from school to work.

A Strategic Commitment by Governments

A strategic commitment by governments to human resource development will be the essential underpinning for a coherent and comprehensive policy designed to enable all youth to gain access to employment that sets them on a course for a productive working life. There is some evidence that this recognition is growing within both the federal and provincial governments. The federal government in its 1989 Throne Speech emphasized human resource development as a key priority. In Ontario, the Premier's Council on Technology is currently reviewing how educational and skill requirements will change for Ontario's labour force as a result of changing technology and growing international competition. In the context of this broad government commitment, specific policies must be developed which actively support and facilitate the transition of Ontario's youth into the work force.

A Basic Education for All Youth

A renewed and strengthened commitment to providing a basic education for all youth in Ontario is an urgent policy priority. While providing all youth with a basic education has long been established as a fundamental objective of education policy, there is ample evidence that the education system in Ontario has failed to achieve this. The high rate of drop-outs from the secondary school system is one example of failure within Ontario's education system; the inadequacy of basic literacy and numeracy skills is another.

The Government of Ontario has recognized the high drop-out rate as a major problem, and in 1987 it commissioned the Ontario Study on the Relevance of Education and Drop-outs. But the remedy for the problem must go well beyond commissioning studies. The education system must respond with explicit measures which increase the retention rate of students in the secondary school system.

Changes in curriculum, standards and teaching process are actions which could improve not only the quality of education, but the perceptions of youth of its value. In addition, specific measures which identify at-risk youth and cause them to rethink their decision to leave the school system before graduation have proven to be successful, not only in reducing the drop-out rate, but in encouraging students to pursue education beyond the high school level.

Higher Level and More Relevant Skills

Providing more young people with higher level and more relevant skills should also become an explicit goal of school to work transition policy. A priority of raising the level of skills and educational attainment for young people should be to increase the proportion of young people who further their education beyond the secondary level.

Increasing the proportion of young people who pursue further education will be one measure of success for public policy. Ensuring that the higher levels of education and training are in areas that fulfil the skill requirements of employers should be another explicit goal. There is a rapidly increasing need to attract more young people to post-secondary education in the scientific, technical and techno- logical disciplines. The foundations for post-secondary education and training in these areas must be laid within the elementary and secondary education system with teachers who are qualified and motivated. Within the post-secondary sys- tem, instructors and educators must have up-to-date skills themselves and access to appropriate teaching aids, such as instruments and equipment that incorporate the latest technologies.

While attracting more young people to the types of education and training that will enable them to work in technical and technological occupations should be a major policy role generally, attracting more women will be a greater challenge. The growing demand for technical skills makes it essential to increase the repre- sentation of females in scientific and technological areas. This will not only ensure equitable access to the types of jobs which are likely to have the greatest opportunities, but will also ensure that there are sufficient numbers of skilled workers, either male or female, to fill the jobs of the future.

Better Linkages between School and Work

Strong and effective linkages between educational institutions and the work- place are of considerable benefit to both young people making the transition from school to work and to prospective employers. Young people will be faced with a growing and changing array of educational options and employment opportunities. The quality of their decisions will be determined, in part, by the quality of the information and guidance they receive, and they will increasingly need access to information, counselling and job placement services.

While counselling and placement systems exist within both the secondary and post-secondary educational systems, it is timely to review the focus of those services and their capacity to meet the demands of the future. It is also important to ensure that young people who have left the institutions of education have access to counselling and placement services that enable them to make appropri- ate choices about employment opportunities as well as about opportunities and options for further education.

More Opportunity for Direct Work Experience

Increasing the extent to which direct work experience is combined with for- mal education should be another policy goal to facilitate the transition from school to work. Cooperative education programs at the university level have been extremely successful, both for students and employers. While these pro- grams are more expensive to operate, they receive little or no special treatment in funding levels by governments. Government and the institutions of education should both be challenged to find ways of increasing the number of students who are able to take advantage of post-secondary cooperative education.

At the secondary school level, the School to Work Apprenticeship Program is also proving to be an effective bridge between formal education and the workplace. Increasing the availability of these types of programs can facilitate the entry of young people, and in particular those who do not pursue post-secondary education, into working life.

Increased participation in apprenticeship training should also be a goal for public policy. Apprenticeship should be an important means of facilitating the transition from school to work as well as of developing high level technical skills for youth. The low rate of participation by youth in apprenticeship programs combined with a drop-out rate of about 50% suggests the need to evaluate the effectiveness of the current system as a means of training youth for the skilled trades.

Opportunities for a Second Chance

A key policy goal must be to ensure that the entire youth population has equitable access to labour markets and, as much as possible, equitable opportunities. The current programs offered by both the federal and Ontario governments aim to reduce the barriers to entry for young people who have experienced long periods of unemployment by offering a combination of training and work experience. These programs, with their specific target groups of disadvantaged, unemployed youth, will continue to be important in the future and will require the ongoing commitment of governments.

In an economy where there will be increasing demands for higher educational attainment and higher level skills, programs which allow young people to return for educational upgrading, while at the same time having the means to support themselves, should be given greater emphasis. In particular, it may be timely to build on the experience of the "part-time/part-time" option of Ontario's FUTURES program, which allows young people to work part-time and attend school part-time.

The Commitment of Employers and Individuals

The focus of this agenda for public policy has been on the role and responsibility of government and the institutions of education to create the appropriate policy environment and educational framework within which the school to work transition can be best facilitated in the future. Government and institutional action alone is unlikely to be sufficient. Employers are important participants in the process. Once educators have provided youth with a basic education, and with a base upon which to build skills that will be in demand in the future, employers must be prepared to provide the training that will make the new entrant to the work force a productive and valued employee.

Youth and their families must also take increasing responsibility in preparing for the workplace. While youth express a recognition of the importance of education and its increasing value, there is much evidence to suggest that these opinions are not being translated into a commitment to higher education or to the development of the types of skills that ensure them access and opportunity to the workplace of the future.

8

ONTARIO'S FIRST PEOPLE
Native Children

Wayne Warry

This chapter examines a range of policy issues concerning Native children, youth and families against the background of the central goal of Native people in Canada today: self-determination and self-government. I am less concerned with specific policy initiatives, although I provide examples of these, than with the fundamental premises that must guide the development of policies and research throughout the 1990s. I first describe the nature of Native communities in Ontario and explain why the categorization of Native people poses unique problems for policy development. I then outline the current status of Native child health and welfare, and discuss the concept of self-government within a tripartite policy process. This broad overview is followed by discussion of two critical policy fields: Native child welfare and health care systems. The chapter concludes with a brief discussion of the need for community-based research projects that enable Native people to pursue their long-term objective of self-determination in order to secure the future for Native children and youth.

First Nations: Ontario's Native Communities

Like aboriginal people throughout the world, Native people have experienced the common historical process of colonialism, which has resulted in the marginalization of their communities. Underdevelopment is not simply a condition; it is also a process. The obstacles faced by Native people are inextricably linked to the social, economic and political structures of a dominant, colonial power, as represented by the Government of Canada. Native communities, particularly in Northern Ontario, face socio-economic conditions which closely parallel those of Third World nations. Statistics demonstrate that Native people clearly constitute a distinct population on the basis of needs. But more fundamentally, they constitute a unique population with regard to policy as a result of colonial history. Dispossessed of their traditional land base, Native people have been forced to the periphery of Canadian society, and have been deprived of political rights which were implicitly recognized in the treaty making process. These political rights, which were affirmed but not defined in the Canada Act of 1983, separate aboriginal peoples from other minorities.

Ontario's Native population is estimated at 185,000.[1] Of this number, approximately 77,000 are status Indians. In 1987, there were 126 Indian communities in Ontario designated as "bands" under the Indian Act, the legislation that defines the federal government's responsibility toward status Indians. The average size of reserve communities is just over 600 people—approximately one-third of whom live off-reserve. These communities refer to themselves as "First Nations", as an assertion of their inherent right to self-determination.[2] Status Indians maintain that the federal government retains ultimate responsibility for a wide range of services, including the provision of health, education, and welfare services which, for other citizens, fall under provincial jurisdiction. In their view, provincial legislation does not detract in any way from this federal trust; First Nations have consistently called, without success, for the inclusion of non-derogation clauses in key pieces of provincial legislation (OISSC, 1984).

Significant differences exist between northern and southern reserves. Many fly-in communities are extremely under-serviced, lacking basic amenities such as running water or indoor toilets. Many reserves are great distances from hospitals or other critical social services. Southern reserves, in comparison, fare better in terms of basic amenities and access to urban based services, but caution must be used when interpreting north-south distinctions. The recognition that remote communities are especially under-serviced should not lead to complacency with regard to southern communities that suffer from problems of high unemployment, insufficient housing, contaminated water supplies, and a lack of adequate sanitation. Indeed, the belief that southern Indians are somehow advantaged is an exceptionally dangerous and misplaced stereotype.

Métis (descendants of Indian and European parents) and many "non-status" Indians living off-reserve are not technically Indians under the Indian Act. (The make-up of the Métis and non-status population is changing as members of these groups apply for and gain status under the Act to Amend the Indian Act, 1985 (Bill C–31). In Ontario, people of aboriginal descent who are not registered as Indians are represented by the Ontario Métis and Aboriginal Association (OMAA), under a regional zone structure. Status Indians who have lived off-reserve for more than 12 months, non-status Indians and Métis who are not currently under the jurisdiction of the Indian Act, constitute the majority of Natives in Ontario and are serviced as ordinary citizens under provincial policy. They have neither special status, nor official recognition as distinct political communities (OMAA, 1988).

Patterns of Native migration to urban centres are clearly related to poor socioeconomic conditions found on reserves. Native migrants are generally a highly

---

[1] This figure includes status, non-status and Métis people and is based on Asbury (1987). Estimates of Ontario's Native population range from 110,000 according to Statistics Canada (1983) to a high of 355,000 (Maidman, 1981).

[2] This fact is not lost on provincial legislators, who continue to ignore all-chiefs political resolutions which would result in the substitution of the words "First Nation" for "Bands" in provincial legislation (OISSC, 1984; Resolution 86/3).

mobile population, often moving to cities to obtain temporary employment and health services and returning to the reserve after several months or years (Maidman, 1981; McCaskill, 1981). Non-status Indians and Métis comprise approximately two-thirds of the Native urban population. Maidman (1981: 34) has projected a current urban Native population of 104,387; an estimated 28,184 are children aged 0–14 years.

Four political organizations represent status Indians in Ontario: Grand Council Treaty Number Three, Nishnawbe-Aski Nation, the Union Of Ontario Indians, and the Association of Iroquois and Allied Indians. Authority in these organizations flows from the bottom up, from band members to chiefs, through regional councils of chiefs and, finally, to provincial and national organizations (Castellano, 1982: 116). This authority system produces a holistic understanding of needs in the community which shapes the design of Native policies; this community-based knowledge often runs contrary to the government's sectoral analysis of local needs. Native organizations' responses to these needs are hampered by inadequate staffing in research and policy analysis. The Nishnawbe-Aski Nation, for example, has a single health policy researcher/coordinator who is responsible for 25,000 Native people living in remote northern communities.

Government bureaucracies, in comparison, are highly compartmentalized, and are premised on decision making structured from the top down, limiting flexibility in meeting locally defined needs. In addition, service responsibilities for related needs are distributed among various departments. Indian health services, for example, are administered under the Medical Services Branch, Health and Welfare Canada, while other closely related areas such as housing and sewage facilities are administered by the Department of Indian Affairs and Northern Development. Interdepartmental divisions create delays in dealing with issues as well as a segmented vision of local needs (ibid.).

In Ontario, the Ontario Native Affairs Directorate (ONAD) is charged with the coordination of provincial policies from various line-ministries. With only five policy advisors, staff time is easily consumed, and the Directorate faces great difficulties in attempting to coordinate a range of provincial policies concerning Native people. The result is a fragmentation of policies concerning Native people similar to that found within the federal government.

Native people are caught in a jurisdictional quagmire which easily produces gaps in services at both the local and regional levels. Funding and evaluation of Native programs are subject to separate federal or provincial government guidelines and to the vagaries of decision making at two bureaucratic levels. Who, for example, is responsible for funding a preventive substance abuse program proposed by a Band for the numerous students living off-reserve attending high-school? More importantly, who is responsible for the design and content of such a program? If a program is operated in a provincial school, must it be subject to the provincial educational authorities? If so, how can Bands ensure that the program is culturally appropriate for its children?

The federal government retains responsibility for funding a number of social services to status Indians in Ontario under the *Indian Welfare Agreement* of 1965. The federal government funds, on average, 95% of all services delivered on-reserve under the General Welfare Assistance Act and the Child and Family Services Act (henceforth CFSA) (MI *Transitions*, 1988: 438). Newer federal initiatives, in the fields of substance abuse, family violence, and day care, commonly contain special allocations for status communities. Thus, for example, a recent federal family violence initiative costing $40 million, contained an allocation of $3 million over four years to enhance existing departmental programs within DIAND by directing funds to Bands for community based initiatives. While not decrying the obvious need for such programs, this degree of financial commitment falls short of Native expectations and totally fails to address the needs of Native people living off-reserve.

The major agencies providing services to urban Natives are the number of Indian Friendship Centres across the province. Core support for Friendship Centres is supplied by the Secretary of State, Canada. Specific programs, for example, Native courtworker programs, are partially funded through provincial ministries (in this case, the Attorney General) on the basis of demonstrated need. The provincial government retains responsibility for the administration of many federal programs, but has been reluctant to develop any new Indian-specific services—however necessary—for reserve residents, unless they are cost-shared by the federal government (*Transitions*: 452).

Native Children At Risk

There is a paucity of Ontario-specific data concerning the status of Native children and youth. To date, there has been little child-specific data gathered by First Nations or Native communities at the local level. This situation will only be remedied through the development of community based research projects which are supported and controlled by First Nations.

The social conditions of Native communities in general, however, are well documented. Insomuch as community and family environments directly affect the lives of children, general statistics will be cited to provide a profile of Ontario's Native children.

Because of high fertility rates and low life expectancy, the Indian population is extremely young. Fifty-eight percent of Natives in Canada are under 24 years of age, as compared to 39% for the Canadian population as a whole (AFN, 1988). The proportion of Indian youth will continue to be high for the next decade; about 40% of Native people are below age 15. (*Native People in Canada*, 1984).

In Ontario, an estimated 74,000 Native children are below the age of 15. Ontario is home to more status Indian children (0–18 years) than any other province: 28,427 children or 21% of all status Indian children in Canada (*DIAND*, 1987a: 12). About three-quarters of these children live on-reserve. Native families are larger than non-Natives families, and a considerable number of Native families are headed by a lone parent: 19% as compared to 11% for non-Natives. The majority of Native single parents are women (87%) (Nicholson, 1987: 15–16). About 45% of births occur outside of registered marriages, five times the national rate (Price, 1987: 91).

These demographics should be considered when interpreting information concerning Native health and welfare. If Native children and youth are at risk, then Indian culture as a whole is at risk. Aboriginal peoples clearly see children as "precious commodities", integral to nation-building and central to the future of a self-sustaining Indian culture (ONWA *et al*, 1983; 8).

Every social indicator affirms that Native people are the most disadvantaged population in Canada. Sixty percent of Indians living on reserve receive social assistance or general welfare assistance (DIAND, 1982: 70). Indian reliance on General Welfare Assistance in Ontario is 9 to 10 times higher than that of other Ontarians (*Transitions*, 1988: 437–438).

Only 44% of adults living on reserve received employment income compared to 64% of non-Indians living in similar remote or northern locations. Unemployment is especially acute among Indian adolescents. Only 24% of Indians aged 15–24 are employed (AFN, 1988). Annual income is 50% that of non-Natives and is well below the statistics Canada poverty line: 83% of Indians who work have incomes of less than $10,000 per year. Native women earn about 36% of the average Canadian male income; single mothers are under enormous financial pressures to feed, clothe and house their children adequately (Nicholson, 1987: 14–16; NWAC 1986).

High unemployment rates are in part related to the poor educational experiences of Native youth. Until recently, the main thrust of Indian education was to assimilate Native children and youth into mainstream society (see Barman *et al*, 1986, 1987; DIAND 1982b). Despite improvements in Indian education during the past decade, the educational system remains ineffective in meeting the unique needs of Native students. According to the 1981 census, drop-out rates at various educational levels are two to four times the national average. Fifteen percent of Indians surveyed had less than a grade five education. More than 40% of Native people have never been to high school, only one-quarter have completed high school, and only 2% of Natives hold university degrees (the non-Native figure was 8%) (Maidman, 1981: 17–18). Cultural differences in learning and teaching styles, a lack of culturally appropriate curriculum, and outright discrimination have combined to make the educational experience of Native children painfully difficult. There continues to be a dearth of Native language programs; over half of status Indians in various school systems have no contact with their aboriginal language (Phillips, 1985). Poor educational experiences translate directly into a lack of skilled Native professionals in medical and social service fields (Weller and Manga, 1988; see also Castellano, 1982).

Standards of living on many reserves and in cities are desperate. Twenty-three percent of all houses on reserve in Canada are in need of repair; 73% of houses are inadequate; 37% have inadequate bathroom facilities and 3% have no bathroom at all. Thirty-four percent of houses lack a piped waste disposal system or septic tank, 18% have no kitchen sink; the number of dwellings lacking central heating is more than 50% (AFN, 1987).

These living conditions produce higher than average incidence of death due to fire as Indians rely on cooking stoves and wood stoves (Young, 1979). Indians are at increased risk for infectious and parasitic disease because of poor water supplies and unhygienic domestic environments (ibid.; see also Barnes, 1985; Young, 1979; Penner, 1983).

The infant mortality rate among Native children is 60% higher than the national rate (Penner *et al*, 1983). Young cites a crude infant mortality rate for infants in Northern Ontario of 2–3 times the national average. Ontario also has the highest rate of Native stillbirths in the country: 16.9 per 1,000, a figure more than double the non-Native average. In the Sioux Lookout area of Northern Ontario, 43% of Native infant deaths occurred at home, before the health care system became involved (Young, 1983). The leading causes of death during the post neo-natal period are gastroenteritis and pneumonia, diseases that are largely preventable (Weller and Manga, 1988: 142).

Fetal Alcohol Syndrome (FAS) is generally regarded to be more prevalent in Native populations. Although as Muir (1985: 130) notes, the prevalence of FAS in the Native and general Canadian population has not been well documented, more than one-half the documented cases in two western provinces involved Natives. Perinatal death rates and neonatal death rates are also higher than the Canadian average (Muir, 1985: 36–40). Post neonatal death rates are 3.6 times the national average. Sudden infant death syndrome is three times more prevalent in Native children. Other infant deaths arise from a variety of causes including pneumonia, injury and poisoning. Such deaths reflect not only poor environmental conditions, but also acute problems concerning access to medical care (Muir, 1985; Young, 1983).

In Southern Ontario, Indian infants had rates of pneumonia that were more that 17.6 times greater than non-Native children (Evers and Rand, 1982, 1983). Indian children were also at twice the risk of *otitis media* and at greater risk for iron deficiency anaemia. The relatively recent (post World War II) dietary shift among Natives from traditional to processed foods has resulted in an increased risk of a variety of health problems in children including irregular birth weights, nearsightedness, iron deficiency, and obesity (Young, 1979; Gazu, 1978).

Young's (1979) historical survey of Indian health in Northwestern Ontario shows that immense strides have been made in arresting the development and spread of epidemics since the turn of the century, but the number of deaths caused by accidents and violence has corresponding increased. Thus, what Young calls the "mortality experience" of Native people has not changed substantially during the past three decades. Young concludes that although:

> improvements in certain indices have undoubtedly occurred in recent years, the most significant health problems of [Native] people will not diminish unless the

deficiencies in housing, sanitation, nutrition and overall socio-economic conditions are corrected (1979: 218).

The three leading causes of Indian deaths in the 1–19 year category are injuries and poisoning (78.%), diseases of the respiratory system (3.8%) and circulatory system (2.7%) (Muir, 1985: 50). Mortality rates among 5–19 year-olds are triple the national average. Native children are five times more likely than non-Natives to die before they reach the age of 16 (*Toronto Star*, 29 November, 1986: G8).

Native adolescents, aged 10–14, commit suicide at a rate that is almost nine times the national average (Muir, 1985: 27). Among 15–24 year-olds the suicide rate is five to seven times the national average (Muir, 1985). The incidence of violent and accidental deaths which are often related to substance abuse is also exceptionally high (cf. Young, 1979; Shkilnyk, 1985; Jarvis *et al*, 1982). From 75–90% of all childhood and adolescent deaths result from accidents and violence. It is estimated that 70% of suicides, 80% of homicides, 52% of motor vehicle accidents and 54% of other accidents are alcohol related (ibid.)

Native rates of alcohol abuse vary dramatically from community to community; it is estimated that 50–80% of some adult Indian populations have alcohol related problems (Heidenrich, cited in Merskey *et al*, 1986: 46). But in the absence of a single, generally excepted definition of alcoholism it is impossible to suggest that, overall, Indian alcoholism rates are higher than in comparable non-Native populations (Leland, 1976; Muir, 1985: 130; Warry, 1987). Factors associated with substance abuse include physical and geographic isolation, unemployment, and lack of recreational opportunities: common features of northern communities in general, and Native communities in particular.

Reliable statistics on substance abuse among Native children and youth are unavailable. However, solvent abuse, including gas sniffing, is generally regarded as a significant problem in many Native communities. According to reliable informants, this problem is of epidemic proportions, involving 30–40% of all Native youth living on particular northern reserves. Solvent and inhalant abuse is learned behaviour: parental patterns of substance abuse are passed to younger generations. Solvent abuse is a temporary substitute for alcohol; but early reliance on solvents also pre-conditions Native youth to lead lifestyles that rely heavily on the use of alcohol to obtain rapid, severe states of intoxication.

Patterns of Native substance abuse are highly influenced by social and cultural factors (see Leland, 1976; Westermeyer and Neider, 1984; Westermeyer and Peake, 1983). A loss of cultural esteem is often at the heart of Native alcohol abuse, and culturally appropriate programs emphasizing traditional Native values are the most successful treatment strategy (Warry, 1987).

Generally, information concerning the physical, sexual or emotional abuse of Native children is lacking, but according to several studies Native child abuse rates are lower than national American or Canadian averages (see Yates, 1987: 1136; Painter, 1986; Leung and Carter, 1983; Duguay, Williams and Associates, 1988). The issue of sexual abuse, however, is a sensitive one which has only recently been discussed openly in Native communities. Family violence is a well recognized, if little researched, problem in many Native communities. The physical neglect of children is often attributable to highly stressful family environments resulting from a combination of social and health conditions.

Native youth also experience legal conflicts at an early age. From Saskatchewan comes the shocking information that an Indian boy turning 16 in 1976 had a 70% chance of at least one stay in prison by the age of 25. For Métis males, the figure was 34%, for non-Native boys, only 8% (Hylton, 1983). Comparable figures are unavailable for Ontario, but Native admissions in the 16–25 age range account for almost half of male admissions and 44% of female admissions to Ontario Correctional facilities (Asbury, 1986: 25). A third of Native adults incarcerated were first convicted as juveniles—the first conviction on average occurring at 16.5 years. Children between the ages of 7–11 represent a high risk category with conflict rates eight times greater than non-Indian youth (Jolly, 1983).

A general pattern of potential risk emerges from these figures which includes a variety of health problems during infancy and a great risk of early childhood death through illness or accidents related to impoverished socio-economic environments. As Native children mature, physical health problems decrease somewhat, only to be displaced by a variety of mental health problems. Exceptionally poor educational and employment opportunities, and a cross-generational susceptibility to various forms of substance abuse, combine with poor social conditions to make for teenage years where violence against both self and others all too often ends in conflict with the law, suicide or "accidental" death.

These statistics reveal a picture of Native children as perhaps the single most disadvantaged group in Canadian society. On the basis of need alone, Native children and families constitute a unique population for policy research. However, the recognition of the Native children's distinct needs is also premised on the inherent rights and sovereignty of First Nations.

First Nations: Self-Determination

Given the nature and context of the problems cited, improvements in the health and welfare of Native children can only be accomplished by improving the total environment of Indian people and by attacking the underlying conditions which lead to social and medical problems: poverty, poor housing, lack of clean water, inadequate sewage and garbage disposal and poor diet (cf. Penner, 1983: 33). The need for major, self-sustaining, economic development at the reserve level is central to the re-vitalization of Native communities. Such development will be enhanced by the resolution of outstanding land claims and with shared decision-making in the management of natural resources. The enormous complexities involved in the search for such changes are clearly illustrated in the recent breakdown in negotiations between the Teme-Augama Anishnabi and the Provincial government concerning the development of the Wakimika Stewardship Council in the Temagami wilderness area. Solutions, therefore, lie fundamentally in the political realm with the exercise of the inherent rights of aboriginal people—rights that First Nations maintain have been neither extinguished nor surrendered through existing treaties.

The problems that Native youth face do not solely stem from poor socio-economic conditions but are directly attributable to low individual and cultural esteem which is produced when individuals and communities are unable to control their future. Psychologists have used such concepts as "learned helplessness" and "acculturative stress," to explain a variety of Native mental health problems. Native professionals, well versed in colonial history, more properly describe these psychological conditions as resulting from "internalized oppression", the psycho-social process whereby individual Natives internalize the collective experience of colonization and experience feelings of powerlessness, low cultural esteem and poor self-image.

The goal of self-determination, in concert with its political counterpart self-government, involves the recognition of inherent and sovereign rights. It encompasses political control, rather than simple administrative authority over community affairs. The control and ownership of intellectual property, as well as natural resources, is intrinsic to this process. At an individual level, Native control over community development reinforces personal esteem and cultural identity and potentially addresses the root cause of psychological and behavioural problems that Native families and youth experience. The concept of self-determination, therefore, remains integrally connected to the social, physical and mental health of individuals and Native communities as a whole.

The idea of self-determination has been legitimized in The Report by the Special Committee of the House of Commons on Indian Self-government (the Penner Report), which identified child welfare and health care as areas of "critical concern." Since this report was tabled, a series of constitutional conferences between First Ministers and representatives of Native political organizations focusing on the entrenchment of the right to aboriginal self-government in the Canadian Constitution have occurred. The last conference, held in March 1987, ended without a federal-provincial accord and with no provision for future conferences.

From a Native perspective, the failure of these negotiations resulted from government intransigence created, indirectly or directly, by an influential "foundation policy" as represented by the Nielsen report—a policy which was, at its best, antithetical to the position of Native political organizations, and at its worst, a hidden agenda for assimilation (see Weaver, 1986a, 1986b; Erasmus, 1986). Constitutionally, therefore, the issue of self-government is "on hold." Native political organizations continue to insist on the entrenchment of a self-government provision before proceeding to define, in detail, individual models of self-government that may be appropriate to individual First Nations. The federal government, and a majority of provinces, while supporting the principle of self-determination, seek clarification of the precise nature of self-government before agreeing to entrenchment, and argue for a degree of political authority similar to that exercised by municipalities.

The Ontario government has supported amendments to the Constitution recognizing aboriginal self-government where aboriginal rights are set out in negotiated agreements. The province has definite concerns about jurisdictional matters, about the potential provincial costs of any new initiatives in Native services, and about the potential for divergence in standards of service in Indian communities under any self-government model. Regarding social services, the province's current position is that Native specific services should be developed in response to the particular needs of Native people, and not in response to generally recognized rights to be exercised in any circumstance. For this reason, the province is attempting to coordinate the development of specific social agencies within existing provincial service networks—a policy approach which severely limits the nature of innovative solutions to Native problems.

The Ontario government has attempted to consult with Native people when drafting new legislation or policy; such was the case in the development of the CFSA. As yet, however, there is no coordinated working relationship between the Ontario Native Affairs Directorate and Native constituencies that would facilitate policy development with regard to self-government. Such a relationship need not compromise the trust relationship between Native people and the federal government. Whatever the shape of self-government, the province will have to establish linkages between policies operating in aboriginal institutions and those policies prevailing in the surrounding environment. Without a commitment toward a coordinated policy-making approach a variety of Native-specific initiatives, such as those recommended in the SARC report, will fail to be realized.

The current stalemate in constitutional negotiations is related to the potentially sweeping implications—and financial costs—associated with constitutional entrenchment of an undefined concept. Until recently, the concept of self-government remained, in the words of Weaver, at the level of a "value notion" (1984). The ultimate nature and cost of self-government is unquestionably vague.

The potential parameters of Native self-government, however, are exceptionally clear, and have been defined by many studies. The Penner Report recommends that First Nations governments be granted authority to legislate in areas such as social and cultural development, resource use, family relations, law, revenue raising and economic development. The Ontario Métis and Aboriginal Association has recently ratified an agenda for tripartite negotiations concerning off-reserve Natives. The jurisdictional menu for their constituents includes a number of specific provisions, including control over medical clinics, hospitals and educational institutions; the formal recognition of traditional curricula; and the integration and recognition of traditional medicine into the Ontario Health Insurance Plan (OMMA, 1988: 95–96).

Two recent reviews, one by the Canadian Bar Association concerning the judicial system, and another by the Ontario Social Assistance Review Committee call for major changes in line with Native perspectives on self-government (Jackson, 1988; *Transitions*, 1988). The authors of *Transitions* eloquently argue for a transfer of legislative control over a variety of social programs to aboriginal government. Noting the groundwork provided by two earlier tripartite working group reports (MCSS, 1979, 1980), they restate the need for a three stage implementation process:

> The first step would be more flexible interpretation of the Indian Welfare Agreement and existing provincial social assistance legislation. The next step suggested was the adaptation of provincial legislation to meet the needs and requirements of Native communities. The final step involved constitutional recognition of the self-governing rights and powers of Indian bands. (*Transitions*, 1988: 441)

Self-government entails the dismantling of the Indian Act and, concurrently, the development of a wide range of new Native legislation. The development of appropriate Native child welfare laws (similar to one existing in the United States), or other forms of social welfare legislation would enable bands to assume direct control and jurisdiction over child welfare matters. (The Spallumchean Band in British Columbia has declared its jurisdiction over child and family services by passing a Band By-Law; its constitutional legality, however, has not been tested; see DIAND, 1987a: 51–58; Wharf, 1989).

For many federal and provincial policy makers, the concept of self-government remains a radical notion. Bureaucrats insist on legislative fine tuning, even as Indian organizations call for fundamental structural change. The politics of incrementalism, prevalent in government circles, serve as a barrier to the development of innovative policy initiatives which would propel the self-government process along its inevitable course.

What is not needed, for example, are policies that make the justice system more "responsive to the needs of Native and visible minority youth"—a statement that fails to recognize Native people on the basis of their inherent rights (see LaPrairie, cited in Bala this volume). Rather, what is required are policies and enabling legislation that allow Native control of legal services, correctional services and the development of a parallel or alternative court system (Jackson, 1988).

The cause of self-government is not advanced by interpreting existing legislation in the light of the unique needs of Native communities. Rather, what is required are policies that proceed from a philosophical base that is in line with the notion of self-government. Such policies must be developed in full consultation with Native communities, or preferably, by Native policy makers. Further, control over research, development and program evaluation must be vested in Native communities.

Native leaders are realistic in their expectations concerning self-government. They realize that constitutional entrenchment of the right to self-government will require much further negotiation, and that years of tripartite negotiations must occur before the implementation of fully self-sustaining institutions is possible.

As the SARC review notes, the province could potentially take a lead role in the self-government process by developing new legislation directed at Native communities, and by giving Native people greater discretionary powers to design and deliver social programs (*Transitions*: 445). The province, while recognizing its legislative authority, could begin to respond to the philosophical demands of First Nations in drafting legislation that includes non-derogation clauses and recognizes the long-term objectives of the self-government process.

Pragmatically, little can be accomplished unless Native people maximize their involvement in all phases of social reform, from research to the drafting of legislation. The development of appropriate services will also require a concomitant financial commitment to Native political organizations and social agencies to facilitate research and policy development at the local level. In short, the current atmosphere and bureaucratic relations between Native and government organizations must be modified to enhance the policy making process. Such a commitment must be accompanied by greater coordination between federal and provincial ministries so as to improve the search for holistic solutions to Native problems. Obviously, multi-faceted approaches are required to solve the systemic problems faced by Native communities. Given this premise, it is possible now to review two specific policy areas, and to suggest how holistic approaches to Native child welfare and health might serve as incipient models for Native self-government.

Native Child and Family Services

Despite major improvements in the child welfare system during the past decade, Ontario Native children continue to be placed in care at a rate four times the non-Native rate (DIAND, 1987a: 14–15). This trend reflects the continuing intervention of Children's Aid Societies—a trend only now beginning to reverse. The percentage of Native children in care has decreased during the past eight years, in part due to the development of Native child and family services and to closer cooperation between non-Native CAS agencies and Native communities. The numbers of Native placements could be further increased, but the current Ministry of Community and Social Service guidelines for foster care placements, when literally interpreted, designate First Nations houses and amenities as inadequate. Obviously new foster care standards must be developed to respond more effectively to Native needs and to reserve conditions (MCSS, 1985: 18–19, Appendix D).

Native child apprehensions by outside agencies, or, conversely, the repatriation of Native children to their home communities, epitomizes the need for Native control over child welfare laws. Interventions by Children's Aid Societies have fragmented, rather than reinforced, Native family life. The apprehension of Native children has had the cumulative effect of eroding the notion that Indian communities have a right to determine their own membership (AFN, 1988).

What has been termed "Native child abuse by the child welfare system" has been well documented by many authors (Bagley, 1984, 1985; Andres, 1981;

Hudson and McKenzie, 1981; Homenuck *et al.*, 1984; Johnson, 1983; Sullivan, 1985). When removed from their communities, Native children are at great risk. Indian culture must be experienced by the child: it can not be learned second hand from well-meaning, non-Native parents. As Nelson and Kelly note, courts have proceeded from a CAS perspective: agencies have had to demonstrate only parental neglect, but have not had to prove that the apprehending authority could do a better job in raising the children (1984: 1) Child welfare advocates now recognize that non-Native CAS workers often remain ignorant of Native culture, misinterpret Indian childrearing practices or fail to recognize the significance of the extended family and community. Native children, reared away from their home communities, lose touch with their cultural background and, as a result, often experience extreme emotional and psychological distress as young adults (see Novosedlik, 1983; Homenuck *et al.*, 1984; Ross, B., 1983; Johnson 1983). The apprehension of Native children negatively affects the emotional, spiritual and cultural health of the extended family and community by reinforcing a sense of collective powerlessness. Loss of children to placement may lead to poor parenting skills, a fear of emotional attachments and increased use of alcohol by members of the extended family (Homenuck *et al.*, 1984).

Non-Native models of child abuse and neglect stress individual pathology. Life histories of abusive parents are often gathered, as are psychological and emotional characteristics of neglectful adults.

> Intervention with Native Canadians shows a distinct pattern and is distinctively different from that with non-Native groups. Native people come into contact with the CAS, less as a result of direct physical abuse by a care-giver, than as a result of neglect and self abuse (Wichlacz and Kempe, 1978).

Homberg states that neglected Native children are often "technically abandoned by intoxicated parents" (1984: 60) and cites a number of personal characteristics of the abusing Native parent, including low self-esteem and poor parenting skills.

In addition to ignoring the social and environmental factors that contribute to child neglect or abuse, non-Native child welfare practices remain rigidly focused on the nuclear family. The extended family or wider Native community is peripheral to a view of child welfare that is parent focused.

These old style, often clinical, models of neglect ignore larger sociological and historical forces. Native people do not deny that low self-esteem, poor parenting skills, or alcoholism are contributing factors to child neglect. Nor do they deny that abusive parents may have themselves suffered from childhood neglect. But Indian models of child abuse stress social and institutional processes originating outside the individual and community (Metcalf, 1978: 4–12). Loucks and Timothy provide an historical perspective on Indian child welfare:

> The systematic destruction of the Native family through the residential school system separated parents from children, broke down the extended family and created a generation of people who never had the opportunity to learn parenting skills ... The unavailability of appropriate social services, both on and off reserve (i.e. personal and family counselling, alcohol and drug abuse programs,

etc.) has created a situation in which Native family life has been allowed to deteriorate ... (1981: 13–14).

Native child apprehensions, therefore, stem in part from non-Native attitudes toward Indian social and environmental conditions and a misunderstanding of the structure of Native communities. This point is diacritical in that it provides the moral justification for the "protection" of Native children: protection against an allegedly destructive environment that impedes the socialization of children and adolescents. Outsiders often fail to recognize that a sense of community spirit remains fundamentally intact despite undeniable problems existing both on and off reserve (Nelson and Kelly, 1984: 12).

This sense of community begins with the extended family. It includes what Nelson and Kelly call a social network of caring helpers who have the child's best interest at heart and who bring community resources to bear on the needs of children who are at risk. Government policy must continue to encourage research into child care practices within Native communities. The development of pilot programs that could lead to the implementation of "customary care" systems is long overdue. Such programs could be used to develop appropriate guidelines for such complex issues as the financial subsidization of customary care relationships according to local practice (see Homenuck et al, 1984: 96–104; Ross, 1988).

In 1961, 65% of adopted Indian children were cared for by registered Indian parents. By 1970–73 this figure had dropped to between 13–16%; by 1981 it had risen again to 27.3%. In other words, almost three-quarters of status Indian children who are adopted are adopted by non-Indian parents. The status of adopted Indian children is subject to legal debate. Status Indian children retain their status under federal law, even if adopted by a non-Indian family. Adoption by non-Indian parents under provincial law has the effect of interfering with the child's rights under federal law (Rhys Jones, 1986: 15). The federal government is currently preparing for negotiations on Native "management" of child welfare services, but to date has refused to provide funds to Indian organizations to locate adopted Indian children (AFN, 1988). Provincially, the identification of Native adoptees, particularly those living off-reserve, who may be entitled to band status raises complex jurisdictional problems. Although Bands have the right to determine their membership under the Indian Act, provincial legislation concerning the disclosure of adoption information continues to limit a Band's ability to identify prospective members. Nor does provincial legislation place any onus on non-Native agencies to inform Indian adoptees of their eligibility for Band status under the Indian Act (see MCSS, 1987).

Homenuck notes that the legal concept of adoption as terminal and irreversible has no counterpart in Indian culture and language (1984: 102). The development of truly Native child and family services can only be based on traditional values which can be reflected and codified in Native child welfare legislation. Research which is designed to document and explain Native traditional concepts as a prelude to the development of appropriate child welfare legislation must be a priority.

Customary care is recognized under Section 194 and 195 of the CFSA, but remains an ill-defined concept. The Ministry of Community and Social Services adheres to a much more restricted definition of "customary care" than that held by Native organizations. The question of subsidies under the Act is permissive, not obligatory, and Bands, according to Rhys Jones (1985: 18) can expect MCSS policies to assert the need for screening before granting subsidies. Likewise, the government requires that customary care arrangements be consistent with the foster allowance rate under the Family Benefits Act and the General Welfare Assistance Act (MCSS, 1987: 28–29). This is but one example of "restricted control" which will continue to plague Indian communities unless federal enabling legislation is passed to allow Indian agencies to operate autonomously outside provincial legislation (see AFN, 1988; Ross, 1988; Rhys Jones, 1985).

There are six Indian Child and Family Service Agencies in Ontario: two located in cities (Thunder Bay and Toronto), the remaining four serving communities in northern Ontario. To date, organizations representing southern reserves have chosen not to develop agencies under provincial legislation. Consequently, intervention by CAS agencies continues to pose problems for southern reserves, and for a large number of urban Native communities. The provincial government has refused to designate Indian communities off reserve even though this is possible under Part X of the Act. The Ministry maintains this section was included only to cover a small number of northern communities that have since been recognized as having Band status by the federal government. The Ontario Métis and Aboriginal Association, in contrast, has proposed the designation of regional Native communities encompassing the entire province, with a Native child and family service authority in each (Rhys Jones, 1986: 17; OMAA, 1988). Thus, the government accepts that, where numbers warrant, special Native services are needed in off-reserve settings and has, for example, agreed to fund the development of Native Child and Family Service in Toronto. But the province is unprepared to recognize that urban based agencies represent a particular Native community and are acting on their behalf in providing such services.

The development of Native child care agencies in urban centres has been identified as a special priority by Native women (NWAC, 1986); one that remains peripheral to recent federal child care initiatives. As previously stated, single mothers are a special subgroup within the city. There is an essential need for affordable, culturally appropriate day care facilities that would allow Native women to pursue employment while protecting their children's culture and language.

Northern Native Child and Family Service agencies vary in terms of local autonomy, and as yet, have not assumed full statutory control for the protection and adoption of children. The emphasis on prevention and community development also varies markedly in the priorities set variously by Native agencies and communities (see *DIAND*, 1987a: and DEL, 1985, for summaries of these organizations).

Native agencies seek federal delegation of authority and envision a range of holistic services that are beyond the Child and Family Services Act (*DIAND*, 1987a: 22–24; see also Wharf, 1989). The concept of customary care, for example, is a holistic one, encompassing not only child protection but also strategies for education in traditional skills and knowledge. The provision of culturally appropriate child care facilities, both on and off reserve, which would incorporate language and cultural instruction, is an important aspect of such a holistic delivery model, as is the development of parenting and recreational programs (OFIFC, 1983; NWAC, 1986).

Native organizations are unanimous in stressing the progressive nature of the Child and Family Services Act. The CFSA is an example of leading legislation that might potentially advance Native aspirations. However, Native service providers note that despite the Act's Indian-specific provisions, the government has not moved to develop policy initiatives that would add impetus to the development of truly holistic services for Native communities. Many Native professionals increasingly feel as if they are brown faces locked in white institutions as they are forced by ministry guidelines into traditional CAS service models. As a result, they express concern that they are distanced from the needs and aspirations of the communities they are attempting to serve. For instance, Native agencies have mandates that naturally restrict them from tackling the problem of youth substance abuse. Counselling services funded by the Medical Services Branch under the National Native Alcohol and Drug Abuse Program (NNADAP) focus on adult alcoholics. Youth prevention programs are nowhere to be found. Native youth, and their substance abuse problems, remain totally unaddressed: for example, in the Fort Francis-Rainey River area (serviced by Wee-chi-it-te-win Child and Family Services), there is not a single worker offering counselling, substance abuse programming, or health promotion for Native youth.

Section 206 of the CFSA permits the Lieutenant Governor in Council to exempt an Indian agency, Band or Bands from the CFSA and thereby affords the government the opportunity to proceed with policies that could produce community-based child welfare models. This section could also be used to assist bands in moving beyond delegated authority to produce legislation in the child welfare area. However, the Ministry is awaiting the conclusion of negotiations concerning self-government before proceeding in these areas. The government is also concerned about the potentially precedent setting implications of holistic service models for non-Native CAS agencies throughout the province. This attitude is indicative of the incrementalist approach and points out the difficulties faced by First Nations in attempting to convince governments of the need for innovative and creative solutions to problems confronting Native children and families at the community level.

Federal and provincial policies which recognize and encourage the development of community-based approaches to Native child problems must be considered a priority for the 1990s. In addition to current CAS activities, a truly Native child welfare agency would include a variety of preventive programs, including family counselling, parenting skills, crisis intervention, substance abuse programs, child care, and early childhood education in culture and language. Guided by a council of Elders and administered through a social services board linked to Band or Tribal councils, such transitional agencies could ultimately prove to be a model for Native controlled services that would operate under child care procedures and guidelines that were community based, and supported by First Nations legislation.

Child Health Care: Holistic Approaches

Holistic approaches to health care contain two separate and related conceptual strands. First, according to traditional Indian health beliefs, the pathology of individual illnesses result from an imbalance in a person's mental, physical, emotional, and spiritual states. Native concepts of "disease" emphasize the functional unity of body and mind (see Lane *et al*, 1984a; 1984b; Hagey, 1984; Jilek, 1982; Warry, 1987). The separation of physical and mental health issues, is, therefore, distinctly non-Native. Second, the provision of health care to Native communities necessarily implies a commitment to community health.

Much knowledge of traditional Indian health practices has been lost as a generation of Indian students have been educated in southern institutions (Gibson, 1988: 115). Still, Native healers continue to practice in many communities, usually without support from the medical establishment. Increasingly, medical researchers are recognizing the efficacy of traditional medical interventions which include, for example, the use of Native ceremonial practices as part of the treatment process (Jilek, 1982). Despite the presence of a Native Healers Program at Lake Of the Woods Hospital in Kenora, Ontario lags behind other provinces in encouraging the use of traditional Indian health practices. Elsewhere, Indian healers and Native medical interpreters have been successfully used in conjunction with, or as an alternative to, orthodox medical treatments, in reserve settings and in urban-based hospitals (Gregory, 1988; Hanson, 1988; O'Neil, 1988; McCormick, 1988).

The link between individual and community health has also been well established. Problems such as teenage solvent abuse, suicide, or family violence do not simply result from chronic unemployment and poverty, but also stem from feelings of powerlessness and cultural dislocation. Many Native communities suffer from an inability to act on their own behalf: a kind of collective paralysis which has been imposed by outside forces. Community development and empowerment, therefore, are central components of any child health care strategy. Policy makers must recognize that lasting improvements in Native children's health will require a concentrated effort in the environmental health field. Specifically, the government must commit itself to a concerted effort to improve basic services such as water and sanitation,—an effort which is in line with existing provincial and federal policy but has as yet been accompanied by a realistic financial commitment.

The small size of Indian reserves, and their kin-based structure, creates a unique health environment. Solvent abuse, suicide or family violence have communal causes and consequences. Studies of psychiatric problems in Indian communities have shown that individual acts can have damaging fallout for a wide network of family and friends (Berlin, 1985; Ward and Fox, 1977; Timpson, 1983). Anniversaries of suicides become major events, marked and remembered by community members (Long, 1986). Individual suicides, or attempted suicides produce a ripple effect and generate further attempts and suicide epidemics among adolescents. Such was the case at Grassy Narrows during the mid-seventies when violent death, conflict with the law and attempted suicide became normative behaviour (Shkilnyk, 1985: 13–14; see also Timpson, 1983).

Such behaviours must be viewed within the context of community pathology. The same forces that generate suicide epidemics or endemic mental health problems among youth, if properly harnessed, can be used to prevent alcohol abuse, risk taking and other socially disruptive behaviours (Lane, 1986). It makes no sense to institutionalize, or to incarcerate, an abusive teenager without addressing the underlying issue of the youth's familial or community environment.

A wide range of American and Canadian studies attest to the efficacy of preventive health approaches which contain community development and health promotion as central components (see Mayfield and Davies, 1984: Berlin, 1985; Gilchrist, 1987; Long, 1986; Schinke, 1986). Holistic child health programs must begin with pre-natal care and include nutritional and substance abuse education. Proven preventive approaches to Native child health care are based on integrated approaches to health education: parenting and infant stimulation programs, immunization, early detection of developmental delays, as well as child care programs that include culture and Native language instruction (Mayfield and Davies, 1984).

The long-term needs of Native youth will only be met through the development of culturally appropriate educational curricula and through the provision of meaningful employment opportunities. The more immediate needs of Native youth are tragically apparent: programs are required to enhance life skills, to prevent teenage suicide and substance abuse and to improve recreational programming. Clearly, there is a need for specialized and culturally appropriate mental health intervention among Native youth. A wide range of Canadian and American studies clearly demonstrate that cultural differences in child rearing, responses to anxiety and peer pressure, and the psychological and behavioural dislocation that results from "acculturative stress", produce a uniquely Native pattern of mental illness (see Angel, 1987; Brant, 1983; Berlin, 1985, 1982; Canadian Psychiatric Association, 1988; Yates, 1986). These mental health problems will require culturally appropriate measures to assess and diagnose Native adolescents (see Borzeki et al, 1988; Homenuck et al. et al, 1984: 22–27; Schinke et al, 1986; Warry, 1987). In the absence of such solutions, inappropriate, and often traumatizing institutionalization of Native youth will continue to occur.

Youth cultural programs emphasizing traditional skills such as hunting, trapping and spiritual awareness have already proven to be successful (see for example, Gilchrist, 1987; Berlin, 1985). There is also a dire need for community-based crime prevention programs, and, for youth who will for the foreseeable future continue to transgress community norms, alternatives to incarceration (Havemann et al, 1985; Clarke, 1987; Jackson, 1988).

From a community perspective, programs involving peer counselling, family therapies and communal grieving are needed to address the enormous impact of community pathology evidenced by family violence, suicide and alcohol abuse. The development and coordination of these program initiatives can only take place within a policy framework which is sensitive to the concept of holistic models of Native health.

These issues are not confined to rural or remote communities. As previously mentioned, the stresses associated with living in urban centres are accompanied by a range of health problems among urban Natives. Given the reluctance of urban Natives to utilize many non-Native social and medical services, the development of Native controlled health centres that include community health promotion, alcohol counselling and referral should be a priority (see Maidman, 1981). Provincial and municipal governments have recently demonstrated willingness to proceed with the funding of one such centre, Anishnawbe Health Services, in Toronto. Medical Services Branch is also funding the development of Native alcohol treatment centres, located on-reserve but proximate to major towns and cities. The need for culturally appropriate programs off-reserve must be guided by a recognition that the Native cultural values and ways often remain uncontaminated and uncompromised by the urban milieu (see for example, McCaskill, 1984, 1981). The development of Native urban health centres must be coordinated through provincial policies which recognize the viability of traditional health practices for urban settings.

The funding of such innovative programs will necessarily take place within an atmosphere of severe financial restraint. Policies will also have to be developed in face of an ethnocentric medical system which continues to be dominated by an acute care mentality emphasizing clinical interventions by highly specialized professionals rather than prevention and health promotion.

Native organizations are, of course, committed to improving the quality of acute care in their communities through the development of Native controlled medical clinics. Improvements in acute care are dependent on the development of long-term policies that will attract doctors, psychiatrists and other specialized professionals to work in Native communities. The shortage of doctors is especially acute in Northern Ontario where doctor-patient ratios are well below World Health Organization standards (McNeill and Nelson, 1988). Concomitantly, Medical Services Branch must also encourage the recruitment and training of Native health practitioners. The lack of trained Native practitioners remains an overwhelming obstacle to the delivery of appropriate health care on reserve. Preventive programs can only be developed through the adequate training and funding of Native infant care workers and/or prevention workers. As Weller notes, policy makers must begin to encourage the development of training models based on local needs (1988: 148). The Union of Ontario Indians and the Association of Iroquois and Allied Indians, in collaboration with two community colleges, have developed one such accredited program for Community Health Representatives, based on a distance education model. In addition, future provincial policies should include special provisions to increase access of Native people into regular programs—programs not only geared to health related professions but to the administration of health services (ibid.: 148). The development of adequate training models will inevitably produce tensions between academic priorities and community expectations concerning the educational requirements of health professionals or paraprofessionals (Castellano et al, 1986: 176). But Native political leaders, in part because of their experiences with social workers and other academically trained professionals, now demand a degree of participation in academic planning processes (ibid.).

Given the lack of Native health professionals, interim policies must be developed to improve primary health care and the use of Native paraprofessionals in local communities. Appropriately trained paraprofessionals, such as Community Health Representatives, NNADAP workers and medical interpreters, in addition to providing preventive services, ensure coordination of non-Native services on reserves and can be instrumental in breaking down the cultural barriers which lead to misdiagnosis, inappropriate treatment and referrals (see Castellano, 1982, 1986; O'Neil, 1988).

Community-based health and mental health workers effectively prevent a range of problems while consuming a smaller percentage of resources and servicing large populations (Sarsfield, 1988: 125; Timpson, 1984). To date, government policies have reflected the attitudes of a highly orthodox establishment and have tended to de-value the role of paraprofessional programs; the result has been a lack of financial commitment for salaries, training and program evaluation for frontline health workers in Native communities.

This medical colonialism is nowhere more evident than on northern reserves which continue to be serviced by urban-based institutions located, in many instances, in southern Ontario. The inappropriateness—and inherent fiscal limitations—entailed in providing psychiatric care, outreach services, or medical training for remote Cree and Ojibway communities from Toronto, Hamilton and London would seem to be obvious. But provincial policy has perpetuated just such a southern bias (Wellar and Manga, 1988; see also Armstrong, 1978; Timpson, 1984). The creation of innovative solutions to the complex health problems of Native people will only be accomplished through the creation to regional health care systems as advocated by Weller and Manga (1988) and by the establishment of community health planning, management and evaluation at the reserve level.

If Indians are to achieve substantive participation in the policy process they need to seek ways of breaking through the exclusiveness which has characterized the Medical Services bureaucracy where administrative interpretation, budget planning and program evaluation take place. (Castellano, 1982: 118)

Ultimately, the challenge of securing the health of Native children rests with the Native community itself, with the devolution of power to First Nations and communities and with the identification of appropriate models of health care at the local level. Federal initiatives have begun in this regard with the funding of health care needs assessments under pre-transfer planning projects. But as Sarsfield notes, government notions concerning the devolution of health services do not necessarily translate into direct control (1988: 124). Sarsfield concludes with a statement consistent with the views expressed here.

If it is accepted that the main obstacles to the health of rural and remote communities are in fact social and political, not medical, then it becomes obvious that what is needed is social and political change. Specifically, communities must be given control of local budgets, as well as the right to hire and fire all employees, management of all local facilities, and institutions, ownership of regional traditional use lands, control of sub-surface resources, and the setting of policy in such areas as wildlife management and education. The right to control in all these areas is vital to community health, and if constitutional change is required to extend such rights to communities then this must be done (1988: 124–125).

Participatory Research: A Model for the 1990s

It remains only to discuss the shape of future policy research that is required to propel the self-determination process forward. Native people often state that their communities have been "researched to death". This statement is perhaps perplexing given the obvious need for further research on a variety of issues concerning the health and welfare of Native children and youth. But this "research lament" is easily understood within the self-determination context. Information is power, and Native people must demand the ownership and control of the research process in order to initiate meaningful change in their communities.

Until recently, Native people have had no control over the research process. A host of academics have entered Native communities to probe, prompt and prod Native people without directly consulting Native communities as to the purpose and implications of their work. Research findings, cloaked in jargon, have been unintelligible to communities or have been largely irrelevant to community needs. Academic reputations, so the argument goes, have been built on the backs of Native subjects and at the political and economic expense of Native communities.

Social research is an intrinsically political process; policy research, even more so, because it concerns alternative strategies for action which must be developed within a political arena where competition for scarce resources is an ongoing reality (van Willigen, 1986: 143–146). Native communities demand applied research that affords them the opportunity to develop strategies to address immediate and long-term goals. Ideally, Native communities must initiate research in order to identify local needs. Increasingly, communities are approaching Native and non-Native academics in order to initiate the research process.

> Although the community based pressure to produce "applied research" is increasing, the responsiveness of researchers and funding agencies to locally defined priorities still lags far behind (Sarsfield, 1988: 123).

When research is initiated outside the local community, Native people require researchers to consult with community leaders from the earliest stages of research design through to the public disclosure of findings.

The research model that has gained widespread acceptance as appropriate for Native communities has been called community-based, participatory research (see Castellano, 1986; Jackson, 1982; Price, 1987). This approach attempts not only to give Native communities control over the research process, but to produce a research environment that enables individuals to obtain skills in survey research, program development, and evaluation. Outside researchers become trainers and facilitators rather than isolated owners of what, from a community perspective, is esoteric knowledge. Native communities must also initiate research that is guided by a realistic awareness of government policy and planning procedures. Castellano states:

> Involvement in a participatory process of research and development will require that Indians acquire a number of specific skills. Information on particular features of community experience must be selected and organized to support new initiatives. Proposals must be written with pragmatic attention to the values, procedures and constraints which operate in the realm of bureaucracy and the public domain. The hopes and needs of the community must be interpreted in terms of specific goals, cost forecasts and projected outcomes. Evaluation must be applied as a tool for development, not evaded as a threat to program survival (1982: 125–126).

For participatory research to be effective, foundations, universities and government ministries must more closely communicate with Native political organizations and service providers. The development of research projects which are jointly undertaken by governments and aboriginal communities, according to mutually acceptable criteria, should provide an important information base for program initiatives at the local level. Policy formation is greatly enhanced by involving front line workers as key informants, or by designing programs that have information gathering as a key component of service delivery (see for example, Homenuck, 1984: 52).

As a minimum, participatory research provides the type of information that communities need to establish priorities for service development and to set appropriate measures for program evaluation. Optimally, participatory research enhances the community development process itself. Community members are brought together to share information, communal consensus is reached, and cooperative solutions to social or medical problems suggested. Throughout this process, skills are learned that enable Native people to take control over the future research and evaluation needs of their community.

Given that local communities must determine the context of community based research, it would be presumptuous and misplaced for me to suggest specific areas of research that should be pursued in the 1990s. However, several broad research areas, arising naturally as priorities from this discussion, can be outlined.

Customary Care. Research into traditional child-rearing practices and Native values has already begun (see Ross, 1988). Further investigation could serve as the basis for new program initiatives and pave the way for Native-appropriate child welfare legislation.

Environmental Health. Those involved in the documentation of the environmental conditions affecting the health of Native children should examine the prevalence of existing medical services, and physical and cultural reasons influencing utilization rates, as well as existing sanitation services, housing conditions, and recreational facilities.

Traditional Health Practices. Investigation of Native approaches to health care, traditional medicines, and the efficacy of traditional healing is required, as well as policy research to suggest methods for incorporating such practices into existing provincial health regulations. The development of community-based programs that attempt to integrate alternative and orthodox treatments of mental health problems faced by Native youth should be a priority.

Community Health Promotion and Prevention. A wide range of Native-specific health promotion and public education materials are needed. Specifically, there is a great need to disseminate more effectively, through the use of videos and Native language materials, information concerning preventive approaches to child and youth health care which have proven to be successful in particular communities.

Education. Appropriate training models for Native health care, and for child welfare practitioners and administrators must be developed. The development of distance education programs and accredited training programs for Native paraprofessionals should also be a priority. Culturally based curricula addressing such issues as substance abuse and suicide is also required.

Alternative Measures/Mental Health. There is a dire need for the funding of research and the development of community-based programs aimed at Native youth in conflict with the law. A variety of approaches, including community crime prevention and alternatives to incarceration, offer enormous potential. Such programs should be supported by the design of culturally appropriate assessment and treatment models that can be used by Native counsellors and mental health professionals. The development of both assessment and treatment techniques will require a commitment to longitudinal studies by Native practitioners and planners.

Evaluation Research. As a special area of research, policy makers should encourage and fund local communities to develop and evaluate holistic child and family service models. Specifically, government policies must be flexible enough to allow existing Native Child and Family Services to develop pilot projects or ongoing programs that are in keeping with locally determined needs. It is imperative that evaluation criteria be developed on the basis of Native values, and that service providers be allowed to evaluate new programs at arms length from bureaucrats responsible for the on-going administration of orthodox programs.

This is by no means an inclusive overview of potential research areas; obviously, the needs of Native communities, both urban and rural, are profound and varied. The development and evaluation of meaningful child health and welfare programs is dependent on sound information; the foundation required to establish such a data base are policies which recognize Native people's right to control the research process.

I have tried to convey some of the current realities and the sense of vision which must guide the development of policies concerning Native children and youth in the 1990s and beyond. The message, I believe, is clear: on the basis of need alone, Native families, youth and children have a legitimate claim to priority policy initiatives and applied research. The vision that is required to guide such policy and research is also clear. It derives from the recognition of the unique and inherent right of Native people to self-determination. It is a vision of the critical role that healthy and empowered Native families, youth and children have to play in the revitalization of First Nations.

THE PSYCHOSOCIAL NEEDS OF CHILDREN IN CARE
Policy Issues for the 1990's

David A. Wolfe and Peter Jaffe

This paper has the unique purpose of stimulating the thinking of professional groups and policy makers about children in care of the province. Our definition of children in care refers to children who come to the attention of our provincially mandated child welfare authorities (the Children's Aid Societies or Family & Children's Services) and are deemed by the provincial court (Family Division) to be in need of protection under the *Child and Family Services Act*. The extent to which these children enter the care of the state may vary from supervision within the home to temporary or crown wardship, in which the province becomes legal guardian on a temporary or permanent basis. The current paper addresses this population, with the recognition that children may also receive equally intrusive intervention by other systems (i.e., juvenile justice, mental health) on a voluntary or involuntary basis.

Much confusion presently exists between the needs and rights of children and families. The early, unseasoned view of alternative care was that the state was seen as providing benevolent interventions when families had failed. This view has been challenged more recently by the realization that not all interventions are beneficial and, in fact, can do more harm than good in some cases by introducing further victimization and disruption into the child's life.

This awareness of potential harm to the child has led to the development of an increasing focus on children's rights and some fundamental safeguards regarding their entry into the care of the state and ongoing review of the state's intervention. However, this shift in focus has lost its initial attractiveness because of the awareness that procedural complications may create delays or that a sequence of failed "least intrusive" measures may not be in the child's best interests.

The emerging policy questions relate to the need to strike a balance between the two related concerns of children's developmental needs and the state's responsibility to provide them with the least intrusive intervention. The real issue, in our opinion, is providing the most effective intervention for children at the right time and in the right place. Part of conceptualizing these policy questions requires an examination of key developmental periods for children and the extent to which current state interventions into the lives of children and families may be inappropriate to their level of development. To analyze this conflict one needs to review reasons for state interventions by each of the major systems that provide services to high-risk children and adolescents: the Child Welfare system, the Children's Mental Health System, and the Juvenile Justice system. The following chapter includes background and review of current policy and data related to children in care, a description of children in care in Ontario, and a detailed discussion of key policy issues that emerge from current theory and practice in the field of child welfare. We plan to look at a broad range of issues concerning the way children come into care and the way in which they are looked after.

BACKGROUND PHILOSOPHY AND INFORMATION REGARDING CHILDREN IN CARE

In July, 1982 the Social Services Committee in the British Parliament decided to undertake an inquiry into children and care. In so doing, they stated unequivocally the dual challenge facing policy makers:

> The state has an overriding responsibility to protect children and ensure satisfaction of their basic needs if those caring for them are failing to do so. In the exercise of that responsibility, the greatest caution has to be exercised. State intervention is a last resort. The state can never be a substitute for real parents. But when it is necessary, our communal responsibility to protect children must outweigh everything (House of Commons, 1984; p. xiv).

In a perfect world no children would be in care of the state. Every child would have his or her basic needs addressed by parents, an extended family system, and/or a caring community. However, the daily reality in North America falls short of this ideal for a sizeable proportion of our child population. Professionals who are agents of the province are mandated to find alternative care for children who are at risk in terms of abuse, neglect, serious emotional or behavioral disorders, or who engage in acts that threaten the safety of the community.

It would be naive to consider interventions by the state simply as beneficial or damaging. State intervention to remove children from their families is generally accepted in North America as an essential last resort for aiding children in families with major difficulties. Such action, however, presents several important dilemmas and policy concerns, such as:

- Are there underlying social and economic factors that need to be addressed in order to reduce the number of children coming into the care of the state?
- Can we properly identify those children who need, and would benefit from, alternative placement?
- What other types of interventions will maximize effectiveness and reduce further trauma and victimization?
- What are our minimal standards and expectations of caregivers for the appropriate care of children, and can these standards be developed in accordance with each community's norms and expectations?

- Is a child's removal from his/her home consistent with the values and perspectives of different cultural and ethnic groups?

In a recent paper, Garbarino (1988) suggested that a very fundamental question related to alternative care was society's view as to who holds the major responsibility for the care of children. On the one hand (according to the laws of Ontario), parents have full custody of their children and the state intervenes only in the event of an extreme violation or disruption in care. A more recent, and controversial, view posits that the family has custody but the community has visitation privileges to ensure that the family is looking after the needs of the child appropriately and/or to assist family members in their role (beyond a protective services supervision order). Further along the continuum, Garbarino suggests that the state and the family have "joint custody" of children, thereby sharing the fundamental responsibility of caring and providing for all children.

In view of the above, we need to reexamine our basic philosophy and policy concerning the welfare of children, as well as the role of the alternative care system and its ability to handle the expanding and increasingly ambiguous demands made on it.

A Description of Children in Care

Although much effort has gone into attempting to develop an adequate computerized information system on children receiving care from the province, the lack of consistent cooperation from local agencies has prevented such a system from being realized. In the preparation of this chapter, descriptive data relating to children in care and the services they received were limited. For example, information concerning how many children on any given day are not in the primary care of their parents and what types of problems they may be experiencing was largely unavailable. This issue is most apparent in reviewing the nature of foster placements across Ontario. Brian Raychaba, in his detailed analysis of the foster care system in Canada, reflected on the informational problems existing throughout this system: "At present, the inadequacy of child welfare data collection stands as a major impediment to effectively addressing the special needs of youth presently and formerly in care" (1988, p. 24). Although bits and pieces of information are available to suggest some patterns, the common data base and necessary classification system remains incomplete.

One notable exception to the general lack of comprehensive information about the children who are presently in care of the province of Ontario is the annual compilation of statistics prepared by the Ontario Association of Children's Aid Societies. Based on a recent summary of pertinent statistics (*The Future of Foster Care,* 1988), children in the care of the province of Ontario can be described as follows:

- 60% of the children in care reside in foster homes (a figure that appears to be relatively stable over years and across jurisdictions).
- 52% of the children in care as of June 30, 1987 were adolescents 13 years and older.

- the majority of elementary (55%) and secondary (61%) school children in care are behind one or more years in school.
- 48% of the children in care are described as having significant behavior problems.
- Based on a random sample of 150 cases across the province, the most common permanent plan for children in care was long-term substitute care (41.3%), followed by preparation for independence (23.3%), return to their own family (18.7%), assessment and stabilization (8.7%), or transfer to an adult facility (4.0%).

Number of Children per Service Category

Children come into the care of the state through a number of service systems. Children who are deemed to be in need of protection (under the Child and Family Services Act) enter through the child welfare system. Children who are experiencing emotional and/or behavioral problems may enter through the children's mental health system. Children between the ages of 12 and 18 years may enter through the correctional system as defined by the Young Offenders Act.

The most comprehensive study of prevalence of childhood disorders and service utilization in Ontario was completed by a team of researchers in the Department of Psychiatry at McMaster University in Hamilton (Boyle & Offord, 1988). The Ontario Child Health Study (OCHS) found that very few children across the province (1.13%) are actually in the care of the state. The majority of this sub-population of children (approximately 65%) are in the care of Children's Aid Societies. The other two systems (i.e. mental health and corrections) demonstrate a clear trend away from residential services. Children's mental health centres, which account for approximately 10% of those children in the care of the state, have 13 times as many children receiving non-residential counselling as they have residing in treatment centres. The same trend is apparent overall in the number of secure custody beds in the province, which declined from 1,563 training school beds in 1970 to 405 beds in 1982. The overall figure for secure custody beds in 1986–87 was 221 for young offenders 12 through 17 years of age. (Note: open custody appears to be an increasingly popular disposition, but there are no comprehensive statistics available that combine MCSS and MCS data; Sullivan & Colfer, 1988.)

There are several striking features of the OCHS data regarding children in care (after Boyle & Offord, 1988):

(1) The number of children receiving significant interventions by the state is very small in comparison to estimates of childhood psychiatric disorders in the population (1.13% versus 18.10%). Yet, as noted previously, a significant proportion (48%) of children in care have been described as displaying major problems in behavioral adjustment. It is becoming apparent that the foster care system assumes much of the responsibility for "treating" children's adjustment problems.

(2) Mental health, social service, and correctional interventions represent a very small percentage (6%) of specialized services requested for children. It is noteworthy that the number of children in care has actually *declined* by 20% between 1976 and 1986, despite the 46.3% *increase* in the number of children served in protection services over the same period of time (Child Advocacy Information System, cited in *The Future of Foster Care*, 1988). The major service providers for children are, in fact, special education professionals and family doctors.

(3) Although there are no significant differences amongst the four regions in the province for the prevalence of childhood disorders, there are major differences in the level of expenditures for children across the regions. That is, service delivery and the rationalization of funding are not consistent with the actual incidence of child behavior problems.

Are children in the care of the state different from those in the care of families?

Important questions emerge in the discussion of who is most likely to be placed into the alternative care of the state. That is, are children placed into care on the basis of a rational, consistent decision-making process, or on a more arbitrary basis according to circumstances that are unrelated to the level of need of their families? These questions remain problematic because case finders and decision makers (including judges) may vary quite significantly from one community to another. Despite the lack of careful record keeping, some general trends relating to who is admitted to care seem consistent from the literature and the experiences of children's services in Ontario:

(1) A great deal of variation in admitting to care appears to be related to the discrepancy amongst clinicians and other "gatekeepers" in terms of their perceived needs of children and their individual decision-making tendencies (MCSS, 1988).

(2) Alternatives to care are most likely to be considered when the resources are available to make such alternatives a meaningful choice.

(3) Courts are generally responsive to the kinds of assessment information and recommendations that are suggested in regard to children who are entering the care of the state (Sullivan & Colfer, 1988).

(4) There are consistent risk factors that, by themselves and in combination with others, seem to affect which children will enter the care of the state. These factors include poverty (i.e. being from a family on welfare), living in public housing, and children of single mothers (MCSS, 1988).

One glaring finding that emerges from these available data is that the choice of who is admitted to the care of the state is significantly driven by the resources possessed by each individual family in comparison to those resources that may be alternatively available in the community. Not surprisingly, children from families who lack the most in fundamental resources are those that are most likely to be seen as in need of placement. Furthermore, children and youth from poor families are twice as likely to return to care after being returned home on a trial basis and, thus, end up spending longer periods of time in care than do children from families with adequate income (Loo, 1972; cited in Raychaba, 1988). Yet, we have very little information at present as to whether the *children* in care (as opposed to their families of origin) demonstrate distinct needs and symptoms from the children who remain with their families. Decisions to place children into the care of the state often appear to be based on individual interpretations and predictions of each family's future direction and present resources, rather than on the basis of a more uniform, unbiased policy derived from empirical validation and equal opportunity (MCSS, 1988).

MAJOR POLICY ISSUES FOR CHILDREN IN CARE

The number of pressing issues in the field of child welfare is almost over-whelming, leading one to pause and think carefully about identifying a manage-able number of "key" issues. In reflecting on the above information, in conjunction with personal interviews and discussions with several experienced individuals familiar with the child welfare system in Ontario, we have identified five major areas of concern pertaining to policy formation. These areas corre-spond to: (1) decision-making and services surrounding the admission of chil-dren to care; (2) the provision of adequate services to children, parents, and foster parents after a child has been admitted to care; (3) the need to coordinate the different systems servicing multiproblem children and youth; (4) the prepara-tion of children who are leaving care (and the gap in services for 16–17 year-olds); and, (5) the growing need for research and evaluation of services.

Admission to Care: Decision-making and Child Support Services

Policies regarding the care and servicing of children in the care of the state could benefit from the following considerations:

Clarifying our community values and our prevention orientation

Some policy planners have been advocating the establishment of "minimum standards of care" for each community. Such standards would balance profes-sional expertise and knowledge, on the one hand, and community standards, values, and culture, on the other hand (e.g. Garbarino, 1988). Proponents of such an endeavour believe this information would provide a more well-defined guide-line for establishing what the minimum standards of care should be, and when state intervention is viewed by the community as a necessary step.

Similarly, policy planners need to look at the community's willingness to implement family support programs at a broad and more comprehensive level. Such programs are aimed at preventing the breakdown of families who require alternative care, and evidence is emerging as to their efficacy and impact on positive child and family development (e.g. Olds, Henderson, Chamberlain, &

Tatelbaum, 1986). Social scientists emphasize that social support systems are the mechanisms by which corrective measures for families are naturally provided, yet such systems may require deliberate planning and implementation to insure that families receive adequate nurturance and feedback on childrearing (Wolfe, 1987).

Determining who is most likely to be helped in care versus at home

The answer to this key policy issue can be determined on the basis of empirical findings, yet to date we have made little systematic effort to evaluate the impact of our services. Understanding who is most likely to benefit from care will maximize our future efforts to keep children out of care unnecessarily by allowing us to target early those families and children who are most "at-risk" of family breakdown.

One comprehensive U.S. study that addressed this crucial issue of whether maltreated children benefit more from foster care or from home care was recently reported by Wald, Carlsmith, & Leiderman (1988). By enlisting the cooperation of state and county protective service agencies, these researchers were able to compare children in two jurisdictions who had been placed in either home care or foster care. Children in one jurisdiction who qualified for foster care placement were matched with a comparable group of at-risk children in another jurisdiction who received home care services. The researchers assessed the children's development on a wide variety of measures, including physical development and health status, cognitive development, academic performance, emotional problems, social behavior, parent-child relations, and the child's satisfaction with self, peers, and school.

The results of this four-year investigation have important policy implications, while recognizing that additional studies must be conducted to generalize the findings to other jurisdictions. The authors found that improved services to families can help to keep abused and neglected children in their home residences, but not without significant costs. That is, children in both settings showed signs of emotional stress and adjustment difficulties that related to the dilemmas in their respective environments. At home, they had to deal with continuing family disorganization and conflict, and in foster care settings children had to confront disruption and adapt to a new family system. Therefore, the impact of either placement must be evaluated not only in terms of the children's personal safety but also in reference to their social, emotional, and intellectual development. In either home care or foster care these children require a high level of services for many years to cope with the trauma that they have experienced.

In their conclusions, Wald et al. (1988) state "The services cannot be short-term or inexpensive. In many instances, both the children and the family may require several years of assistance. Although we cannot be certain that new services will alleviate their problems, current efforts are not adequate" (p.200). One is left to speculate as to whether or not these findings would be the same for Ontario in 1990s.

Currently, our system functions on a principle of reaction (to crises and conflicts), and consequently little effort is directed toward the "front-end" of the child welfare system. Those families who are most in need often receive very little support and assistance until they commit a major violation of child care practices. Policy planning, therefore, needs to consider more seriously the possibility of building in a "two-tiered" system for aiding families. The first tier would consist of prevention activities and services for families aimed at assistance and education in child care issues, which would be expected to have a positive effect on the incidence of admitting children into care. The second tier would consist of the more familiar child welfare/protection efforts that are designed to ensure that community standards are upheld and children's needs are adequately met.

We also need to take a closer look at the available data on prevention derived from similar jurisdictions. The rising costs of foster care, the concern about the possible harmful effects of care, and the belief that some placements could be prevented add up to a demand for more adequately planned prevention activities. Our knowledge of families developed over the past three decades has confirmed that family problems tend to occur in patterns rather than randomly or in isolation. Typically, the functioning of family members is interrelated and tied to factors such as income and housing needs.

A recent study of 142 families with 243 "at-risk" children lends some insight into the interrelationship between the functioning of family members and the subsequent admission of children to care, and offers useful suggestions for the development of prevention policies. In "A Second Chance for Families," Jones (1987) reports on an early intervention effort in which families were provided with multiple services, including counselling, financial assistance, medical services, and help with housing problems. Children's entry into care could be significantly predicted among this sample on the basis of seven family background and family problems, such as mother or father's functioning, income and housing, and child health. The researcher further discovered that predisposing factors (i.e. those that increase the risk of entering foster care) tend to consist of family background characteristics (e.g. income, housing, etc.), whereas it was the family problems that precipitate the actual entry into care. The four major areas comprising these predisposing and precipitating factors included: (1) the unavailability of the mother; (2) limited backup resources; (3) problems in the child's functioning; and, (4) lateness of intervention. It would appear from these results that each of these factors signifies vulnerability for entry into care, and provides valuable clues to enhancing service effectiveness.

Because the mere presence of the parents (particularly the mother), and not the quality of their functioning per se, was the key to the child's remaining in the home, the author argues that just "being on the job," and not necessarily being very good at it, is an important resource for the child. Added to this factor is the importance of backup resources—such as social support, relatives, mother's education, and financial adequacy—that provide indirect assistance to the developing parent/child relationship.

Provision of Adequate Services to Children, Parents, and Foster Parents

Once a child has been admitted to care the state has a clear responsibility not only to the child who is admitted, but also to the child's family and to the alternative caregivers (usually foster parents) who will help to fulfill the state's mandate. Historically, it has been assumed that the services being offered by the state were preferable to the child's existing home care, and that a voluntary foster care program would suitably meet the demands on the system. Yet, there has been considerable attention in Ontario in recent years directed towards the "crisis in foster care," in reference to the lack of adequate compensation, training, and support provided to foster parents, and the general deficiency in the number of homes available throughout the province.

Moreover, considerable concern has been raised over the transiency of both social workers and foster home placements, an issue that was recently raised by youth delegates to a OACAS conference. As reported by Raychaba (1988), Ontario statistics for 1984 indicate that over 81% of Crown wards had gone through more than one worker, and almost half (48.7%) had over three (not including worker changes made prior to granting of Crown wardship). Similarly, Ontario figures reveal that over 34% of Crown wards had lived in three or more placements (*The Future of Foster Care*, 1988). It is often the exception, rather than the rule, when one finds a child who has remained in a stable placement throughout his/her wardship. Moving the child to another placement appears to be the most frequently chosen option for dealing with the "hard to serve" child or adolescent, an option that may be made more attractive due to the general lack of support and assistance made available to the social worker to address the child's needs effectively (e.g. current level of caseloads and professional development opportunities).

Several policy considerations arise from this discussion of improving services for children and families once the state has assumed responsibility:

How do we ensure continuity of care by the state?

The belief that early life experiences strongly influence subsequent adult functioning and vulnerability to psychopathology has been widely supported by empirical findings confirming the importance of early childhood attachment (for review, see Paterson & Moran, 1988). One of the major tenets of attachment theory is that once an attachment is established, the infant uses the parent as a secure base from which to explore and learn from the environment. The attachment system is inactive during low stress periods, but can become reactivated at any time—causing the infant to attempt to reestablish contact with the secure attachment figure. Considerable research has demonstrated the importance of this attachment process in the development of the child's cognitive and social competence. Early attachment is most clearly disrupted when no primary attachment figure is available or when the attachment figure becomes physically or psychologically unavailable.

In light of this important developmental process, our current policy of foster care needs to consider how its operation may be counter-productive in terms of ensuring the continuity of attachment figures for the child. Although children can have more than one attachment figure, they usually cannot thrive in an environment where such figures are inconsistently available or frequently changed. In clinical practice, we often see older children who would much prefer to live with the parent(s) they know or to whom they have a biological attachment than to live with a surrogate parent, despite the latter's greater availability and consistency. Accordingly, we must form a policy that is more in tune with the developmental needs of children at various ages. Similarly, we must recognize the long-term impact of placing a child with a foster parent without constant contact with the natural parent or attachment figure. Frequently the decision to place a child in temporary care can have ramifications that extend far beyond the immediate six-month plan, and our policy must be sensitive to this important issue.

Foster care is designed to be a temporary placement, yet researchers note that children too often remain in foster care until the age of majority (Tuma, 1989). This growing tendency for children to remain beyond the intended six-month period has been described as "foster care drift," in which temporary placements become permanent, without the benefit of suitable planning. This phenomenon has led to the promotion of permanency planning, which refers to the policy of taking prompt, decisive action that is aimed at either placing the children with a permanent foster family or maintaining him/her in the family with the provision of adequate services. With the growing acceptance of permanency planning, policy planners will need to design suitable evaluation studies to determine the long-range impact of this shift in foster care utilization.

Do we want a voluntary or a paraprofessional model of fostering?

One of the policy issues that emerges most clearly from the recent movement to improve services for children in care is how to redesign the foster care system more effectively. The recent research study commissioned by the OACAS, entitled *The Future of Foster Care* (1988) reported that the current foster care system in Ontario is moving from a voluntary to a professional model of service delivery "in a haphazard, uncoordinated way," without the benefit of policy planning or guidance. The report found that over half of the foster parents surveyed already considered themselves to be professionals. In addition, social workers tend to view the role of the foster parents as demanding a professional status, recognition, training, and benefits.

The foster care system was originally built on the premise that providing voluntary parent "surrogates" for children in the care of the state would be an inexpensive alternative to institutional care or no care at all. Moreover, such an approach was more in line with what developmental psychologists were discovering—positive family care, through its provision of attachment figures and emotional support, has a major impact on the child's developing cognitive, emotional, and behavioral abilities (Appathurai, Lowery, & Sullivan, 1986). Although the foster care system may have value to the "average" client, foster parents, foster children, and social workers alike are clamouring to upgrade the service in order to meet the needs of those children who are more difficult to serve and who often create the most stress on the existing system (*The Future of Foster Care*, 1988).

In parallel, a growing research consensus supports the "collegial" working relationship between foster parents and support staff, whereby foster parents are compensated for their role at a level that is more in line with the demands made on them (Appathurai et al., 1986). Clearly, to maintain the important role that foster parents are playing in providing a family environment for children we need to take a closer look at what changes can be made to attract and sustain their commitment. On the other hand, one can argue that extrinsic reward *alone* for such personal commitment may not be as straightforward as it appears - foster parenting will most likely continue to attract individuals who are *intrinsically* rewarded for their efforts. Policy planners, therefore, will need to address the question of how we define (and therefore attract, train, and compensate) the role of the foster parent.

Are we providing proper support and training to substitute caregivers?

Substitute care was intended to be an interim solution to family crisis. In conjunction with the removal of the child from the home, the state (through its representatives) plans for the needs of the child and family in order to reunite them as soon as possible. However, critics (e.g., House of Commons, 1984) have charged that the current policy does not adequately avoid the "trap" of allowing the child to remain in care beyond the stated goal. Due to many practical and realistic circumstances (such as heavy caseloads, lack of treatment services, changes in child or family member's behavior, etc.) the goals of fostering often have to be postponed and reassessed. However, many experts believe that six months in care (or less) should be set as a realistic target, and that fostering contracts should be prepared to specify the length and plans during the fostering agreement (House of Commons, 1984). Although such practices are familiar to many agencies, the extension of care beyond the desired goal is commonplace. Policy planners need to determine more realistically whether the state is providing the proper support and training necessary to avoid this trap of extended care.

In *The Future of Foster Care,* the investigators found that the foster children themselves raised several policy considerations that could have a bearing on the type of service being provided during the period of care. In particular, these children requested that agencies provide them with greater opportunity to play a meaningful part in their plan of care, to deal with their foster-care experience through greater peer support and worker contact, and to permit them to have greater "consumer input" into the system for the benefit of contributing productively to the foster-care program.

At a similar level the foster parents' reports indicated that agency support was variable (possibly across agencies)—only a third of the sample in the OACAS study were satisfied with such support. Many foster parents are fearful of child abuse allegations, and their increasing role confusion, expectations, and responsibilities point to the need for agencies to provide more clear job descriptions, training, evaluation, and feedback. Policy development, furthermore, should take note of the finding that foster parents who think of themselves more as partners or co-workers are more satisfied in their role.

As important as these above findings have been in helping to understand the "crisis in foster care" from the perspective of the foster child and the foster parent, it is noteworthy that the child's natural family members were not interviewed for their input. The child's parents may also be dissatisfied with the conditions or follow-through of the fostering agreement. Although a contract may be discussed and agreed upon, often the parents lack the resources, education, and support necessary to follow through realistically on the stated goals. Consequently, the fostering contract is extended and all parties involved feel betrayed, disappointed, or angry. In some cases, the only "intervention" for the child's family of origin is the passage of time, so the requisite skills and modifications needed to return the child are incomplete. Many agency social workers cannot implement the ideal policy because of the constant crises amongst their client families which detract from planned strategies to avoid admission to care.

Coordinating Different Systems for Multiproblem Youth

Although children may enter the care of the state through the child welfare, mental health, or correctional system, the reality of children's needs is that they defy any boundaries between service providers. For example, abused children who are involved in the child welfare system have needs that simultaneously involve the children's mental health system, and may also engage in acting-out behavior problems that may involve the Youth Court. A recent study of young offenders in the province of Alberta found that 47% had previously been in need of protection and 18% had received mental health services (Thompson, 1988). This study pinpoints the importance of a high level of communication, cooperation, and coordinated interventions by different professionals and systems representing care by the state. Several of the topical concerns that comprise this key issue of coordinating different systems for multiproblem youth are delineated below.

Crisis management or treatment?

Part of the frustration experienced by service providers may be based on unrealistic expectations of the state representatives' role and abilities to "cure" the psychological and behavioral problems exhibited by children in care. Can policy be directed toward the full utilization of all community services, including those that are needed as well as those that are currently in existence? Rather than attempting to repeat the services that may presently be available in the community, the needs of many children and adolescents can be best met by immediate crisis intervention or the recognition of an ongoing pattern of crises that requires long-term planning.

A crisis event or situation has long been recognized as offering a valuable opportunity for a meaningful intervention based on both the child's immediate instrumental needs and his/her greater willingness to express genuine feelings and acceptance of help. Successful crisis intervention can sometimes assist children in coping with future crises. Early identification of childhood disorders and referrals to proper resources can begin at an earlier stage if policy planning is aimed more at the training of "front-line" service providers to identify such problems. For example, the police department in every municipality offers a 24-hour "crisis intervention" that can be of considerable assistance to children and families in locating help for family problems (Jaffe, Thompson, & Wolfe, 1984). We need to form a more clear-cut policy on crisis management because this activity appears to be the most frequent demand placed on the mental health, law enforcement, social services, and related service divisions.

Organizing Serial Interventions

Many children in the care of the state remain apart from their families for longer periods of time than initially expected. Studies have suggested that a period exceeding 18 months in care is a critical sign of the likelihood of ongoing care (House of Commons, 1984). Such children may have experienced a series of failed "least intrusive" interventions, rather than a long-term planning process. A series of failed interventions leaves clients and professionals pessimistic, frustrated, and searching for alternative programs for their clients. Some authors (e.g. Wolf, Braukmann, & Ramp, 1987) have suggested that professionals may underestimate the complexity of children's needs and the extent to which a long-term plan is necessary.

For example, young offenders who are conduct disordered may have a long history of violence in their families as well as significant learning problems and failure experiences in the school system. Although no clear label exists for their problems, they can best be described as "socially disabled" (Wolf et al., 1987), and they require a long-term plan to deal with treatment issues related to family, educational and vocational, and emotional needs. Without a long-term plan, the children will be exposed to a disjointed series of short-term programs that only touch the surface of expressed needs. All too often, children from broken homes are placed into "broken helping systems" that inadvertently promote more conflict and rejection rather than cooperative planning.

Formation of a Ministry for Children and Youth

Consideration should be given to the reorganization of government ministries to reduce conflict over services and funding. The creation of a Ministry for Children and Youth may be central in coordinating the services necessary for special needs children. Because all children are in the care of the school system on a mandatory basis until age 16, this system offers a central focus for identifying children at risk and providing appropriate interventions. Several reasons for the creation of services for children and youth that is more closely link to the educational system can be highlighted:

(1) the existing gap between identified disorders and specialized services suggests that the school system may form a more meaningful distribution point for resources;

(2) prevention programs for a wide range of mental health and social services could more easily be school-based;

(3) considerable conflict over funding and mandate could be reduced by having a more common framework (e.g., "Shared Visions," A discussion paper from the 1988 Ontario Association of Children's Mental Health Centres Conference);

(4) funding could be more suitably equalized throughout the province;

(5) less stigma could be attached to specialized services, since they would be seen as a normal part of the community and the school system; and,

(6) mental and social health promotion could be more accessible to all children, rather than having a limited number of resources focused on high-risk children (Peters, 1988).

Leaving care: Preparation and gap in service for 16–18 year-olds

Current foster care policy apparently is insufficient in providing services for youth during later adolescence. As stated by the Youth In Care organization (Raychaba, 1988):

A normally disruptive period in the lives of all young people is made even more disruptive for youth in the process of leaving care. All formal support networks are dismantled with termination of care: the result is added instability during a period of fast-paced changes. The young person must leave the group home or institution regardless of how long he/she has called it 'home' (p. 54).

Little policy planning to date has been directed toward the ease of transition of children back into their families or independent living. Although a number of Canadian provinces have passed legislation that provides for extended care benefits until age 21 for youth with special needs, these funds have not resolved the dilemma faced by many young people who are suddenly faced with the termination of financial and social support. What is particularly alarming is that very little data currently exists as to what happens to these children once they leave care. The limited study of this problem, however, reveals a picture of young adults who are quite transient, under-employed, unhappy, and poor (Raychaba, 1988). From a cultural standpoint certain ethnic groups, such as Native Americans, may return to their communities after discharge from care lacking in any cultural identity and understanding.

There is a move underway to strengthen "post-care support systems" (e.g., National Youth in Care Network), yet little systematic study and approach to this issue has been undertaken. There is significant reason to believe that these children and youth not only deserve to be assisted by the state beyond the care agreement, but in addition may represent a "high-risk" population that will create further mental health and family problems if left unattended. Therefore, services for 16–18 year-olds, both while in care and upon departure, warrant careful review and expansion.

Research and Evaluation

The existing published literature concerning children in care of the state is scanty, and lacks critical evaluation, methodological sophistication, and adequate follow-up of experimental programs (Appathurai et al., 1986). This is so despite our belief that foster care programs do lend themselves to empirical verification. An important policy direction, therefore, is to plan the design and implementation of innovative services for children in care in a rigorous, quasi-experimental fashion.

Perhaps the reason why so little reliable information exists on the effectiveness of different forms of care rests on the lack of emphasis placed on proper program evaluation. The cost-effectiveness of our current and planned interventions, in terms of actual expenses and short- and long-term benefits, needs to be addressed systematically. Rather than assuming that our current system will "fit" any client, we need to explore which client characteristics respond most favorably to which specific programs (e.g., group homes, individual foster homes, etc.). In effect, the state is operating a very crucial "psychotherapeutic" intervention for each and every child, and therefore we should profit from the methodological and procedural advances that have been discussed in this literature. The "active ingredients" of various forms of intervention by the state, such as supportive peers, concerned adults, or other children with comparable life situations may lead to the design of effective programs that maximize the value of each intervention plan.

Beyond the need for better record-keeping and evaluation of services, the OACAS (*The Future of Foster Care*, 1988) has identified several additional research issues that merit discussion. Most notably, this group feels research is needed regarding:

- the level of disturbance or difficulty of children in care
- the Native children in care
- ethnicity of children in care

The OACAS recommendation to establish a Child Welfare Research Centre to conduct studies into the treatment and placement services of children in care throughout the province is a first step in confronting these research and policy needs.

Summary

This chapter has raised some key policy issues for children in care that warrant the consideration of policy planners. The first issue dealt with the need for more coordinated and effective decision-making policies for admission to care. We focused on the importance of clarifying our community values and conducting research on the overriding question of who benefits most from foster placement versus home placement. The second key issue raised questions regarding the provision of adequate services to children and foster families once a child is in care, especially our lack of permanency planning and our failure to recognize the professional role of the foster parent. The third issue dealt with the dilemma of the lack of coordination amongst the different systems involved with multi-problem youth, and many concerns were raised as to the provision of adequate planning and services for these populations most at risk. Finally, we highlighted as a key policy issue the importance of preparing children for leaving care, noting in particular the wide gap in service for 16–18 year-olds.

Children who are taken into the care of the state present many complex challenges for society. At one extreme is the underlying social conditions that are responsible for abuse and neglect of the most vulnerable members of our communities. At the other is whether our response to these children is adequate to meet their needs. A basic question raised in this examination is whether the state has been concerned enough about effectiveness and interventions that ensure the rights of children and parents. The modest proposals contained in this chapter will assist in developing more coordinated and effective interventions for children in care.

REFERENCES

Abramovitch, R., 1987. *An overview of rural child care needs 1988.* Ministry of Community and Social Services.

Achenbach, T.M., 1980. DSM-III in light of empirical research on the classification of child psychopathology. *Journal of the American Academy of Child Psychiatry, 19,* 395–412.

Achenbach, T.M., McConaughy, S.H., and Howell, C.T., 1987. Child/adolescent behavioral and emotional problems: Implications of cross-informant correlations for situational specificity. *Psychological Bulletin, 101,* 213–232.

Achenbach, T.M., Conners, C.K., Quay, H.C., Verhulst, F.C., and Howell, C.T., 1989. Replication of empirically derived syndromes as a basis for taxonomy of child/adolescent psychopathology. *Journal of Abnormal Child Psychology, 17,* 299–323.

Advisory Council on Adjustment, 1989. *Adjusting to win,* Report of the Advisory Council on Adjustment, March.

American Psychiatric Association, 1980. *Diagnostic and statistical manual of mental disorders.* (3rd ed.). Washington, DC.

American Psychiatric Association, 1987. *Diagnostic and statistical manual of mental disorders.* (3rd ed. rev.). Washington, DC.

Andres, R., 1981. The apprehension of Native children, *Ontario Indian,* (January), 32–46.

Angel, Ronald, 1987. Mary Day Ward: The socio-cultural dimensions of mental health: A curriculum and practice model. *Contemporary Sociology, 16*(1), 101–102.

Angold, A., 1988. Child and adolescent depression. I. Epidemiological and aetiological aspects. *British Journal of Psychiatry, 152,* 601–617.

Appathurai, C., Lowery, G., and Sullivan, T., 1986. Achieving the vision of deinstitutionalization: A role for foster care? *Child and Adolescent Social Work, 3,* 50–67.

Armitage, A, et al, 1988. *Champagne/Aishihik child welfare, pilot project evaluation and recommendations.* University of Victoria.

Armstrong, Harvey, 1978. Providing psychiatric care and consultation in remote Indian villages. *Hospital and Community Psychiatry, 29*(10), 678–680.

Asarnow, J.R., Goldstein, M.J., Carlson, G.A., Perdue, S., Bates, S., and Keller, J., 1988. Childhood-onset depressive disorders: A follow-up study of rates of rehospitalization and out-of-home placement among child psychiatric inpatients. *Journal of Affective Disorders, 15,* 245–253.

Asbury, C., 1986. Fact sheet on the disproportionate imprisonment of Native people in Ontario, 1984–1985. Toronto: The Ontario Native Council on Justice.

Assembly of First Nations, 1987. *Indian housing and living conditions.*

Assembly of First Nations, 1988. *Assembly of First Nations initial response to task force report on child and family services in Canada.*

Avison, William R., 1988. *Parental and child health in the single-parent family.* London, Ont: Centre for the Study of Health and Well-Being, University of Western Ontario.

Axel, H., 1982. *Workplace issues and the family: How the corporation responds.* New York: Conference Board.

Axel, H., 1985. *Corporations and families: Changing practices and perspectives* (Report No. 868). Ottawa: The Conference Board of Canada.

Bagley, Chris, 1984. Child protection and the Native child: A case study. *Perception, 8*(1), 17–20.

Bagley, Chris, 1985. Child abuse by the child welfare system. *Journal of Child Care, 2*(3).

Banting, Keith G., 1987. The welfare state and inequality in the 1980s. *Canadian Review of Sociology and Anthropology, 24,* 309–338.

Barman, Jean, Hebert, Yvonne, and McCaskill, Don (eds.), 1986. *Indian education in Canada: The legacy.* Vancouver: University of British Columbia Press.

Barman, Jean, Hebert, Yvonne, and McCaskill, Don (eds.), 1987. *Indian education in Canada: The challenge.* Vancouver: University of British Columbia Press.

Barnes, Gordon. E., 1985. Canadian Indian health: A needs assessment project. *The Canadian Journal of Native Studies, 5*(1), 44–60.

Beaujot, Roderic, 1987. The Family. In James J. Teevan, (ed.), *Introduction to sociology: A Canadian focus.* Scarborough, Ont: Prentice-Hall, 225–264.

Benimadhu, P., 1987. *Hours of work: Trends and attitudes in Canada.* (Compensation Research Centre Report No. 18–87). Ottawa: The Conference Board of Canada.

Berlin, Irving N., 1982. Prevention of emotional problems among Native American children: Overview of developmental issues. *Journal of Preventative Psychiatry 1*(3), 319–330.

Berlin, Irving N., 1985. *Prevention of adolescent suicide among some Native American tribes.* Chicago: University of Chicago Press.

Berman, P., 1985. *The next step: The Minnesota Plan.* Phi Delta Kappan, (November).

Bill C–144, *Canada Child Care Act,* 2nd Session, 33rd Parliament, 34–36–37 Elizabeth II, 1986–87–88.

Birch, M., 1974. *Statement to the legislature announcing day care services for children.* Toronto, Ontario.

Bluestone, Barry, and Harrison, Bennett, 1982. *The de-industrialization of America.* New York: Basic Books.

Borzecki, M., Wormith, J.S., and Black, W.H., 1988. An examination of differences between Native and non-Native psychiatric offenders on the MMPI. *Canadian Journal of Behavioural Science, 20*(3), 287–301.

Bowen, G.L., 1988. Corporate supports for the family lives of employees: A conceptual model for program planning and evaluation. *Family Relations, 37,* 183–188.

Boyle, M.H., and Offord, D.R., 1988. Prevalence of childhood disorder, perceived need for help, family dysfunction and resource allocation for child welfare and children's mental health services in Ontario. *Canadian Journal of Behavioural Science, 20*(4), 374–388.

Boyle, M.H., Offord, D.R., Hofmann, H.G., Catlin, G.P., Byles, J.A., Cadman, D.T., Crawford, J.W., Links, P.S., Rae-Grant, N.I., and Szatmari, P., 1987. Ontario Child Health Study: I. Methodology. *Archives of General Psychiatry, 44*, 826–831.

Bradshaw, J., 1972. The taxonomy of social need. *New Society, 19*, 496, 640–642.

Brant, C.C., 1983. *The Native family: Traditions and adaptations.* Transcribed and edited proceedings of the Canadian Psychiatric Association, Section on Native Mental Health, 30–36.

Britton, James, 1982. *Prospect and retrospect.* Pradl, G.M. (ed.), Boynton/Cook Publishers, Inc.

Bronfenbrenner, U., and Weiss, H.B., 1983. Beyond policies without people: An ecological perspective on child and family policy. In E.F. Zigler, S.L. Kagan and E. Klugman (eds.), *Children, families and government: Perspectives on American social policy.* Cambridge MA: Cambridge University Press, 393–414.

Bryson, S., Clark, B., and Smith, I., 1988. First report of a Canadian epidemiological study of autistic syndromes. *Journal of Child Psychology and Psychiatry, 29*, 433–445.

Bullock, A. (Committee), 1975. *A language for life.* Department of Education and Science, London: HMSO.

Burden, D.S., and Googins, B., 1985. *Balancing job and homelife study: Summary of findings.* Boston, MA: Boston University School of Social Work.

The Bureau of National Affairs, 1984. *Employers and child care: Development of a new employee benefit* (A BNA Special Report). Washington, DC: The Bureau of National Affairs.

The Bureau of National Affairs, 1986. *Work and family: A changing dynamic.* Washington, DC: The Bureau of National Affairs.

Burnaby, Barbara, 1982. *Language in education among Canadian Native peoples.* Toronto: O.I.S.I.E. Canadian Psychiatric Association.

Burnaby, Barbara, 1984. English and Native languages: integration not competition. *Canadian Journal of Native Education, 11*(2), 7–13.

Burt Perrin Associates, 1986. *A review of training and educational programs for social assistance recipients entering the labour force.* Prepared for the Ontario Social Assistance Review Committee, March.

Business Task Force on Literacy, February, 1988. *Measuring the cost of illiteracy.* Toronto, Ontario.

Canadian Advisory Council on the Status of Women, 1987. *Integration and participation: Women's work in the home and in the labour force.* Ottawa: Canadian Advisory Council on the Status of Women.

Canadian Education Association, 1984. *Speaking out: The 1984 CEA poll of Canadian opinion on education.* Toronto, Ontario.

Canadian Psychiatric Association, 1988. *Native adolescents: Stepping stones to the future.* Proceedings from CPA section on Native health.

Canadian Youth Foundation, 1988. *Canada's youth ready for today, (A Comprehensive Survey of 15–24 Year Olds).* Ottawa.

Cantwell, D.P., 1980. The diagnostic process and diagnostic classification in child psychiatry—DSM III. *Journal of the American Academy of Child Psychiatry, 19*, 345–355.

Cantwell, D., 1986. Attention deficit disorder in adolescents. *Clinical Psychology Review, 6*, 237–247.

Casey, R.J., and Berman, J. S., 1985. The outcome of psychotherapy with children. *Psychological Bulletin, 98*(2), 388–400.

Castellano, Marlene Brant, 1982. Indian participation in health policy development: Implications for adult education. *Canadian Journal of Native Studies, 11*(1).

Castellano, Marlene Brant, 1986. Collective wisdom: Participatory research and Canada's Native people. *IRDC Reports, 3*, 50–53.

Castellano, Marlene Brant, Stalwick Harvey, and Wein, Fred, 1986. Native social work education in Canada. *Canadian Social Work Review 86*, 166–184.

Chang, W.C., 1985. A cross-cultural study of depressive symptomology. *Culture, Medicine and Psychiatry, 9*(3), 295.

Children's Defense Fund, 1988. *A children's defense budget, FY 1989*, USA.

Clark, B., 1985. Cited by Goodlad, J., Phi Delta Kappan. (December).

Clarke, G.S., 1987. *Developing crime prevention activities in Native communities*. Solicitor General Canada.

Class, N.E., 1980. Some reflections on the development of child day care licensing. In S. Kilmer (ed.), *Advances in early education and day care*. Greenwich, CT: JAI Press, Inc.

Clayton, S., 1983. Social need revisited. *Journal of Social Policy, 12*, 215–234.

Coleman, J., 1985. *High school achievement*. New York: Basic Books.

The Conference Board of Canada, 1987. *Canadian work environments and changing family structures: A proposal to conduct research*. Ottawa: The Conference Board of Canada.

Cooke, K. (Chair), 1986. *Report of the task force on child care*. Ottawa: Minister of Supply and Services.

Costello, E.J., 1989. Developments in child psychiatric epidemiology. *Journal of the American Academy of Child and Adolescent Psychiatry, 28*, 836–841.

Council of Ontario Universities, 1988. *Attracting and retaining women students for science and engineering*. A report from the Committee of the Status of Women in Ontario Universities, June.

Crouter, A.C., 1984. Spillover from family to work: The neglected side of the work-family interface. *Human Relations, 37*(6), 425–442.

Crouter, A.C., and Perry-Jenkins, M., 1986. Working it out: Effects of work on parents and children. In M.W. Yogman, and T.B. Brazelton (eds.), *In support of families*. Cambridge, MA: Harvard University Press, 93–108.

Davis, W., 1984. *Speech to the Legislature*. Reprinted, Queen's Printer.

Day Nurseries Act, 1983. (Regulation R235).

DEL Support Centre Inc., 1985. *To protect and preserve: A case study in planning Indian community services for children and their families*. Toronto, Ontario.

Denton, Margaret, et al, 1987. *Employment survey of 1985 graduates of Ontario universities*, Report of major findings. Ontario Ministry of Education and Ministry of Colleges and Universities.

Doherty Social Planning Consultants, 1987. *A survey of child care support services*. Ontario Ministry of Community and Social Services.

Dooley, Martin D., 1988. *An analysis of changes in family income and family structure in Canada between 1973 and 1986 with an emphasis on poverty among children*. McMaster University: QSEP Research Report No. 238.

Driben, P., and Gummer, Burton, 1985. The Native interface: An emergent role in government-Native relations. *Native Studies Review 1*(2), 33–45.

Dryden, Ken, 1986. *Report of the Ontario Youth Commissioner*. Ottawa: Queen's Printer for Ontario.

Dulcan, M., 1986. Comprehensive treatment of children and adolescents with attention deficit disorders: The state of the art. *Clinical Psychology Review, 6*, 539–569.

Dumas, C., 1986. *Occupational trends among women in Canada: 1976–1986* (Reprint No. 9). Ottawa: Labour and Household Surveys Analysis Division.

Duncan, Greg J., and Rogers, Willard, 1987. Single-parent families: Are their economic problems transitory or persistent? *Family Planning Perspectives 19*, 171–178.

Easterlin, Richard, 1978. What will 1984 be like? *Demography 15*, 397–432.

Easterlin, Richard, 1980. *Birth and fortune*. Chicago: University of Chicago Press.

Easterlin, Richard A., 1987. The new age structure of poverty in America: Permanent or transient? *Population and Development Review 13*(2), 195–208.

Economic Council of Canada, 1985. *Towards Equity: Proceedings of a colloquium on the Economic Status on Women in the Labour Market, November 1984*. Ottawa: The Economic Council of Canada.

Economic Council of Canada, 1987. *Innovation and jobs in Canada*. Ottawa: The Economic Council of Canada.

Edelbrock, C., Costello, A.J., Dulcan, M.K., Kalas, R., and Conover, N.C., 1985. Age differences in the reliability of the psychiatric interview of the child. *Child Development, 56*, 265–275.

Edelbrock, C., and Costello, A.S., 1988. Convergence between statistically derived behavior problem syndromes and child psychiatric diagnoses. *Journal of Abnormal Child Psychology, 16*, 219–231.

Edmonds, R., 1979. Effective schools for the urban poor. *Education Leadership*, (October), *37*(1).

Eichler, M., 1988. *Families in Canada today: Recent changes and their policy consequences*. (2nd edn.) Toronto: Gage Publishing Co.

Ellis, Robert J., 1987. *Post-secondary cooperative education in Canada*. Ottawa.

Emlen, A.C., and Koren, P.E., 1984. *Hard to find and difficult to manage: The effects of child care on the workplace*. Portland, OR: Regional Research Institute For Human Services.

Englander-Golden, P., and Barton, G., 1983. Sex differences in absence from work: A reinterpretation. *Psychology of Women Quarterly, 8*(2), 185–188.

Epp, J., 1988. *Mental health for Canadians: Striking a balance*. (Cat. H39–128/1988E). Ottawa: Minister of Supply and Services Canada.

Epstein, J.L., 1986. Effective schools for the urban poor. *Education Leadership*, (October), *37*(1).

Epstein, J.L., 1986. Parents' Reactions to Teacher Practices of Parent Involvement, *Elementary School Journal, 86*(3).

Erasmus, George, 1986. Native studies review comment. *Native Studies Review*, 2(2), 53–63.

Evers S.E., and Rand, C.G., 1982. Morbidity in Canadian Indian and non-Indian children in the first year of life. *Canadian Medical Association Journal 126*, 249–252.

Evers S.E., and Rand, C.G., 1983. Morbidity in Canadian Indian and non-Indian children in the second year. *Canadian Journal of Public Health 74*, 191–194.

Fernandez, John P., 1986. *Child care and corporate productivity.* Massachusetts: Lexington Books.

Fiene, R., 1986. *State child care regulatory, monitoring and evaluation systems as a means for ensuring quality child development programs.* Pennsylvania: Office of Children, Youth and Families.

Fiene, R., and Kontos, S., 1986. *Predictors of quality and children's development in day care.* Manuscript of paper obtained from authors.

Finn, P., 1981. The effects of shift work on the lives of employees. *Monthly Labor Review, 104*(10), 31–35.

Fleming, J.E., and Offord, D.R., 1989. *Childhood depression.* Unpublished manuscript, McMaster University, Department of Psychiatry, Hamilton, Ontario.

Fleming, J.E., Offord, D.R., and Boyle, M.H., 1989. Prevalence of childhood and adolescent depression in the community. Ontario Child Health Study. *British Journal of Psychiatry, 155*, 647–654.

Foot, David, 1986. Youth unemployment in Canada: A misplaced priority. *Policy Politiques*, (September), *XII*(3).

Frankel, M., 1988. *The families at work research project.* Unpublished manuscript.

Friedman, D.E., 1985. *Family-supportive policies: The corporate decision-making process* (Report No. 897). Ottawa: The Conference Board of Canada.

Friedman, D.E., 1986. Child Care for employees' kids. *Harvard Business Review*, (March-April), 4.

Friendly, M., 1989. *Flexible child care services: An overview of extended hours, sick child and emergency child care and child care in rural areas.* Manuscript in preparation. The Centre for Urban and Community Studies, University of Toronto, Toronto, Ontario.

Fullan, M., and Connelly, F.M., 1982. *The meaning of educational change.* Toronto: OISE Press.

Fullan, M., and Connelly, F.M., 1988. *Teacher education in Ontario.* Ontario Ministry of Education/Ministry of Colleges and Universities.

Galinsky, E., 1986. Family life and corporate policies. In M.W. Yogman, and T.B. Brazelton (eds.), *In Support of Families.* Cambridge MA: Harvard University Press, 109–272.

Galinsky, E., Hughes, D., and Shinn, M.B., 1986. *The corporate work and family life study.* New York, NY: Bank Street College of Education.

Garbarino, J., 1988. The role of social policy in the health and welfare of young children. *The Journal of Childcare, 3*, 1–13.

Garber, J., Kriss, M.R., Koch, M., and Lindholm, L., 1988. Recurrent depression in adolescents: A follow-up study. *Journal of the American Academy of Child and Adolescent Psychiatry, 27*, 49–54.

Gazu, Cliff, 1978. Native foods give Natives health and oneness with the land. *Native Perspective, 2*(8).

George, Rosemary, 1987. *Youth policies and programs in selected countries.* The William T. Grant Foundation Commission on Work, Family and Citizenship, Washington, DC., August.

Gibson, Nancy, 1988. Northern medicine in transition. In David Young (ed.), *Health Care Issues in the Canadian North.* Edmonton: Boreal Institute for Northern Studies, University of Alberta, 108–117.

Gilchrist, Lewayne D., Schinke, Steven P., Trimble, Joseph E., and Cvetkovich, George T., 1987. Skills enhancement to prevent substance abuse among American Indian adolescents. *The International Journal of the Addictions, 22*(9), 869–879.

Gittelman, R., 1986. Childhood anxiety disorders: Correlates and outcome. In R. Gittelman (ed.), *Anxiety disorders of childhood.* New York: The Guilford Press, 101–125.

Gittelman, R., Mannuzza, S., Shenker, R., and Bonagura, N., 1985. Hyperactive boys almost grown up: I. Psychiatric status. *Archives of General Psychiatry, 42,* 937–947.

Goldsmith, H.F., Lin, E., Jackson, D.S., Manderscheid, R.W., and Bell, R.A., 1988a. The future of mental health needs assessment. In H.F. Goldsmith, E. Lin, R.A. Bell, and D.J. Jackson (eds.), *National Institute of Mental Health. Series BN No. 8, Needs assessment: Its future.* (DHHS Publication No. ADM 88–1550). Washington, DC: U.S. Government Printing Office, 79–93.

Goldsmith, H.F., Jackson, D.L., and Hough, R.L., 1988b. Process model of seeking mental health services: Proposed framework for organizing the research literature on help seeking. In H.F. Goldsmith, E. Lin, R.A. Bell, and D.S. Jackson (eds.), *National Institute of Mental Health. Series BN No. 8, Needs assessment: Its future.* (DHHS Publication No. ADM 88–1550), Washington, DC: U.S. Government Printing Office, 49–64.

Goodlad, J.I., 1983. *A place called school.* New York: McGraw-Hill Book Co.

Goodlad, J.I., 1985. *The great American schooling experiment.* Phi Delta Kappan, (December).

Gould, M.S., Wunsch-Hitzig, R., and Dohrenwend, R., 1981. Estimating the prevalence of childhood psychopathology. *Journal of the American Academy of Child and Adolescent Psychiatry, 20,* 462–476.

Government of Canada, 1980. *Indian conditions: A survey.* Department of Indian Affairs and Northern Development.

Government of Canada, 1982a. *Indian social welfare.* Indian and Northern Affairs Canada.

Government of Canada, 1982b. *Indian education paper, phase 1.* Ministry of Indian Affairs and Northern Development.

Government of Canada, 1983. *Indian self-government in Canada.* Report of the Special Committee on Indian Self-Government (the Penner Report).

Government of Canada, 1984. *Canada's Native people 1981 census of Canada.* Supply and Services Canada.

Government of Canada, 1986. *Human resources automotive study: Why people count.* Employment and Immigration Canada, Ottawa.

Government of Canada, 1986. *Task force on Indian economic development.* Summary Report to the Deputy Minister, Indian and Northern Affairs Canada.

Government of Canada, 1987. *Adoption and the Indian child.* Indian and Northern Affairs Canada.

Government of Canada, 1987. *Indian child and family services in Canada, final report.* Department of Indian and Northern Affairs.

Government of Canada, 1988. *Inventory of income security programs in Canada.* Ministry of National Health and Welfare.

Government of Canada, 1988. Department of Indian and Northern Affairs Communique 1–8810.

Government of Ontario, 1976. *Advisory Council on Day Care* (Progress report, January 1975, progress report II, June 1975, final report, January 1976). Ministry of Community and Social Services.

Government of Ontario, 1978. *Program priorities for children's services.* Ministry of Community and Social Services.

Government of Ontario, 1979. *Funding of children's services in the 1980s.* Standards and Information Unit, Children's Services Division, Ministry of Community and Social Services.

Government of Ontario, 1979. *Ontario assessment instrument pool.* Ministry of Education.

Government of Ontario, 1979. *A starving man doesn't argue: A review of community social services to Indians in Ontario.* Ministry of Community and Social Services.

Government of Ontario, 1979. *H.S.I.* Ministry of Education.

Government of Ontario, 1980. *Community care: Toward Indian control of Indian social services.* Ministry of Community and Social Services.

Government of Ontario, 1980. *Day nurseries services: Proposed standards and guidelines.* Ministry of Community and Social Services.

Government of Ontario, 1981. *Day care policy: Background paper.* Ministry of Community and Social Services, Program and Policy Division.

Government of Ontario, 1981. *Report of the secondary review project.* Ministry of Education.

Government of Ontario, 1982. *The Renewal of Secondary Education in Ontario.* Ministry of Education.

Government of Ontario, 1984. *Ontario Schools: Intermediate and Senior Divisions* (Grades 7–12/OAC's), Program and Diploma Requirements. Ministry of Education.

Government of Ontario, 1984. *Women in rural life: The changing scene.* Ministry of Agriculture and Food.

Government of Ontario, 1984–85. *Statistical summary.* Ministry of Colleges and Universities.

Government of Ontario, 1985. *A policy statement on standards for foster care.* Ministry of Community and Social Services.

Government of Ontario, 1985. *Report of the early primary education project.* Ministry of Education.

Government of Ontario, 1985. *Tentative policies for Indian provisions of The Child and Family Services Act.* Ministry of Community and Social Services.

Government of Ontario, 1986. *Demographic outlook and implications for training in Ontario.* Unpublished report, Ontario Manpower Commission, Ministry of Skills Development.

Government of Ontario, 1986. *Education statistics, Ontario.* Ministry of Education.

Government of Ontario, 1986. *Indian and Native child and family services under The Child and Family Services Act, 1984, a discussion paper.* Ministry of Community and Social Services.

Government of Ontario, 1987. *Child and Family Services Act, 1984.* Ministry of the Attorney General.

Government of Ontario, 1987. *Child care: Annual statistics.* Ministry of Community and Social Services.

Government of Ontario, 1987. *New directions for child care.* Ministry of Community and Social Services.

Government of Ontario, 1987. *Ontario Statistics 1986.* Ministry of Treasury and Economics.

Government of Ontario, March, 1987. *Out of school youth in Ontario: Their labour market experience.* Ontario Manpower Commission, Ministry of Skills Development.

Government of Ontario, 1987. *Training for technological change.* Ministry of Skills Development.

Government of Ontario, 1987. *Vital statistics for 1985.* Registrar General.

Government of Ontario, 1987a. *Service planning: Services and resources data base for children's services.* A consultation paper. Children's Services Branch, Community Services Division, Ministry of Community and Social Services.

Government of Ontario, 1987b. *Corporate plan: Ministry of Community and Social Services.* Ministry of Community and Social Services.

Government of Ontario, 1987b. *Response to Indian and Native services under the child and family services act (1984): A discussion paper and proposed recommendations.* Ministry of Community and Social Services, Children's Services Branch, Community Services Division, 63.

Government of Ontario, 1988. *Adjusting to change: An overview of labour market issues in Ontario.* Ministry of Skills Development.

Government of Ontario, 1988. *Employment Standards Act.* Ministry of the Attorney General.

Government of Ontario, 1988. *Final report of the teacher education review steering committee,* Ministry of Education/Ministry of Colleges and Universities.

Government of Ontario, 1988. *Investing in children: New directions in child treatment and child and family intervention.* Ministry of Community and Social Services.

Government of Ontario, 1988. *New directions for child care—report on year one: 1987/88.* Ministry of Community and Social Services.

Government of Ontario, 1988. *Select Committee on Education First Report.* Legislative Assembly, Queen's Park.

Government of Ontario, 1988. *Transitions report of the social assistance review committee.* Ministry of Community and Social Services.

Gregory, David, 1988. An exploration of the contact between Indian healers/traditional healers on Indian reserves and health care centres in Manitoba. In David Young (ed.), *Health Care Issues in the Canadian North.* Edmonton: Boreal Institute for Northern Studies, University of Alberta, 39–43.

Grubb, W.N., and Lazerson, M., 1982. The frontiers of public responsibility: Child care and parent education. In *Broken promises: How Americans fail their children.* New York: Basic Books, Inc., 208–232.

Gutterman, E.M., O'Brien, J.D., and Young, J.G., 1987. Structured diagnostic interviews for children and adolescents: Current status and future directions. *Journal of the American Academy of Child and Adolescent Psychiatry, 26,* 621–630.

Hagey, R., 1984. The phenomenon, the explanation and the response: Metaphors surrounding diabetes in urban Canadian Indians. *Social Science and Medicine, 18*(3), 265–272.

Hargreaves, D.H., 1984. *Improving secondary schools.* London, England: Inner London Education Authority.

Harris, L., and Associates, 1981. *Families at work: Strengths and strains.* Minneapolis, MN: General Mills Inc.

Havemann, P, Couse, K., Foster, L., and Matonovich, R., 1985. *Law and order for indigenous people.* Regina: Prairie Justice Research, School of Human Justice, University of Regina.

Hersov, L., 1985. Emotional disorders. In M. Rutter and L. Hersov (eds.), *Child and adolescent psychiatry: Modern approaches* (2nd. ed.). London: Blackwell Scientific Publications, 368–381.

Homberg, R., Cameron, G., and Rothery, M., 1983. *The nature and effectiveness of family support measures in child welfare.* Prepared for the Ministry of Community and Social Services by Canadian Sociotelic Limited.

Homenuck, Peter, 1984. *The social and psychological effects of separation from family and community on Native children: A research proposal.* Toronto: Native/Canadian Relations Theme Area, York University, Faculty of Environmental Science.

Hope, J.A., Commissioner, 1950. *The report of the Royal Commission on education in Ontario.* Toronto: Published, Baptist Johnson.

House of Commons, 1984. *Second report from the Social Services Committee: Children in care.* London: Her Majesty's Stationary Office.

House of Commons, 1987. *Sharing the responsibility.* Ottawa: Special Committee on Child Care.

Hudson, P.,and McKenzie, B., 1981. Child welfare and Native people. The extension of colonialism. *The Social Worker, 49*(2), 63–81.

Hudson Institute, Inc., 1988. *Workforce 2000: Work and workers for the 21st century.* Washington DC: U.S. Dept. of Labor.

Hughes, D., and Galinsky, E., 1988. Balancing work and family lives: Research and corporate applications. In A.E. Gottfried, and A.W. Gottfried, (eds.), *Maternal employment and children's development: Longitudinal research.* New York: Plenum Press, 233–268.

Human capital: The decline of America's work force. *Business Week,* September 19, 1988.

Hylton, J., 1983. Locking up Indians in Saskatchewan: Some recent findings. In T. Fleming and L.A. Visano (eds.) *Deviant designations, crime, law and deviance in Canada.*

Institute of Medicine, 1989. *Research on children and adolescents with mental, behavioral and developmental disorders: Mobilizing a national initiative.* Washington, DC: National Academy Press.

Irving, Allan, 1987. *From no poor law to the social assistance review: A history of social assistance in Ontario, 1791–1987*. Research report prepared for the Social Assistance Review Committee, Ontario.

Jackson, Michael, 1988. *Locking up Natives in Canada*. A Report of the Committee of the Canadian Bar Association on Imprisonment and Release.

Jackson, Ted, 1982. Learning for self-determination: Community-based options for Native training and research. *Canadian Journal of Native Studies 2*(1).

Jaffe, P., Finlay, J., and Wolfe, D.A., 1984. Evaluating the impact of a specialized civilian family crisis unit within a police force on the resolution of family conflicts. *Preventive Psychiatry, 2*, 63–73.

Jarvis, George K.,and Boldt, Menno, 1982. Death styles among Canada's Indians. *Social Science and Medicine, 16*(14).

Jencks, C., 1972. *Inequality*. New York: Basic Books.

Jilek, W, 1982. *Indian healing*. Surrey B.C.: Hancock House.

Johnson, Patrick, 1983. *Native children and the child welfare system*. Toronto: Canadian Council on Social Development, James Lorimer and Company.

Johnson, L., 1986. *Working families: Workplace supports for families*. Toronto: Social Planning Council of Metropolitan Toronto.

Johnson, L., and Abramovitch, R., 1987. Rush hours: A new look at parental employment patterns. *Social Infopac, 6*(4). Toronto: Social Planning Council of Metropolitan Toronto.

Johnson, L., and Abramovitch, R., 1989. *The relations between employment and parenting*. Paper presented at the Biennial Meetings of the Society for Research in Child Development, Kansas City, Kansas.

Jolly, Stan, 1983. *Our children our hurting: Fact sheet on the disproportionate involvement of Indian young people in the juvenile justice and child welfare systems of Ontario*. Ontario Native Council on Justice.

Jolly, Stan, 1985. *Indian children in Ontario's juvenile justice and child welfare systems 1983–84*. Ontario Native Council on Justice.

Jones, M.A., 1987. *A second chance for families: Five years later—Follow-up of a program to prevent foster care*. New York: Child Welfare League of America.

Jones, Rhys W., 1986. *Practicing family law for Indian and Native clients: Child protection proceedings under the child and family services act, 1985*. 1986 Annual Institute on Continuing Legal Education. Canadian Bar Association, Ontario.

Kamerman, S.B., 1980. Child care and family benefits: Policies of six industrialized countries. *Monthly Labor Review* (November), 23–28.

Kamerman, S.B., 1983. Child care and family benefits: Policies of six industrialized countries. In R.G. Genovese (ed.), *Families and change: Social needs and public policies*. Massachusetts: Bergin and Garvey Publishers, Inc.

Kamerman, S.B., and Kahn, A.J., (eds.), 1978. *Family policy: Government and families in fourteen countries*. New York: Columbia University Press.

Kamerman, S.B., and Kahn, A.J., 1981. *Child care, family benefits and working parents*. New York: Columbia University Press.

Kamerman, S.B., and Kingston, P.W., 1982. Employer responses to the family responsibilities of employees. In S. B. Kamerman and C.D. Hayes (eds.), *Families that work*. Washington, DC: National Academy Press, 144–208.

Karp, Ellen, 1988. *The drop-out phenomenon in Ontario secondary schools.* A report to the Ontario study of relevance of education and the issue of drop-outs. Ontario Ministry of Education.

Kazdin, A.E., 1983. Psychiatric diagnosis, dimensions of dysfunction, and child behavior therapy. *Behavior Therapy, 14,* 73–99.

Kazdin, A.E., 1987. Treatment of antisocial behavior in children: Current status and future directions. *Psychological Bulletin, 102,* 187–203.

Kendell, R.E., 1988. What is a case? Food for thought for epidemiologists. *Archives of General Psychiatry, 45,* 374–376.

King, A.J.C., 1986. *The adolescent experience.* Ontario Secondary Teachers' Federation.

King, A.J.C., and Hughes, J., 1985. *Secondary school to work, a difficult transition.* Ontario Secondary Teachers' Federation.

Klerman, G.L., 1988. The current age of youthful melancholia: Evidence for increase in depression among adolescents and young adults. *British Journal of Psychiatry, 152,* 4–14.

Knopf, I.J., 1984. *Child psychopathology: A developmental approach* (2nd ed.), Englewood Cliffs, NJ: Prentice Hall.

Kovacs, M.E., and Paulauskas, S., 1986. The traditional psychotherapies. In H.C. Quay and J. S. Werry (eds.), *Psychopathological disorders of childhood* (3rd ed.), New York, NY: Wiley, 496–522.

Kovacs, M., Feinberg, T.L., Crouse-Novak, M., Paulauskas, S.L., Pollock, M., and Finkelstein, R., 1984. Depressive disorders in childhood: II. A longitudinal study of the risk for subsequent major depression. *Archives of General Psychiatry, 41,* 463–649.

Krett, Karen, 1985. Maternity, paternity and child care policies: A new survey on benefit policies. *Personnel Administrator, 30*(6).

Kutchins, H., and Kirk, S.A., 1986. The reliability of DSM-III: A critical review. *Social Work Research and Abstracts,* (Winter), 3–12.

Kuttner, Bob, 1983. The declining middle. *The Atlantic Monthly* (July), 60–72.

Lane, P. Bopp, J., and Bopp, P., 1984a. *A wholistic curriculum can contribute to health.* Lethbridge: Four Worlds Development Project. Discussion Paper Seven.

Lane, P. Bopp, J., and Bopp, P., 1984b. *Wholistic educational evaluation for community transformation.* Lethbridge: Four Worlds Development Project.

Lane, Phil (Producer), 1986. *The honour of all.* (Video) Lethbridge, Alberta: Four Worlds Development Project.

Langner, T.S., Gersten, J.C., Greene, E.L., Eisenberg, J.C., Herson, J.H., and McCarthy, E.D., 1974. Treatment of psychological disorder among urban children. *Journal of Consulting and Clinical Psychology, 2,* 170–179.

Leah, R., 1981. Women's labour force participation and day care cutbacks in Ontario. *Atlantis, 7*(1), 36–41.

Leithwood, K.A. and Bradley, James, 1988. *Fostering inequality in Ontario secondary schools: The implementation of O.S.I.S.* OISE Field Development Newsletter, (January), *18*(1).

Leland, J., 1976. *Firewater myths.* New Brunswick, NJ: Rutgers Centre of Alcohol Studies.

Lero, D.S., Pence, A., Goelman, H., and Brockman, L., 1985. *Parents' needs, preferences, and concerns about child care: Case studies of 336 Canadian families.* Background paper prepared for the Task Force on Child Care. Ottawa: Status of Women.

Lero, D.S., Pence, A., Goelman, H., and Brockman, L., 1988. *National child care study*, University of Guelph, Guelph, Ontario. Study in progress.

Leschied, A., Jaffe, P., Suderman, M., Austin, A., and Willis, W., 1988. *The changing profiles of young offenders with special needs: trends and critical issues.* London, Ont: London Family Court Clinic, Inc.

Leung, Sophia, and Carter, James, 1983. Cross cultural study of child abuse among Chinese, Native Indians and Anglo-Canadian children. *Journal* for *Psychiatry Treatment and Evaluation, 5*, 37–44.

Lewinsohn, P., Hops, H., Williams, J.A., Clarke, G., and Andrews, J., 1987. *Cognitive-behavioral treatment for depressed adolescents.* Paper presented at the Annual Meeting of the American Academy of Child and Adolescent Psychiatry, October, Washington, DC.

Liberal-NDP Accord, 1985. Toronto, Ontario.

Lightfoot, M., and Martin, N., 1988. *The word for teaching is learning.* Essays for James Britton. London: Heinemann Educational Books Ltd.

Lind, G., and Wiseman, C., 1978. Setting health priorities: A review of concepts and approaches. *Journal of Social Policy, 7*, 411–440.

Livingstone, D.W., 1979. *Public attitudes toward education in Ontario 1978.* Toronto: OISE Press.

Livingstone, D.W., Hart, D.J., and McLean, L.D., 1983. *Public attitudes toward education in Ontario: Fourth OISE survey.* Toronto: OISE Press.

Lombardi, J., 1988. Now more than ever ... It is time to become an advocate for better child care. Public Policy Report. *Young Children, 43*(5).

Long, Kathleen Ann, 1986. Suicide intervention and prevention with Indian adolescent populations. *Issues in Mental Health Nursing, 8*, 247–253.

Loucks, Bryan, and Timothy, Arnette, 1981. *Justice related children and family services for Native people in Ontario.* Toronto: Ontario Native Council on Justice.

Luria, A.R., and Yudovich, F.I., 1971. *Speech and development of mental processes in the child.* Penguin Books.

Magid, R.Y., 1983. *Child care initiatives for working parents: Why employers get involved* (AMA Survey Report). New York: American Management Associations.

Maidman, Frank, 1981. *Native people in urban settings. problems, needs and services, a report of the Ontario Task Force on Native people in the urban setting.* Toronto, Ontario.

Marockie, H.L, and Jones, H.L., 1987. *Reducing dropout rates through home-school communication.* Education and Urban Society *19*(2), 200–205.

Mayfield, Margie, and Davies, Gayle, 1984. An early intervention program for Native Indian infants and their families. *Canadian Journal of Public Health 75*, 450–453.

McCaskill, Don, 1981. Migration, adjustment, integration of Indians in Toronto, Winnipeg, Edmonton and Vancouver: A comparative analysis. *Culture 1*(1).

McCaskill, Don, 1984. When cultures meet: Indians in Canada. *Bridges 1*(5).

McCormick, James, 1988. To wear a white coat: Options for traditional healers in a Canadian medical future. In David Young (ed.), *Health Care Issues in the Canadian North*. Edmonton: Boreal Institute for Northern Studies, University of Alberta, 8–14.

McIntosh, A., and Rauhala, A., 1989. Who's minding the children? Toronto: *The Globe and Mail*. (February 3, 4, 5, 6, 7, & 8).

McNeil, John, and Nelson, Eric, 1988. Call of the wild proves weak lure. *Globe and Mail,* (Nov. 5), D5.

McQuillan, Kevin, 1988. *One-adult and two-earner households and families: Trends, determinants and implications*. Part II: Family change and family income in Canada. Report prepared for the Review of demography and its implications for social and economic policy. Ottawa: Minister of Health and Welfare.

Merskey, H., Brant, C.C., Malla, A., Helmes, E., and Mohr, V., 1986. Symptom patterns of alcoholism in a northern Ontario population. *Canadian Journal of Psychiatry 33*, 46–51.

Metcalf, Ann, 1978. *Urban Indian Child Resource Centre*. Oakland, California.

Michelson, W., 1985. *From sun to sun: Daily obligations and community structure in the lives of employed women and their families*. Totowa, NJ: Rowman and Allenheld Publishers.

Miller, J. Thomas, 1984. The effects of employer-sponsored child care on employee absenteeism, turnover, productivity, recruitment or job satisfaction: What is claimed and what is known. *Personnel Psychology, 37*, 277–289.

Moen, P., and Dempster-McClain, D.I., 1987. Employed parents: Role strain, work time, and preferences for working less. *Journal of Marriage and the Family, 49*(3), 579–590.

Morgan, G.G., 1980. Can quality family day care be achieved through regulation? In S. Kilmer (ed.), *Advances in early education and day care*. Greenwich, CT: JAI Press, Inc.

Morgan, G.G., 1986. Supplemental care for young children. In M.W. Yogman and T. Berry Brazelton (eds.), *In support of families*. Cambridge, MA: Harvard University Press, 156–170.

Moss, P., and Brannen, J., 1987. Discontinuity in daycare arrangements for very young children. *Early Childhood Development and Care, 29*, 435–449.

Moynihan, Daniel Patrick, 1986. *Family and nation*. New York: Harcourt Brace Jovanovich.

Muir, Bernice, L., 1985. *Current health status of Indians and Inuit compared to other Canadians*. Report to Sub-committee on Community Health.

Murray, Charles, 1984. *Losing ground: American social policy, 1950–1980*. New York: Basic Books.

Myles, J., Picot, G., and Wannell, T., 1988. The changing wage distribution of jobs. *The Labour Force* (October), 83–138. Cat. No. 71–001.

Nakamura, C.Y., McCarthy, S.J., Rothstein-Fisch, C., and Winges, L.D., 1981. Interdependence of child care resources and the progress of women in society. *Psychology of Women Quarterly, 6*(1).

National Council of Welfare, 1988. *Poverty profile 1988*. Ottawa: Minister of Supply and Services.

National Task Force on Suicide in Canada, 1987. *Suicide in Canada*. Ottawa: Mental Health Division, Health Services and Promotions Branch, Health and Welfare Canada. (Cat. No. H39–107/1987E).

National Council on Welfare, 1981. *Poverty in Canada*. Ottawa: Minister of Supply and Services.

National Council on Welfare, 1988. *Child care: A better alternative*. Ottawa: Minister of Supply and Services.

National Day Care Information Centre, 1987. *Status of Daycare, 1987*. Ottawa: Department of Health and Welfare.

Native Women's Association of Canada (NWAC), 1986. *Our children are our future*. Presentation to the Special House Committee on Child Care.

Nelson, C.H., and Kelly, M.L., 1984. *Wichiwin 'come along beside me' insights into Indian helping*. Paper prepared for the Fifth International Congress of Child Abuse and Neglect, Montreal, Canada, September 16–19, 1984, 35.

Nett, Emily M., 1988. *Canadian families past and present*. Toronto: Butterworths.

Niagara Children's Services Committee, 1988. *Child and adolescent mental health care services in Niagara: A proposal*. Fonthill, Ont: Niagara District Health Council, 1440 Pelham St., P.O. Box 1059, L0S 1E0.

Nicholson, Philip J., 1987. *Economic status of Native women in Ontario*. Prepared for the Ontario Women's Directorate, Government of Ontario.

Novosedlik, Stephen G., 1983. Native children white law. *Perception 6*(8), 27–29.

Ontario Secondary Schools Teachers' Federation (O.S.S.T.F.), 1988. *Present challenges, new directions*. A Discussion Paper, Ontario.

O'Malley, P.M., Bachman, J.G., and Johnston, L.D., 1984. Period, age and cohort effects on substance use among American youth, 1976–1982. *American Journal of Public Health, 74*, 682–688.

O'Neil, John, 1988. Referrals to traditional healers: The role of medical interpreters. In David Young (ed.), *Health Care Issues in the Canadian North*. Edmonton: Boreal Institute for Northern Studies, University of Alberta, 29–38.

Oakes, J., 1985. *Keeping track: how schools structure inequality*. New Haven: Yale University Press.

Offord, D.R., 1987. Prevention of behavioral and emotional disorders in children. *Journal of Child Psychology and Psychiatry, 28*, 9–19.

Offord, D.R., Boyle, M.H., and Jones, B.R., 1987. Psychiatric disorder and poor school performance among welfare children in Ontario. *Canadian Journal of Psychiatry, 32*, 518–525.

Offord, D.R., Boyle, M.H., Szatmari, P., Rae-Grant, N.I., Links, P.S., Cadman, D. T., Byles, J.A., Crawford, J.W., Munroe Blum, H., Byrne, C., Thomas, H., and Woodward, C.A., 1987. Ontario child health study: II. Six-month prevalence of disorder and rates of service utilization. *Archives of General Psychiatry, 44*, 832–836.

Olds, D., Henderson, C., Chamberlain, R., and Tatelbaum, R., 1986. Preventing child abuse and neglect. *Pediatrics, 78*, 65–78.

Ontario Association of Children's Aid Societies. The Future of Foster Care, 1988. *The Journal of the Ontario Association of Children's Aid Societies*, 3–20.

Ontario Institute for Studies in Education, 1985. *Fifth OISE Survey*, Toronto: OISE Press.

Ontario Institute for Studies in Education, 1987. *Sixth OISE Survey*, Toronto: OISE Press.

Ontario Institute for Studies in Education. 1989. *Seventh OISE Survey*, Toronto: OISE Press.

Ontario Métis and Aboriginal Association (OMMA), 1988. *A process and priority agenda for negotiations between Canada, Ontario and OMMA on aboriginal self-government in Ontario.*

Ontario Indian Social Services Council (OISSC), 1984. *Amendments to the CFSA and Response to Indian Child and Native Services Under the Child and Family Services Act.* Toronto, Ontario

Ontario Federation of Indian Friendship Centres (OFIFC), 1987. *Young offenders act manual a Native perspective.* Toronto, Ontario.

Ontario Native Women's Association; Ontario Federation Of Indian Friendship Centres; Ontario Métis and Non-Status Indian Association, 1983. *Remove the child and the circle is broken: A response to the proposed children's act consultation paper.* Toronto, Ontario.

Ontario Task Force on Employment and New Technology, 1985. *Employment and new technology,* Toronto, Ontario.

Ontario Council of Regents, Vision 2000, 1989. *With the future in mind.* Toronto, Ontario.

Ontario Secondary School Teachers' Federation, 1987. *Reducing the dropout rate.* Toronto: OSSTF.

Organization for Economic Cooperation and Development, 1981. *The transition from education to working life.* Paris.

Organization for Economic Cooperation and Development, 1982. *The competences needed in working life.* Paris.

Organization for Economic Cooperation and Development, 1983. *The role of education and training in relation to employment and unemployment of young people.* Paris.

Organization for Economic Cooperation and Development, 1985. *Changes in work patterns and their educational implications.* Paris.

Organization for Economic Cooperation and Development, 1986. *Facets of the transition to adulthood.* Paris.

Painter, Susan Lee, 1986. Research on the prevalence of child sexual abuse: New directions. *Canadian Journal of Behavioural Science, 18*(4), 323–339.

Parsons, Cynthia, 1988. *The bridge, cooperative education for all high school students.* Washington, DC: The William T. Grant Foundation Commission on Work, Family and Citizenship.

Paterson, R.J., and Moran, G., 1988. Attachment theory, personality development, and psychotherapy. *Clinical Psychology Review, 8,* 611–636.

Peters, R. DeV., 1988. Mental health promotion in children and adolescents: An emerging role for psychology. *Canadian Journal of Behavioral Sciences, 20,* 389–401.

Phillips, Sondra B., 1985. *Aboriginal languages in Canada.* Paper prepared for the Secretary of State.

Picherack, J.R., 1989. *1989 Per diem rates for private centres under subsidy contract.* Report to Metro Toronto Community Services and Housing Committee, Toronto, 1–2.

Picherack, J.R., 1989. *Comprehensive review of Metropolitan Toronto's future role in child care.* Report to Metro Toronto Community Services and Housing Committee, Toronto, 2.

Piotrowski, C., 1981. *Work and the family system.* New York: The Free Press.

Pleck, J.H., and Staines, G.L., 1985. Work schedules and family life in two-earner couples. *Journal of Family Issues, 6*(1), 61–82.

Pleck, J.H., Staines, G.L., and Lang, L., 1980. Conflicts between work and family life. *Monthly Labor Review, 103,* 29–32.

Polanyi, M., 1958. *Personal knowledge.* Routledge and Kegan Paul.

Porter, John, Blishen, B.R., and Barados, M., 1977. *Survival of a grade 8 cohort: a study of early school leaving in Ontario.*

Premier's Council on Technology, 1988. *Competing in the new global economy.* Report of the Premier's Council, Volume I, Queen's Printer for Ontario.

Preskorn, S.H., Weller, E.G., Hughes, C.W., Weller, R.A., and Bolte, K., 1987. Depression in prepubertal children: Dexamethasone nonsuppression predicts differential response to imipramine vs. placebo. *Psychopharmacology Bulletin, 23,* 128–133.

Pressser, H.B., 1988. Shift work and child care among young dual-earner American parents. *Journal of Marriage and the Family, 50,* 133–148.

Preston, Samuel H., 1984. Children and the elderly: Divergent paths for America's dependents. *Demography 21,* 435–458.

Price, John A., 1987. *Applied anthropology: Canadian perspectives.* Toronto: York University, Society of Applied Anthropologists in Canada.

Quay, H.C., 1986. Classification. In H.C. Quay and J.S. Werry (eds.), *Psychopathological disorders of childhood* (3rd ed.). Toronto: John Wiley and Sons, 1–34.

Quay, H.C., Routh, D.K., and Shapiro, S.K., 1987. Psychopathology of childhood: From description to validation. *Annual Review of Psychology, 30,* 491–532.

Radwanski, George, 1986. *Ontario study of the service sector.* Ontario Ministry of Treasury and Economics.

Radwanski, George, 1986. *Ontario study of the service sector.* Background papers. Ontario Ministry of Treasury and Economics.

Radwanski, George, 1987. *Ontario study of the relevance of education and the issue of dropouts.* Ontario Ministry of Education.

Rashid, A., 1983. *Evaluation of 1980 income data.* Statistics Canada, Consumer Income and Expenditure Division.

Raychaba, B., 1988. *To Be On Our Own With No Direction From Home. A Report on the Special Needs of Youth Leaving the Care of the Child Welfare System.* Ottawa: National Youth in Care Network.

Regier, D.A., Shapiro, S., Kessler, L.G., and Taube, C.A., 1984. Epidemiology and health services resource allocation policy for alcohol, drug abuse, and mental disorders. *Public Health Reports, 99*(5), 483–492.

Reynolds, W.M., and Coats, K.I., 1986. A comparison of cognitive-behavioral therapy and relaxation training for the treatment of depression in adolescents. *Journal of Consulting and Clinical Psychology, 54,* 653–660.

Richman, A., and Barry, A., 1985. More and more is less and less: The myth of massive psychiatric need. *British Journal of Psychiatry, 146,* 164–168.

Richman, A., Boutilier, C., and Harris, P., 1984. The relevance of sociodemographic and resource factors in the use of acute psychiatric inpatient care in the Atlantic Provinces of Canada. *Psychological Medicine, 14,* 175–182.

Robins, L.N., 1966. *Deviant children grown up: A sociological and psychiatric study of sociopathic personality.* Baltimore, MD: Williams and Wilkins.

Robins, L.N., 1978. Sturdy childhood predictors of adult antisocial behavior: replications from longitudinal studies. *Psychological Medicine, 8,* 611–622.

Rosenberg, M.L., Smith, J.C., Davidson, L.E., and Conn, J.M., 1987. The emergence of youth suicide: An epidemiologic analysis and public health perspective. *Annual Review of Public Health, 8,* 417–440.

Ross, A., 1983. Beatrice. *Canadian Woman Studies, 4*(4), 85–86.

Ross, David, 1987. *Benefit adequacy in Ontario.* Research report prepared for the Social Assistance Review Committee, Ontario.

Ross, H., 1988. *Customary care and the economics of child rearing phase 1: The shape of customary care.* Paper prepared for Payukotayno and Tikanagan Child and Family Services.

Rothman Beach Associates, 1985. *A study of work-related day care in Canada.* Background paper prepared for the Task Force on Child Care. Ottawa: Status of Women.

Rush, J.C., and Evers, F.T., 1986. *Making the match: Canada's university graduates and corporate employers.* Montreal: Corporate Higher Education Forum.

Rutter, M., 1975. *Helping troubled children.* Markham, Ont: Penguin Books.

Rutter, M., 1982. Prevention of children's psychosocial disorders: Myth and substance. *Pediatrics, 70,* 883–894.

Rutter, M., and Graham, P., 1968. The reliability and validity of the psychiatric assessment of the child: I. Interview with the child. *British Journal of Psychiatry, 114,* 563–576.

Rutter, M., Tizard, J., and Whitmore, K., 1970. *Education, health and behavior.* New York, NY: Longman Inc.

Sapir, Edward, 1949. *Culture, language and personality.* University California Press.

Sarsfield, P., 1988. Health issues in northern Canada. In David Young (ed.), *Health Care Issues in the Canadian North.* Edmonton: Boreal Institute for Northern Studies, University of Alberta, 119–124.

Sattes, B.D., 1985. *Parent involvement: a review of the literature.* Charleston, West Virginia: Appalachia Educational Laboratory.

Saxe, L., Cross, T., and Silverman, N., 1988. Children's mental health: The gap between what we know and what we do. *American Psychologist, 43,* 800–807.

Schinke, Steven P., and Schilling, Robert F., 1986. Prevention of drug and alcohol abuse in Amerindian youths. *Social Work Research and Abstracts, 22*(4), 18–19.

Schulz, P.V., 1978. Day care in Canada: 1850–1962. In G. Ross (ed.), *Good day care: Fighting for it, getting it, keeping it.* Toronto: The Women's Educational Press, 137–158.

Science Council of Canada, 1984. *Science for every student: Educating Canadians for tomorrow's world, report 36.* Ottawa.

Seguret, M.C., 1981. Child-care services for working parents. *International Labour Review*, *120*(6), 711–725.

Select Committee on Health, 1987. *Special report: Future directions for child care in Ontario* (3rd session, 33rd Parliament, 36 Elizabeth II). Ontario.

Senate Committee on Youth, 1986. *YOUTH: A Plan of Action.* Ottawa.

Shaffer, D., Schwab-Stone, M., Fisher, P., Davies, M., Piacentini, J., and Gioia, P., 1988. *A revised version of the diagnostic interview schedule for children (DISC-R).* New York, NY: New York State Psychiatric Institute, Columbia University College of Physicians and Surgeons, Division of Child Psychiatry.

Shapiro, S., Skinner, E.A., Kramer, M., Steinwachs, O.M., and Regier, D.A., 1985. Measuring need for mental health services in a general population. *Medical Care*, *23*(9), 1033–1043.

Shaw, R. Paul, 1986. Unemployment and low family income in Canada. *Canadian Public Policy 12*, 368–386.

Shkilnyk, Anastasia, 1985. *A poison stronger than love.* New Haven: Yale University Press.

Smalley, S., Asarnow, R., and Spence, A., 1988. Autism and genetics. *Archives of General Psychiatry*, *45*, 953–961.

Smith, F., 1986. *Insult to intelligence.* New York: Arbor House.

Social Assistance Review Committee, 1988. *Transitions: Report of the social assistance review committee.* Toronto: Queen's Printer for Ontario.

Social Planning Council of Metropolitan Toronto, February, 1989. *Target on training: Meeting workers' needs in a changing economy.* Toronto, Ontario.

Sorbara, G., 1988. Presentation to the Work and Family Conference, sponsored by Ryerson Polytechnical University and the Ontario Ministry of Community and Social Services, Dec. 2.

Southam Inc., 1987. *Literacy in Canada: A research report.* Ottawa.

Spakes, P., 1983. *Family policy and family impact analysis.* Cambridge, MA: Schenken Publishing Company, Inc.

Spitzer, R.L., and Cantwell, D.P., 1980. The DSM-III classification of the psychiatric disorders of infancy, childhood and adolescence. *Journal of the American Academy of Child Psychiatry*, *19*, 356–370.

SPR Associates Inc., 1986. *A national overview of child care arrangements in the workplace.* Toronto: Report commissioned for the Special Committee on Child Care.

Staff, 1985. Towards equity: A report on a recent colloquium held to discuss the economic status of women in the labour market. *Au Courant*, *5*(4).

Staff, 1989. *Toronto Star*, (February 12), A9.

Staines, G.L., 1986. Men's work schedules and family life. *Marriage and Family Review*, *9*(3&4), 43–65.

Staines, G.L., and Pleck, J.H., 1984. Nonstandard work schedules and family life. *Journal of Applied Psychology*, *6*(3), 515–523.

Staines, G.L., Pottick, K.J., and Fudge, D.A., 1985. The effect of wives' employment on husbands' job and life satisfaction. *Psychology of Women Quarterly*, *9*(3), 419–424.

Stallings, J.A., and Stipek, D., 1986. Research on early childhood and elementary school teaching programs. In M.C. Wittrock (ed.), *Handbook of research on teaching*. New York: McMillan Publishing Company.

Stamp, R.M., 1988. *Ontario secondary school program innovations and student retention rates 1920s–1970s*. Ontario Ministry of Education.

Standing Committee on Social Development, 1985. *Recommendations on the day nurseries act* (4th session, 32nd Parliament, 34 Elizabeth II).

Stapleford, E.M., 1976. *History of the day nurseries branch*. Ontario Ministry of Community and Social Services.

Statistics Canada, 1985. *Canada, the provinces and the territories: A statistical profile*. Ottawa: Small Area Data Program.

Statistics Canada, 1986. Families: Part one. In *The Nation*. Ottawa: Population and Dwelling Characteristics, Census 1986.

Statistics Canada, 1987. *Family incomes: Census families. 1985*. Ottawa: Minister of Supply and Services.

Statistics Canada, 1988. *The labour force: Annual averages 1987*. Ottawa: Household Surveys Division.

Statistics Canada, 1988. *Estimates of families for Canada and the Provinces. Census of Canada* (Cat. 91–204). Ottawa: Minister of Supply and Services.

Statistics Canada, 1988. *Education in Canada: A statistical review for 1986–1987*. Ottawa: Education, Culture, and Tourism Division, Projections and Analyses Section.

Status of Women, 1986. *Report of the task force on child care*. Ottawa: Canada Government Publishing Centre.

Stevenson, D.L., and Baker, D.P., 1987. The family-school relation and the child's school performance. *Child Development, 58*, 1348–1359.

Submission of The Board of Education for the City of Toronto to The Ontario Secondary Education Review Project: A Discussion Paper. Toronto, Ontario, 1980.

Sullivan, T., 1988. *Investing in children: New directions in child treatment and child and family intervention*. Ontario Ministry of Community and Social Services.

Sullivan, T., and Colfer, P., 1988. *Secure services in Ontario: An MCSS perspective*. Queen's Park, Toronto, Ontario.

Sullivan, Michael (Decima Research), 1988. *A comparative analysis of drop-outs and non-drop-outs in Ontario secondary schools, a report to the Ontario study of relevance of education and the issue of drop-outs*. Ontario Ministry of Education.

Thompson, A.H., 1988. Young offender, child welfare, and mental health caseload communalities. *Canadian Journal of Criminology, 30*, 135–144.

Timpson, Joyce B., 1983. Indian mental health: Changes in the delivery of care in northwestern Ontario. *Canadian Journal of Psychiatry, 29*, 234–241.

Tiner, T., 1985. Kids at work. *Executive, 27*(7).

Tischler, G.L., Leaf, P.S., and Holzer, C.E., 1988. The direct measurement of need: A clinician's perspective. In H.F. Goldsmith, E. Lin, R.A. Bell, and D.J. Jackson (eds.), *National Institute of Mental Health. Series BN No. 8, Needs assessment: Its future* (DHHS Publication No. ADM 88–1550,). Washington, DC: U.S. Government Printing Office, 13–16.

Todres, E., 1988. Presentation to the Work and Family Conference, sponsored by Ryerson Polytechnical University and the Ontario Ministry of Community and Social Services, Dec. 2.

Toomey, D., 1986. *Home-school relations and inequality in education.* Provo, Utah: Conference on Education and the Family, Feb. 4–6. (ED 269495).

Townson, M., 1987. *Women's labour force participation, fertility rates, and the implications for economic development and government policy.* Ottawa: Institute for Research on Public Policy.

Treas, Judith, 1987. The effect of women's labour force participation on the distribution of income in the United States. *Annual Review of Sociology 13*, 259–288.

Tuma, J. M., 1989. Mental health services for children: The state of the art. *American Psychologist, 44*, 188–199.

Tuma, J.M., and Sobotka, K.R., 1983. Traditional therapies with children. In T.H. Ollendick and M. Hersen (eds.), *Handbook of child psychopathology.* New York, NY: Plenum Press, 391–426.

Union of Ontario Indians, 1987–88. *Native Community Care: Counselling and Development: Curriculum Materials.*

Vaillant, G.E., and Schnurr, P., 1988. What is a case? A 45-year study of psychiatric impairment within a college sample selected for mental health. *Archives of General Psychiatry, 45*, 313–319.

Vanier Institute of the Family, 1986. *Child care options for Canadian families* (brief presented to Federal Special Committee on Child Care).

Voydanoff, P., 1988. Work role characteristics, family structure demands, and work/family conflict. *Journal of Marriage and the Family, 50*(3), 749–761.

Vygotsky, L.S., 1962. *Thought and language.* trans. Haufmann, E. and Vaker, G. MIT Press.

Wald, M.S., Carlsmith, J.M., and Leiderman, P.H., 1988. *Protecting abused and neglected children.* Stanford: Stanford University Press.

Ward, J.A., and Fox, J., 1977. A suicide epidemic on an Indian reserve. *Canadian Psychiatric Association Journal, 22*, 423–426.

Ware, J., 1988. Measuring health status in the well population. *Quality of Life and Cardiovascular Care.* (Winter), 156–163.

Warry, W., 1987. *Breaking the cycle: A report on the Native inmate liquor offender project.* Toronto: The Ontario Native Council on Justice.

Waterloo Region Social Resources Council, 1987. *Development and delivery of children's mental health services in the Waterloo region.* Waterloo Region Social Resources Council, Suite 214, Waterloo Town Square, 75 King Street South, Waterloo, Ontario, N2J 1P2.

Weaver, Sally, 1984. Indian self-government: A concept in need of a definition. In Leroy Little Bear, Menno Boldt and J.Anthony Long (eds.), *Pathways to self-determination.* Toronto: University of Toronto Press, 65–68.

Weaver, Sally, 1986a. Indian policy in the new conservative government, Part I: The Nielsen task force of 1985. *Native Studies Review 2*(1), 1–43.

Weaver, Sally, 1986b. Indian policy in the new conservative government, Part II: the Nielsen task force in the context of recent policy initiatives. *Native Studies Review, 2*(1), 1–43.

Weiss, H., 1983. Introduction. In *Programs to strengthen families: A resource guide.* New Haven: Yale Bush Centre in Child Development and Social Policy. 2–6.

Weissbourd, B., 1987. A brief history of family support programs. In S. Kagan, D. Powell, B. Weissbourd, and E. Zigler, (eds.), *America's family support programs: Perspectives and prospects.* New Haven: Yale University Press, 38–56.

Weisz, J.R., Weiss, B., Alicke, M.D., and Klotz, M.L., 1987. Effectiveness of psychotherapy with children and adolescents: a meta-analysis for clinicians. *Journal of Consulting and Clinical Psychology*, 55(4), 542–549.

Weller, G., and Manga, P., 1988. The feasibility of developing an integrated health care system in the north: The case of northwestern Ontario. In David Young (ed.), *Health Care Issues in the Canadian North.* Edmonton: Boreal Institute for Northern Studies, University of Alberta, 140–150.

Welner, Z., Reich, W., Herjanic, B., Jung, K.G., and Amado, H., 1987. Reliability, validity, and parent-child agreement studies of the diagnostic interview for children and adolescents (DICA). *Journal of the American Academy of Child and Adolescent Psychiatry*, 26, 649–653.

Werry, J.S., Reeves, J.C., and Elkind, G.S., 1987. Attention deficit, conduct, oppositional, and anxiety disorders in children: I. A review of research on differentiating characteristics. *Journal of the American Academy of Child and Adolescent Psychiatry*, 26, 133–143.

Westermeyer, J., and Peake, E., 1983. A ten year follow-up of alcoholic Native Americans in Minnesota. *American Journal of Psychiatry.*

Westermeyer, J., and Neider, J., 1984. Predicting treatment outcome after ten years among American Indian alcoholics. *Alcoholism: Clinical and Experimental Research*, 8(2), 179–184.

Wharf, Brian, 1989. *Toward First Nation control of child welfare, a review of emerging developments in B.C.* University of Victoria.

White, J., 1983. *Women and Part-Time Work.* Ottawa: Canadian Advisory Council on the Status of Women.

Wichlacz, L., and Kempe, H., 1978. Indian child welfare: A community team approach to protective services. *Child Abuse and Neglect* 2(1).

Willigen, John Van, 1986. *Applied anthropology.* Massachusetts: Bergin and Garvey.

Wilson, William Julius, 1987. *The truly disadvantaged: The inner city, the underclass, and public policy.* Chicago and London: University of Chicago Press.

Wolf, M.M., Braukmann, C.J., and Ramp, K.A., 1987. Serious delinquent behavior as a part of a significantly handicapping condition: Cures and supportive environments. *Journal of Applied Behavior Analysis*, 20, 347–359.

Wolfe, D.A., 1987. *Child Abuse: Implications for child development and psychopathology.* Newbury Park, CA: Sage.

Women's Bureau, Labour Canada, 1988. *Leave for employees with family responsibilities* (Labour Cat. No. L0161658/88E). Ottawa: Ministry of Labour. (Report prepared by Monica Townson Associates Inc.)

Women's Bureau, 1982. *Employers and child care: Establishing services through the workplace* (Pamphlet 23). U.S. Department of Labor. (Publication prepared by Kathryn Senn Perry.)

Worswick, G.D.N. (ed.), 1985. *Education and economic performance, National Institute of Economic and Social Research.* UK: Gower Publishing.

Wright, E.N., and Tsujii, G.K., 1983. *The grade nine student survey.* Toronto Board of Education Research Service.

Wright, R., 1985. *Work-site day care in Canada.* Human Resources Management in Canada.

Yates, Alayne, 1986. Current status and future directions of research on the American Indian child. *American Journal of Psychiatry, 144*(9), 1135–1142.

Young, T. Kue, 1979. Changing patterns of health and sickness among the Cree-Ojibwa of northwestern Ontario. *Medical Anthropology 3*(2), 192–220.

Young, T. Kue, 1983. Mortality pattern of isolated Indians in northwestern Ontario: A 10 year review. *Public Health Reports 98,* 467–475.

Ziegler, S., Hardwick, N., and McCreath, G., 1989. *Academically successful inner city children: What they tell us about effective education.* Toronto Board of Education.

Zigler, E., and Muenchow, S., 1983. Infant day care and infant-care leaves: A policy vacuum. *American Psychologist, 38,* 91–94.